ENDANGERED SP

ENDANGERED SPECIES

Diplomacy from the Passenger Seat

MARGARET BULLARD

PRIVATELY PRINTED

2021

Hardback ISBN 978 0 9931898 5 2
Paperback ISBN PAPERBACK 978 0 9931898 6 9

BY THE SAME AUTHOR

Inside Stalin's Russia 2000
ISBN 953 22131 8
Published by Day Books

Bootstraps – A Memoir of Reader William Bullard 2008
(out of print)

No Tennis on Sundays – A Memory of Wartime Childhood 2015
(being reprinted)

Designed by Nick Clarke

In Memory of
Julian

Contents

Prologue

JULIAN enjoyed producing light hearted verse for birthdays and other occasions, and a song he wrote for our children to sing at a Christmas party in Bonn had the final lines:

If you ask us, would we like to be a diplomatic wife
Or a diplomatic husband, we reply:
NOT ON YOUR LIFE

I have tried to give my reasons for taking the opposite view, not to encourage my readers to follow in my path, but to describe what it felt like and what I enjoyed about it. I chose my title because I wondered whether in the future there are likely to be wives who are happy to travel to wherever the spouse should be sent, and not to be financially independent, who would rather not be so far from their children, nor enjoy having to be warm and welcoming to unknown people they may never see again. If one can solve the problem of finding an occupation that can be combined with a peripatetic life, one can escape the embarrassment of having to reply to a question frequently asked in Washington, with the answer, 'Well, I look after the house and the garden and the children, see that they have nice food and suitable clothes, and there are letters to write and holidays to plan' I remember an American explaining to me that as everyone else has a job, if you don't, there is no one to go to exhibitions or excursions with.

I was almost grateful for the arrival of Covid 19 and the lockdowns which gave me the spur I needed to write a sequel to *No Tennis on Sundays*.

Without the help and advice of my children and my Foreign Office friends I should never have written this book, and I am very grateful to everyone who helped me. Those in the Foreign Office will find many mistakes. I ask their forgiveness.

Five decades are an awful lot of time –
To live through, or to try to fix in rhyme:
What comes to mind on looking back
Is not the single and continuous track
Of time, but individually sieved
By memory, the places where we lived.
First Orange Street: the dubious club next door,
The rats that once ran out across the floor,
The spinster sisters in their ancient car
With fresh supplies of Caspian caviar.

'Geneva Conference', to me must spell
The fountain in the Place du Grand Mezel,
The narrow window where we blessed the hours
And watched the Jura change her snow for flowers.
Vienna showed us chandeliers and Schmalz
And skis, and how to (anti-clockwise) waltz
And also Ordnung, Ruhe and Befehl,
Three words at which all German spirits quail:
And we, proud parents, on those polished floors
Outboast all other diplomatic bores.
Jordan was locusts, sun and (far but loud)
The ugly rumble of an Arab crowd
The disco music from across the way
The call to prayer bringing another day,
The heat, the light and Moussa on his knees
Making a lawn beneath the almond trees:
Two children are now added to our slate,
One small and punctual, one large and late.
That phase of Foreign Service at its finish
We scanned the scene and pitched our tent in Greenwich –
And stayed for 20 years! What offered most,
That Tudor mansion on the Dorset coast?
Or Filkins (rural slum!), Belgravian mews,
Where Spanish drivers shined their shoes
Meanwhile, what post to build our life upon?
Unsmart, unfamous, unpretending Bonn.

Julian wrote this for my 50th birthday
What follows is my story.

I

FRANCE

APRIL 1954

GENEVA

APRIL 1954 – JUNE 1954

'Diplomacy is letting someone else have my way'
LESTER PEARSON

I T was April 1954. We were on our honeymoon in the ancient chateau of Carrenac when Julian broke the news to me that the Foreign Office wanted him, as soon as he got home, to join the delegation to a conference to agree terms for peace in Indo China and Korea. I was delighted. I was ready to go anywhere in the world provided I was with Julian. Then he added the bad news: The Foreign Office did not pay for wives to accompany husbands to conferences, but I wouldn't mind being by myself in our flat in Orange Street for a bit would I? I did mind. A lot. Where was the conference? How long did Julian think it would last? 'At the Palais des Nations in Geneva and how long depends how long it takes for terms on which an armistice between North and South Korea can be agreed. One or two months, of course it could be longer.' Was this going to be what being married to a diplomat was like? I learned that it principally means that you have to be prepared for anything.

The chateau at Carrenac had become a hotel, strongly recommended by friends who had stayed there the previous year, but they had been luckier with the weather. Coming into the chateau cold and dripping wet, we asked about a hot bath. *'Only a shower I am afraid, we will call you when it is ready.* '*Ready*' meant that a young girl was standing on a stool with several jugs of water ready to pour them down a pipe ending in a ring round our necks. This appeared to be the only alternative to a jug and basin, so we up-sticked and drove to the Loire, where we sketched many of the chateaux from the front seat of the car as the windscreen wipers swished to and fro. Julian's Rugby classics master had lent us his car as a wedding present. Going up a narrow dirt track we noticed the indicator said 'empty'. But Norman's parting words had been: '*Don't worry if it says empty. There is always a little more left in the tank.*' In turning round, we found ourselves stuck in a ditch. But Julian was a man of many talents and he had skills not possessed by anyone in my family. Somehow, he managed to turn the car so that it faced downhill, allowing gravity to deliver the little petrol there was to the engine. We freewheeled down the hill, and used the last pint of petrol to reach a garage.

We had a flat in Orange Street, a desirable spot between Lower Regent Street and The National Gallery, right in the centre of London, but with one snag. The owner of the flat had a shop on the ground floor which sold caviar and strange bits of dried fish, underneath which was a cellar containing stores of comestibles very tempting to rats. I knew that Westminster Council held an unconcerned view of the rat infestation because I had complained about it earlier. They answered: '*I am afraid getting rid of the rats in Soho sewers would be a labour of Hercules.*'

I did not want to start married life sharing it with rats and no husband, so I counted out my last remaining francs and found I had just enough for a train ticket from Paris to Geneva, so I waved Julian goodbye on the train to London, and took a train to Switzerland. I booked myself for a night in a cheap room not far from the railway station, (knowing that I had not enough money to pay the bill). At the end of the next day, when Julian had arrived with the rest of the delegation at the Beau Rivage Hotel, I was able to tell him that I had a job working for the International Labour Office (at almost twice the salary he was paid by the Foreign Office) and that we had a flat in the Place du Grand Mezel in the old part of Geneva. My work at the ILO was to help in the compilation of a report on the conditions of work in the Persian carpet industry.

Two blissful months followed. Sometimes we joined John Addis in his search for golden orioles in the lower slopes of the Jura. Some weekends we would board a yellow tram and rattle up one of the valleys, Julian carrying *War and Peace* in his pocket. We would lie in the sun reading alternate chapters to each other. As daytime ended, we would climb up over a col and find a tram to take us home, my arms sometimes full of wild orchids. In the evening we would order and re-order raclette at the Café du Midi. Other members of the British Delegation were impressed with my having simply bought a ticket, and managed to find a job and a flat. The only other accompanying wife was Clarissa Eden, the wife of the Foreign Secretary.

Before we were married Julian had been one of four Resident Clerks, who had a flat in the attic of the Foreign Office, taking it in turns to be on duty in the hours when the Foreign Office was closed. Julian said he never received a call as dramatic as that which Frank Roberts did on 2 September 1939, (later he was our Ambassador in Bonn): '*Field Marshal Göring would like to speak to Sir Anthony Eden*' to which he said he had replied '*Too late, Too late.*'

During the day he had the Korean desk in the East Asian Department, so it was appropriate that he should be a member of the delegation representing the UK at the conference which took place in the Palais des Nations, in Geneva, the first headquarters of the United Nations. His role was confined to trying to agree terms on which an armistice could be signed to end the fighting between those parts of Indo China and Korea backed by the Soviet Union and China and those supported by the 'free world.' Julian later described his career as having been a Cold War Warrior, a term first used by George Orwell in 1945 to describe 'a state which is at once unconquerable and in a permanent state of cold war with its neighbours.'

Intervening years may have eroded the memory of the Korean War from everyone's minds. The situation was roughly that at the end of WWII the occupying Japanese forces were evicted and a straight line drawn along the 38th parallel to separate the Communist North from the American supported South, led by Syngman Rhee. This held for five years, but in 1950 Dean Ascherson, U.S. Secretary of State, made a speech in which he unwisely indicated that he no longer considered Korea within the U.S. area of responsibility. Encouraged by this, and supported by Moscow and Peking, Kim II Sung ordered his troops to cross the border line, drive out the American occupiers, and reunite Korea. General McArthur, considered the hero of WWII in the Pacific, rashly declared that he could handle the North Korean attack with two hands tied behind his back, in which he was mistaken. The southern army had no weapons capable of penetrating the North Korean tanks and were forced to retreat until they were almost driven from the peninsula.

Such a slap in the face from the North Koreans was very unpopular in the United States. President Truman persuaded the Security Council to authorise UN action and the Allied forces made a bold pincer movement landing behind the Communist lines. At first their success was startling, but they were defeated as they approached the Chinese border by the terrible icy blast of winter, as was Napoleon in Russia. US soldiers found their machine guns no longer worked. Faced with certain death from the cold they retreated back to the 38th parallel. Much public criticism led Truman to consider authorising McArthur to use the atomic bomb. It was the first occasion when the knowledge of the possibility of using atomic weapons was in policymakers' minds. An alarmed Attlee flew to Washington urging caution. It was agreed to continue the war by air, avoiding troop losses but destroying just about every town, village and installation

3

as a result of indiscriminately dropped napalm. Both countries were reduced to rubble. Syngman Rhee ruled the South ruthlessly, food and resources were scarce, corruption was everywhere. The election of Eisenhower, followed in March 1953 by the sudden death of Stalin, together with the extreme unpopularity of the war, broke the stalemate.

At first the Conference was unable to come to any agreement on the withdrawal of troops, or on regulations for elections, or on acceptance that UN troops should supervise the peace, but after an intervention from the Canadian Prime Minister, Lester Pearson, an agreement was reached on 27th July 1953. This was the first action by the newly established United Nations. A cease-fire came into force, the repatriation of prisoners of war was agreed, and the Korean Demilitarized Zone (DMZ) was established as the *de facto* new border almost exactly where it had been before so many lives were lost and so much devastation pulverized the country. So that was the end of Julian's part in the conference, but before we left we had a long weekend in the Alps.

Shortly after WWII ended, a Swiss boy wanting to improve his English, had come to stay with Julian's family in Oxford. His parents, who knew Julian's father, invited us to make use of their chalet in Grimentz, high in the Alps and not too far from Geneva. My mother had been staying with us, and I persuaded her to stay an extra weekend and come too. In those days it was possible to change the date of one's air ticket, and this she reluctantly did, despite having to miss various meetings of the Church Missionary Society and the Parish Council. Wickedly choosing pleasure over duty had saved Mother's life as the ground staff forgot to fuel the Swiss Air plane, on which she had first booked, and only the pilot and air hostesses were not drowned in the English Channel. I climbed to the Col du Torrent, 2916 metres, in tennis shoes and a sun dress with no hat, sun cream or dark glasses,with Julian pulling me up the final stretch insisting I reach the top. An unbelievable panorama of snowy alps opened up before us – well worth the pain with which we woke next day.

Sadly the Bullards packed their bags for home.

2

BRITISH EMBASSY, VIENNA

1955 – 1956

Fein, fein schmeckt uns der Wein,
Wenn man 20 ist, und auch die Liebe,
Fein, Fein schmeckt uns der Wein,
Wenn man 30 ist, und auch die Liebe.
Wenn man 40 ist, man noch gerne küst,
B'sonders wenn man einst sparsam gewesen ist,
Doch wenn man kälter wird,
Und Langsam kälter wird,
Bleibt allein nur der Wein.

A rough translation: Wine is fine when you're 20 and so is love. It's still fine at 30 and even at 40 one's glad of a kiss, especially when it hasn't come your way often, but when you are older, and get slowly colder, it's only the wine that remains.

Back in London, after a busy few weeks trying to get the better of the rats, Julian was instructed to report to the Embassy in Vienna as Third Secretary. Julian told me I would not have to pack our things myself as it would be done by a firm of professional packers. The civil service way of getting this done cheaply was to tell us to provide three estimates from different packers. When one firm had looked at our modest belongings, I explained that I could not engage them until I had seen two other firms. '*Oh, no one bothers about that: we will supply you with three estimates,*' I couldn't help wondering whether this is the way all government contracts are given.

Before we left London, Julian took me to a cocktail party where most of the guests were his colleagues. Sir Edward Crowe asked me where Julian was to be posted and who the ambassador was. His face fell. '*Fella's a bounder*' was his rather worrying comment. We bought our first car and drove proudly to Vienna. Just across the Austrian border we took a cog railway to the top of an Alp. We decided to walk off our magnificent lunch by going down on foot. Twenty minutes up turned out to be three hours down using unaccustomed muscles. We arrived in Vienna in a crippled state and got out of our car barely able to crawl upstairs to the flat the Embassy had rented for us. The flat would have been pleasant had the owner's taste in décor not been for dark textiles with lurid patterns, and walls hung with large and gloomy pictures. The view from the windows was of two large square anti-aircraft towers – still there today – defying all attempts to demolish them because of the risk to the surrounding houses.

Next morning I kissed goodbye to Julian, lay down on my bed and howled. Suddenly I realised I was without family, friends or job. I had forgotten even the little German I had learned from Ilse, the Jewish refugee in my class at school. How was I to pass the days? Nothing to do and I knew no one. Boredom was all the worse for being unexpected. Foreign travel had seemed so glitteringly romantic to all of us girls imprisoned on our island throughout the war. The first thing to do was clearly to learn German. I put an advertisement for a 'Mädchen für Alles' (maid of all work) in the local paper which produced one reply: a wonderful girl about my age prepared to do whatever was required – cook, clean, stoke boilers, for the schilling equivalent of about £4 a week. We were fortunate. Ella and her parents had just arrived in Vienna as refugees from Tito's Yugoslavia where her family had had a smallholding since the days of the Austro-Hungarian empire. They had fled the communists and found their way mostly on foot, her parents selling the gold from their teeth for food and shelter. We were fortunate that Ella spoke good German without the charming but broad dialect of the local Viennese.

I carried my small red dictionary everywhere, starting by translating the advertisements and the headlines of the newspapers. I was greeted in every shop with some words I could not understand. After listening carefully, I tried returning the same greeting. Roars of laughter. It is not appropriate for the customer to say: '*I kiss your hand gracious lady.*' Julian and I both enrolled for German lessons with a stout Russian emigree in a wheelchair who lived in the attic of the Schönborn palace not far from the Hofburg. She was equally willing to give lessons in Russian, German, French or English but there was something a little odd about the questions she asked. Why was she so interested in the workings of the Embassy, and who worked in which department? I later realised that she must have been under orders from the Russians to collect information for them. No doubt they threatened unpleasant consequences for her relations if she could not tell them who in the Embassy was a spy and who a diplomat.

Vienna had recovered a good deal from the days of *The Third Man*, pre-war yellow trams still rattled through the streets, also Jeeps carrying soldiers in the uniform of the occupying powers, but almost no private cars. We were naturally keen to get to know some Austrians. But this was difficult as we were not ordinary foreigners but occupying powers and our sterling salaries turned us into mini-millionaires. Most Austrians were more concerned with survival than getting to know their erstwhile enemies. An exception were the *Erste Gesellschaft*, the members of the titled and well-connected families who spoke most languages fluently and happily accepted invitations from all the Western ambassadors. We sometimes wondered if perhaps they were ready to go anywhere for a square meal. We were envious of Nicko Henderson, who had the post of information officer and at least got to know the journalists. Mary Henderson introduced me to the Dorotheum, the state auction house founded by Joseph II. We both had an eye for interesting and inexpensive antiques and I much admired the elaborate wall clock which played the Radetzky March on the hour which Mary had found. Through Julian's Oxford landlady we got to know a hospitable elderly couple who invited us to their parties at which they served beer and weisswürst (made with veal). Herr Baumgarten had been interned in France at the beginning of the war, and he told us that he used his English trilby hat to carry water from the standpipe – so well made that it continued not to leak for the whole time of his imprisonment. After the war he went to Lock's in St James's Street and told them the story. Their reaction was not satisfaction, but shame that one of their hats had sunk so low.

Julian's chief work in the Embassy was to work on the Peace Treaty which would bring to an end the four-power occupation of Austria and the restoration of independence. London stipulated that the Austrians must hold free elections, at first unacceptable to the Russians. Luckily for the West, the Russians did not anticipate the landslide victory for the Right, and gave way. They did not make this mistake again and the Germans were left under allied occupation for another 35 years. Julian also had to meet his opposite number from the Embassies of the U.S.A, Russia and France and consider whether any public meetings, concerts or plays were likely to promote Nazi views and should therefore be banned. Since this required all four to agree, not surprisingly no public performances were ever banned. But this gave us an excellent reason to improve our German at the Theater an der Josefstadt or enjoy opera and concerts in the Theater am Wien (where early performances of works by Mozart, Schubert and Beethoven had been given). For the only time in our lives, we had normal friendly relations with Julian's Russian colleague, and from time to time we would actually entertain Russians in our flat, and they would come bringing a present of a small tin of caviar!

Only in Vienna was it Julian's job to greet, on behalf of the Queen, unknown elderly ladies, mostly relations of Commonwealth Heads of State, who came to be treated with cosmetic surgery, often for removal of surplus fat. One day he had to greet the Duchess of Windsor, not I imagine for fat removal. Her carefully tended face scarcely bore witness to the number of winters through which she had lived, but Julian told me he had caught sight of one un-gloved hand which gave a more accurate idea of her age

There were several camps of displaced persons, and sometimes families, in the British zones of Graz and Klagenfurt in the south of Austria, waiting to be returned to their country of birth, as had been agreed between the four powers at the Potsdam Conference. The inmates lived in huts which looked like prisoner of war huts in a WWII movie and were fed on reduced army rations. As none of the Russian prisoners wished to be handed back to communist Russia, this was a problem that took a long time to solve. To raise their spirits at Christmas, the French wife of our 'bounding' ambassador decided to hold a little bazaar to raise money to give presents to all the children. She summoned the Embassy wives to a meeting to explain our roles. '*I think we will give sewing things to the girls and carpentry sets to the boys. I will obtain things to sell from English firms and you will wear your national dress and stand behind the tables and take the money.*' '*You have no national dress?*' (Incredulously) She clearly took a poor view of this. '*Very well: you will wear a little black dress and I will get tartan 'ats and sashes for you all*'. We wore the tartan hats and sashes. In those distant days no one dared do other than obey the Ambassador's wife!

Her social secretary used to telephone me and say '*Lady Wallinger heard that you were seen in the Graben without a hat or gloves,*' (possibly even no stockings as well). Apart from my school hat I had never owned a hat in my life. I had a very small one made for me and wore it next time I was invited to <u>lunch</u> at the embassy. My hat was unfortunately invisible to my very short hostess. Bad marks again! Lady Wallinger went into hospital for a small operation and I was told it was my duty to call on her. I was surprised to see her lying in pink satin sheets, which, were her own, and which she said she always brought with her. I found it hard to imagine our Ambassador in those satin sheets.

To pass the time I took up Bridge again and even got to the finals of the diplomatic championship. During the war I had spent many hours being taught Bridge by American doctors from the nearby military hospital who often used to come round to our house in the evenings. Julian was impatient with my evening Bridge engagements and said '*You've got to choose. It's Bridge or me*'.

I was slightly puzzled one day to be phoned by the social secretary telling me that the ambassador would like us to join him and the secretary, to go skiing on the Rax Alp. I now wonder if we were taken as a cover to avoid gossip had he and the secretary set off alone in the Rolls Since they were both better skiers than us, we were not surprised to see nothing of them until it was time to go home. I was horrified and distressed when I heard that, after we had left Vienna, she had killed herself. Could the bounding Ambassador have been involved? Why else would an attractive girl in her early twenties with a covetable job want to end her life?

I was pregnant and I knew nothing at all about childbirth or babies, and none of the Embassy wives seemed interested in changing this, so I was lucky that I had a Swiss friend, Cleo, married to an American diplomat, who took charge of me, introducing me to Dr. Spock's bible on baby care, which supplied answers for everything. On 22 June 1955 Julian came into my room in the Rudolfinerhaus with a huge bunch of pink peonies to see the newly arrived Antonia. The nurses shook their heads. Roses were the right kind of flowers to bring to a new mother. The two years we spent in Vienna passed quickly as we washed, fed, dressed, admired, and photographed our baby. Dr Spock's advice was that it was unnecessary to buy any special equipment for the baby. She wouldn't care if she was kept in a cardboard box. I have a picture of Antonia having her morning bath in a metal laundry tub.

On summer evenings we would sometimes drive to the XVIIIth district and go to a Heuriger tavern. *Heuriger Wein* means wine made in the year in which you drink it, and is drunk only in the taverns in the outskirts of Vienna as one listens to the traditional songs sung to the sound of the zither. At weekends in summer we sometimes drove into the Wienerwald or to the Wachau with our baby and our painting things. Sometimes we picnicked in the ruins of the castle where Richard the Lionheart had been imprisoned while waiting for his ransom to arrive from England. In winter we would drive to the mountains with our new skis, wedding presents from Julian's brother. My mother flew out for Antonia's christening, but sadly soon afterwards on a very hot day, after a swim and sunbathing while staying in a hotel in the Alps, she suffered a stroke which paralysed her right arm and the right side of her face. I summoned an ambulance and went with her on the long journey to a hospital in Vienna, where she was made to lie in the hospital entrance hall until all her details had been entered in the admissions book: her birth in the West Indies, her missionary parents, and what diseases she had had (about which I knew nothing). With her characteristic courage and strong will power she managed in a few months to train her left hand and arm to take over, and shortly after was writing, cooking and even painting, almost as well as before.

Julian had occasional spells of wondering whether he was cut out for diplomatic life. Was he too good at seeing all sides of a question, and too lacking in firm principles ever to be any good at it?

In a letter to his parents he wrote:

'There are times when the whole game appears not worth being good at. Certainly the world would not lose much if a pest destroyed all cars with diplomatic number plates and their occupants overnight. If I could feel more satisfied on the central question of what it is all worth, I should have a better conscience with which to enjoy the travel and comforts of life and the good company. Vienna is far from being the exciting meeting ground of East and West that I had expected. I have nothing to do more than observe with cynicism the horse-trading between the two coalition parties and the weak-kneed drift towards friendship with Russia'.

In May 1955 Austria's independence was restored at the price of neutrality. The peace treaty was signed and the opera house rose in magnificence from its blackened ruins. Julian was promoted to Second Secretary and told to proceed to the Embassy in Amman at his earliest convenience, but to leave his wife and daughter behind in England 'as the political situation was extremely unstable'. Of this we were aware, because the papers had been full of the dismissal by King Hussain of General Glubb, the British soldier who had commanded the local army, and turned it into a disciplined fighting force to repel possible Israeli raids. Anti-British pressure encouraged by Colonel Nasser of Egypt had resulted in an Arab nationalist being put in his place. I flew to England with Antonia, leaving Julian to drive with our luggage. Half-way home, intending to make a very early start in the morning, and not wanting to disturb people staying in the inn, Julian had left the car in the square rather than bring it into the courtyard. He did not notice until his next stop that our luggage was missing, which meant not only had we had lost almost all the clothes but all our paintings, paints and brushes.

3

AMMAN JORDAN

SEPTEMBER 1956 – DECEMBER 1959

Once years ago
We'd paid a glancing visit to Amman –
I could recall a run-down Roman theatre,
And a still more run-down hotel. Of course
There were some problems; a few months before,
Glubb Pasha had been sacked, but the Embassy
Had a first-class staff, the house was quite agreeable . . .
Next evening someone said 'What about the news?'
We turned it on and caught the tail end of a phrase . . .'
in view of Colonel Nasser's decision to nationalize
The Suez Canal.'. . . This had little relevance for me . . .

CHARLES JOHNSTON (later Ambassador in Amman)

I T was September 1956. Julian kissed me goodbye, and drove off in the direction of Dover. He watched nervously as his new car was hoisted aloft by a crane and unloaded the same way at Calais and later in Beirut. Invited to the Captain's table for dinner he won a bottle of champagne as a prize for dancing (his partner was the captain's wife). Not until he reached the Syrian frontier and the unwelcoming border guards saw he was wearing shorts and that his mother's name was Miriam (both to them indicating Jewishness), did he get a flavour of what was in store for him.

I found it difficult to accept that there was no alternative for me but to occupy my mother's spare room with my little Putzl (Austrian for 'little cherub'). I had been greeted so often in Vienna with '*Wie gehts die kleine Putzl?*' that the name somehow stuck. It was not clear to me that the Foreign Office had any right to prevent me joining Julian. Had I enough money I could have booked myself on a plane, as I had done to Geneva. I was very annoyed that once again care and consideration for wives was not something to which the Foreign Office gave highest priority. Julian was worried less about my situation than that there seemed to be very little money in our bank account. He asked me to be very economical since it was dangerously low.

This was the last straw. I went up to London, found my way to the Foreign Office and firmly asked to see the head of the Middle East Department. A very young man was sent down to calm me. He gave me a distinctly funny look on the money question, hinting that husbands couldn't always be expected to be totally honest with wives over financial affairs. Then, after leaving me for 15 minutes, he returned and somewhat shamefacedly said that it appeared that Julian had been signed off from Vienna but not signed on for Amman, and promised that the missing two months' salary would appear in Julian's account forthwith. Though Julian's bank balance soon contained enough to enable him to buy a few stamps, he told me it was noticably less than he had been paid in Vienna, because the Foreign Office rule was that a diplomat only qualified for a full overseas allowance (an addition of about one third to one's salary) if he had an *accompanying* wife. Some years later these rules were updated. As to the Foreign Office's unjust views about the right of wives to be with their husbands, the young diplomat informed me that: ' *Wives and children not being with their husbands in the Middle East was a very important part of our foreign policy. It was to show Nasser that we mean business.*' I expressed great doubts that anyone in Egypt would notice, still less care if I was or was not in Amman. I felt doubtful that this was the real reason for my not being allowed to join Julian, nor did I like being treated as if I were an employee of the Foreign Office.

Julian's first letters from Amman were not encouraging.

'Amman is a small, hot, dusty town surrounded by desert, inhabited by people who owe everything they have to Great Britain but nevertheless do not like us. The press and politics are crooked. Most of the things that make life agreeable either have not yet reached Amman or come by road from Beirut and cost a fortune. The foreign community is small and know each other all too well. Contact with Jordanians is strained. I hadn't bargained for the anti-British feeling. I am continually stopped by police and asked for my papers and not at all politely considering we supported the country with twelve million pounds last year. Earlier this year the Ambassador's car was stoned, the Head of Chancery wounded and mobs attacked the British Council and the British Bank. A ten foot barbed wire fence has been erected on the town side of the Embassy and steel grilles put on the windows. A substantial armoury has been delivered which we are supposed to be able to use. The whole town is papered with huge pictures of Colonel Nasser with a technicolour grin. My work in the Embassy seems to be mostly keeping an eye on the spending of the money which we pour in. I even have a seat on the Jordan Development Board and can veto pipelines with a wave of the hand.

Antonia being bathed in
the laundry tub

Margaret on wall outside
our House in Amman

I was told that no Arabic was required for being Second Secretary in Amman but all the same I have decided that, by getting up an hour earlier, I can fit in a daily Arabic lesson before breakfast'.

When Julian arrived at the Embassy he found that he was not as keenly expected as he had been led to believe. The Embassy's immediate concern was with a terrible road accident. Just three days before Suez, two members of the Embassy and their wives, together with a Palestinian lawyer with an English wife, had driven over to Jerusalem for a bibulous lunch. On the return journey through the twisty-turny road in the Dead Sea valley, one car went off the road and overturned. The Palestinian wife was killed instantly, the legs of the Second Secretary's wife were broken; her husband, the driver, got off lightly with a broken wrist. The English wife was sent home to England and her husband went with her.

Julian's first task was to to go to the Headquarters of the Arab Legion and collect anything belonging to the dismissed British General Glubb. In spite of a widely held rumour that the General had enriched himself hugely in the 17 years of being in a very powerful position, Julian found only an alarm clock, some well worn clothes and a few books.

Letters from Julian painted the local picture:

28 October 1956

'A General Strike has been proclaimed in all Arab countries in protest against French policy in Algeria. A mob has just straggled past my house on their way to the French Embassy. They looked hot and tired, because the hill is pretty steep and they had a lot of cumbrous banners to carry and were wasting a lot of breath chanting antiphonal slogans. A distant banging suggests that they have reached the Embassy and met the police I am sorry for the French, but at least it is a change to hear someone else abused. As their embassy is presumably not working today, and it is still barely ten o'clock, I am afraid the building maybe damaged, if not sacked. We have the most elaborate scheme for defending the Embassy against hostile mobs, and I keep a little private armoury of tear-gas bombs in my desk, but the plan assumes that everyone will be inside the building when the attack starts, so what happens on Sundays I don't know.*

Later same day.

Awful day, sitting on the balcony listening to the mob smashing up the French Embassy, and I hear that at Jerusalem they actually got into the French consulate, set it on fire and wounded two people. At 3.30 I went for a stroll to see how things looked. There were twenty or thirty policemen lounging about by the French Embassy with shields and riot sticks, and heaps of stones and other missiles all over the road and round the building. The Embassy looked pretty battered. What happens when they attack us I don't know. We are right on the street and vulnerable on all four sides. Brutes – what do they know about Algeria? I suppose the whole thing was organized by the Egyptians out of pique at having been well and truly exposed over the Athos gun-running case. Still, I am sure that Arab nationalism is very soon going to sweep away what remains of the traditional Anglo-Jordan friendship. The king may hope to check the process, but if he doesn't go along with it he will lose his throne.

I could see the political situation in the Middle East was clearly uncertain. Anthony Eden could not accept that Britain was no longer a first-rate power, after all we had nuclear arms, a permanent seat on the UN Security Council, and military forces in both hemispheres. We also had a vital interest in the global free passage of goods. However the war had left us very short of money, and to economize, it was decided to bring our troops home from occupying the canal zone in Egypt. Abdul Nasser immediately announced that he was nationalising the Suez Canal and moving his army in to take their place. An outraged Eden, after top secret negotiations with Israel and France, forged an agreement for joint military operations and on 31 October invaded the canal zone. It was clear to Israel that it was to her advantage to play a major part in the invasion because after 1948 Egypt had denied passage through the canal to any Israeli-flagged or Israel-bound ships. In less than seven days, the entire Sinai peninsula was in Israeli hands.

The Suez venture came as much of a surprise to the staff of the Embassy as to those listening to the news in England. Amazingly, the Foreign Office had not even informed the Ambassadors, including our Ambassador to Washington, Lord Sherfield, about the Suez plan, so perhaps it was not surprising that Harry Truman, President of the US, was also in ignorance. Not until the fall of Eden were amicable UK–US relationships restored. Many people I knew were doubtful that I would ever be able to join Julian. What follows are extracts from more of his letters to me:

Tuesday October 30

Just seen the news of the Israeli attack on Egypt. God knows what happens next. The Americans, who were moving their diplomatic families out yesterday, must have had advance information. If the Jordanians are wise they will lie very low, and the Israelis won't attack them. If the worst comes to the worst (i.e. if Jordan is involved in war with Israel and we all have to clear out) I can pack everything up in the boxes, which fortunately still litter the garden, lock all the doors and windows and tell the landlord to keep an eye on the place. God save us. I hope it won't come to that.

Wednesday October 31

A frustrating day sitting about waiting for some instructions which never come, and trying to get the British community away. The Embassy has been full of missionaries, businessmen etc and their families, who all ignored the advice to leave which we gave them three times and now look to us to get them out in a couple of hours. The extraordinary and comforting thing is that Amman, though pretty tense, is still outwardly normal, with the shops open, the workmen building houses etc and no demonstrations. Of course they haven't yet heard that we are bombing Egypt . A macabre touch has been cast over the whole day by the arrival last night of a man from the Ministry of Labour, to investigate the RAF's problems with their civilian labourers. In the midst of these earth-shaking events he has been ambling about asking for copies of the Workmen's Compensation Act and demanding a car to visit the Ministry of Social Welfare.

Thursday November 1

The worst day. We spent it discovering just what a difficult thing it is to burn an archive.

Friday November 2

Last night, so as to avoid a hostile town on a Friday morning, we conveyed the entire British community, or what remained of it, up to the abandoned RAF station on the edge of Amman during the hours of darkness, They had to spend an uncomfortable night in a collection of wrecked barrack rooms. I shan't forget the spectacle of the seven Church Missionary Society ladies blithely ripping the pin-ups off the wall. The British community had had so many contradictory orders in the course of the last 48 hours that they were in a sort of coma and ready to comply with anything. This kind of thing brings out the best in some people. Mrs Bodger, the wife the Arab Airways engineer and the seven Church Missionary Society teachers accepted their barrack-room with absolute calm and a sort of blithe certainty that it would be very comfortable really, while Mrs Bodger's husband and his Arab Airways colleagues just scowled and showed the utmost scepticism over the number of people that we proposed to cram into the aeroplanes which leave for Beirut this afternoon.

Today, the Moslem day of rest, we all crept into the Embassy at dawn with provisions for a siege, got out the armoury and sat waiting for the onslaught. It never came. Looking back I think that the people were simply stunned by the news. Probably a good deal of old-fashioned fear entered into it as well. It shows how utterly bogus was the agitation about Algeria a fortnight ago. I don't think anyone who hasn't lived through a flap like this can imagine what it is like. One of the unexpected things was the actual physical difficulty of destroying files: Mountains of ash and the smoke filled the corridors. Also the relative importance of things alter strangely: the urgent letter to the Prime Minister takes second place to the problems of Miss X the C.M.S. teacher or Mr Y the local bank manager or Mr Z the man with the water drilling team believed to be somewhere out in the desert towards the north-east.

It is now noon and the amazing thing is that this morning has been completely calm. The people of Amman are either plotting something violent for this afternoon or they have been stunned by the news. Perhaps something like this (the Suez attack) should have been done years ago, and Captain Waterhouse was right all along. Perhaps .I can see the arguments in favour of our action: that in the end it will produce a more stable situation than we have had in the Middle East for seven years, that it will finish Nasser, that it will restore our position in the area etc, but how we justify it on moral grounds I cannot imagine. This is a peak in the history of the Middle East, on a level with the establishment of Israel. Also a peak in the history of imperialism, on a level with the Boer War.

We have a plan for moving the entire Embassy up to the Ambassador's and Head of Chancery's houses on top of a hill next to the king's palace. But for the time being we are all to stay where we are. Our cook and house boy are still gamely complying with the fiction that all is normal. The cook goes about muttering 'Bad people – very bad people' but I don't know who she means. By tonight most of the British subjects will be gone, and we shall be left with all the other British subjects by marriage, adoption, naturalisation etc. We hope that most of these will decide to stay. If they don't we shall have the evacuation problem all over again tomorrow, only twice as large and with people twice as difficult to deal with. Then there are the locally-engaged staff of the Embassy, who have started forming up deputations (which it falls to me to receive) enquiring what will be their position if diplomatic relations are broken off and the Embassy closes down. (The regulations, as usual, are cruelly unhelpful).

This surprising calmness reminded me of Dingle Foot's description of being in Amman at that point in the War when things were looking very black for us in North Africa. He was amazed that the Jordanians hadn't changed sides and decided to support the Germans who must, at that time, have seemed more likely to win the war. After the war he asked them why they had stayed loyal to Britain. Their answer was: 'We watched you walking d own the hill to fetch your paper from *Dar el Kutub* every afternoon looking so calm and confident and we said to each other: '*Wallahi, he must know something we don't*'.

Thursday, November 8

It has been a fascinating week to have lived through, provided that we have indeed got through it. Having clung on until now without either provoking the Israelis or break-ing off relation with us, the Jordanians would be fools to do either of these things now. Not that they are not capable of folly. Since the British Community left, the worst worries have been connected with the RAF. They moved from Amman to Mafraq as a precaution just before the Israelis walked into Egypt. Mafraq is an immense camp in the desert about sixty miles north of Amman. It cost millions to build and can take any known aircraft (today that is) – when a new and heavier type is brought out they just add a few yards to the runway at each end – but it lacks one indispensable thing, and that is water. The villagers along the road are so hostile that the ordinary water-trucks haven't been able to get through. The Jordan Army would send trucks, but they haven't enough for themselves. And the RAF could at a pinch keep themselves supplied from odd springs here and there, only each of these is swarming with grubby Syrians and rather smarter Iraqis. I suppose Mafraq was built on the assumption that the populace would always be friendly. Like a good many of the old assumptions about Jordan, this is not going to hold good in future. Then there has been the problem of the RAF's former civilian employees. To keep the move a secret, these were never told in advance, and they all arrived as usual one morning to find the place deserted. They then of course marched down to the Embassy, about 500 of them, demanding their wages, their pay in lieu of notice, their terminal gratuities and every imaginable kind of small private debt. The RAF are willing enough to pay, but everything has to be arranged through the almost inaudible telephone. The paying officer can't come by road, because he might be lynched; yet he can't come by air, because the Army won't give him permission. He can't come in uniform, again because he might be attacked; yet he can't come in civilian clothes because his C.O. won't allow it. And where is he to pay out? Not anywhere in the town, because that would excite a crowd; but not in the old RAF station, because that is in the hands of the Army, who won't admit civilians. We have been gradually resolving these contradictions, each one by patient yelling down telephones. Then there are the seven RAF horses – too expensive to keep, too precious to sell to farmers, too valuable to put down. Also several hundred pigs, which only a Christian could think of eating. And the little stall where a man used to sell sweets and bootlaces to the airmen; everything that he owns in the world is there, but the Army won't allow him in. And the 41 night watchmen, who were, it is true, on daily rates of pay, but were paid monthly: what gratuity are they entitled to? While the Middle East totters, this is what we have had to think about – and quickly too, or somebody will smash the door down.

The sad thing is the thought that, unless we turn on the Israelis pretty soon, Jordan will never again be a pleasant place for English people to live in. An astonishing amount of good will survives – in the Army, in the top civil servants who used to work for us in Palestine, in dozens of people to whom Britain and British money have done good – but the press and the radio are now simply poisonous, the King is said to be bitter and there are some hostile faces in the streets.

Friday, November 9

The atmosphere in Amman for the past 10 days has been perfectly horrible. I find myself avoiding people's eyes in the daytime and sheering away from them at night. A Cypriot wife has been spat at in the street. It looked yesterday as if the whole thing had fizzled out just too soon for us to get any benefit from our action, but the news this morning is that the Israelis have agreed to withdraw from the Sinai peninsula provided that Egypt ends the state of war. If we can make the Egyptians do this we shall be well away because the other Arab states will all have to follow suit and the other things should then come gradually one by one: recognition, revision of the frontiers, Arab-Israeli trade, use of Haifa by Jordan, re-opening of the Haifa pipeline, settlement of the refuges problem, acceptance of the Johnston Plan etc. But all this may take months or years.

Sunday, 18 November

It really looks as if the crisis were blowing over as far as Jordan is concerned. The King managed to get through the meeting of Arabs at Beirut without putting his name to anything outrageous. From now on things should start to get better provided the with-

drawal of British and French troops from the canal is not delayed. In a way it helps us for Syria and Egypt and Saudi Arabia to have broken off relations, because it means that the FO can consider Amman on its own.

On 24 November the Jordanian parliament unanimously passed a resolution calling on the Government to enter into diplomatic relations with the USSR and China and to abrogate the Anglo–Jordan Treaty, end our £10 million subsidy and remove the military and RAF bases.

In a letter to his father Julian pointed out that:

' provided we don't do anything to make ourselves any more unpopular than we are at the moment, the Government should be able to tell the Parliament in a couple of month's time that the replacement of British by Arab money presents certain practical difficulties, all of course attributable to the dastardly imperialiist attack on Egypt, and for the time being it is necessary to go on accepting the money which the vile Briish for their own sinister purposes are ready to go on paying – that is if we are'.

And a few days later:

'The road accident having decimated the Embassy staff, I have sent more letters and telegrams off my own bat than in two years in Vienna. The new Ambassador Charles Johnston, has arrived and is doing his best to get wives out here by 20 December since the only incident we have had is the explosion of a very small bomb outside the British Bank. This puts us on a level with Beirut where there has also been a small bomb, but way ahead of Baghdad where people have been killed and wounded in riots. Yet the Embassy wives in Baghdad have not been sent home. The atmosphere has been a lot calmer since the fighting stopped in Egypt. Arab Airways (a BOAC subsidiary) has resumed services with British pilots, and the British Council want to return, but I still cross to the other side of the road when I see a crowd listening to a café radio.

I took my gun the other day tramping for miles with Heath Mason over bare hills and up desolate watercourses not caring to shoot the little birds scurrying about among the stones or the pied Bulbul, or the queer kind of songless lark, or two ravens or one owl.

Our ambassador succeeded in persuading the FO that the situation was calm enough for wives to be allowed back, and on 10th December the daily flight from Beirut disgorged a flock of women and children, including me and Antonia, ecstatic to be re-united families again. Also on the same plane was Charles Johnston's wife Natasha, born a Russian princess. Her passport named Princess Marina of Greece as her next of kin. Her mother, a Princess Bagration, was shortly to become the Abbess of the Russian convent on the Mount of Olives. Natasha had charm and style and was full of gusto. The short brown-skinned man sitting next to her on the plane nursing an important looking box we learned was Mo, who had been Charles Johnston's batman during the war in Cairo, and the box contained his fez.

Julian drove me to my new home: a stone house on a hill surrounded by almond and pomegranite trees, overlooking the town, which had once been a Roman settlement called Philadelphia, one of the cities of the Decapolis, complete with temple and theatre. I liked the looks of the servants we had inherited – Julia, a plump Palestinian Christian cook from Jerusalem, and our house boy Moussa, a moslem – though the latter turned out to be more valuable as a tiller of the land than a butler. Towards the end of a dinner party he would do his party piece: cracking nuts by banging them on his skull with his hand. Julian had managed to find a Christmas tree, under which on Christmas morning lay two suspiciously identically shaped parcels. We had each secretly chosen the same present, an inlaid backgammon board from Damascus. Julia produced a turkey from the market. I suppose our Saxon ancestors must have thought Turkey was where the bird had come from. In Austria a turkey is called *Indiana* (the indian bird). In Amman it is called *Habash* (the Ethiopian bird). We gathered enough friends to have a party and taught our guests to play the version of charades which was conveniently common to both our families. It requires a knowledge of the classics and the bible, famous figures of history, nursery rhymes and a good collection of dressing up clothes.

Julian was given the task of master-minding the termination of the Anglo Jordanian Treaty, by which we were allowed Army and RAF bases in Jordan in return for £10 million support to the government. He proposed we withdrew our troops in six months and Jordan pay us 4.5m pounds for what they leave behind. Jordan might pay the first installment on May 1st but he doubted we would ever see the rest. He wrote to his father:

> '*It is a sad ending to the story of Lawrence, Peake, Kirkbride, Glubb and the rest, but I don't see how it could have been avoided, any more than the French departure from Syria or ours from India and Burma. In fact I think that Jordan's services to us and ours to her, were mostly rendered under the Mandate 20 or 30 years ago, when we established the monarchy, the Arab Legion and the beginnings of commerce and government and incidentally trained the Palestinian admnistrators who now keep Jordan going. So I don't shed any tears for the Treaty itself.*'

A week passed and it was dfficult to believe that a country's situation could have changed so quickly. On the domestic front daily life was delightful. I often walked down to the suq to shop with Julia. Most of the Arab women wore beautifully embroidered dresses and balanced a large cauliflower or a sewing machine on their heads as they picked their way gracefully between moth-eaten camels and over-laden donkeys. We would also go to the animal market and collect a sackful of camel and sheep dung to improve the garden soil. When we were ready to go home Julia would choose the toughest of the crowd of smallboys all wanting to carry our purchases back up the hill, all fighting to be rewarded with a couple of dirhams for their toil. From our terrace we could

Julia, our Palestinian Christian cook with Antonia in Amman

see the across the valley to a small encampment of refugees, but most of the Palestinians fleeing from the Israelis across the Jordan river had been sent to Zerka, about 12 miles to the north, where there were empty British Army huts and a river. The plight of the refugees had received much attention in British newspapers, and the retired headmistress of the Girls College in Jerusalem, Winifred Coate, living in the small village of Ottery St Mary in Devonshire, was so deeply moved to think of the girls she had taught being in such a desperate and hopeless situation, that she sold her house and moved to Zerka. When we arrived in Amman she had already found a water diviner who had discovered well sites, and she seemed to be spending the greater part of her money helping the refugees set up small businesses to support themselves. She would tour the suq herself, notice what things were not on sale, and set her refugees to making them. She equipped a carpenters shop, from where I commissioned a simple doll's house for Antonia. I borrowed the Ambassador's picnic basket and wine and thermos holder and had them copied by the basket makers, who also made a crib for Vicky. I still have many tablecloths and napkins embroidered by the women

Amman is perfect in March; within easy reach are the Ajlun woods, a perfect place for a picnic, and not much further away, Jerash, where the almost complete ruins of a Roman city of the 1st and 2nd centuries steadily mouldered in the scrubby earth, a very impressive example of Roman achievement. One of Julian's colleagues told us about the tremendous production of *Julius Caesar* which the British Council put on there a year earlier against a backcloth of the Nympheum. A battalion of the Arab Legion sold programmes, served drinks at the bar, acted any walking-on parts and kept out intruders. Bus loads of children were driven over from every school in Jordan and it was a full house for all four performances.

It was announced that Egypt, Syria and Saudi Arabia had promised to provide Jordan with 12.5m pounds a year for the next ten years. One Sunday, as we drove out along the Jerusalem road, we suddenly saw, 20 yards in front of us, a vast swaying mob carrying cheer leaders on their shoulders bearing down on us. There were no side turnings. We pulled up behind a stationary bus and I tried to look inconspicuous by keeping my eyes on my feet. My heart was thudding as they came abreast and we expected the car to be overturned any minute. But amazingly, although the mob hesitated slightly as they reached us, the river of men passed us by. We learned later that they were on their way to the Iraqi Embassy to protest about the arrest of a Jordanian student. Julian wrote to his father:

16 March 1957:

'The discussions about ending the Treaty continue. Our opponents are pretty cunning

Palestinian lawyers. We discovered that the military stores and ammunition about which we had been arguing, had in fact been stolen by the Jordanian Army last November. One of them had simply removed the fence and everything was carried into their compound. I shall not forget the bland way in which Abdullah Rihani, Minister of State for Foreign Affairs, rose to his feet and asked, spectacles glinting, 'But on what basis exactly do you claim that these installations belong to you at all?' I can't think how the Ambassador remained so calm and kept his temper.

The local inhabitants were very hospitable. Apart from those who have fled from Palestine and the Israelis, there were Circassians who were expelled from Russia a hundred years ago, a few Armenian doctors and dentists, and Arabs of Beduin origin. The Suez debacle did not seem to have discouraged them for long from wanting to throw parties and invite all their friends to meet the newly arrived English diplomat and his wife. Hardly had I settled in before I found myself elected President of the Women's Club, set up by some of the wives of the Americans working for UNRWA (United Nations Relief and Works Agency) to encourage women of different nationalities to get to know each other over coffee and cakes. The previous president had left, and they wanted to have a Palestinian succeed her. Since two candidates were needed, they asked me to stand *'Since no one knows you, the local candidate will be elected'*. They had not realised that the shame of possibly not being elected would be unbearable for an Arab, and so when it came to the vote, I was the only candidate. This is in spite of my arabic being only good enough to negotiate purchases in the bazaar and getting rid of troublesome small boys. It was difficult to learn Arabic because most of the people I met had been at school in Palestine and learnt fluent English. Twice a week I gave English lessons to a girl called Arab Abdul Hadi, a seventeen-year-old who was one of the few who hadn't. My teaching was to have been bargained against arabic conversation for Julian, but the girl's family jibbed at her being with a man without a chaperone – *'not that they would have minded themselves, of course, but one must think of the neighbours'*. Giving a lead in an unpopular direction is not the Arabs' strong point, in politics or in anything else . Gradually we learned to accept their differences in life-style. It was not possible to persuade an unmarried woman to join us for a picnic or go and look at excavations of ancient tombs. They would shake their heads and say they couldn't : *'Someone might talk'*. I remember a guest saying a propos of something I said *'Poor Abdul Harim'* Why poor? I replied. *'His wife. Very thin'* Mostly I thought them grossly overweight from all those sugary cakes. But that was the way their husbands seemed to prefer their wives. I am sure they thought my way of looking after my little daughter was very wrong. Antonia was dressed in orange and blue dungarees made by me, (they thought only suitable for a boy), and she would be playing with whatever rubbish she found while I sat on the ground painting.

While Julian was working in the Embassy I often explored the countryside. Schliemann had discovered Troy by following all the geographic details in contemporary literature. Encouraged by this I consulted the bible for references about the Ark of the Covenant in the same way and found it recorded that it had been carried 'to Kirjath-jearim and given to Abinadab' for safe keeping. I went to Madaba with a spade, confident that this would be a good place to start even if I had no idea what the Ark of the Covenant would look like, nor if Kirjath-jearim and Madaba were one and the same place. Both had fine views of the plains of Jericho and the Dead Sea laid out below. The difficulty was that wherever I dug, after a few centimetres I hit rock. However Madaba was certainly the most likely spot and also the very best place for picnics. I always hoped one day before we left we might find the Ark but we never succeeded.

The lot of the amateur painter in Jordan is not easy. One day I was painting with Julian and we were so pestered by little boys that we retreated into the car, but the crowd of children was so large, that we could no longer see the view at all. When we protested they banged on the windows and scratched the paintwork in retaliation. One day we were invited onto a balcony to paint out of the way of the children, but the larger boys could not be stopped from throwing stones at us. Another day we were with a family from the US Embassy sketching down by the river Jordan, and we were arrested as Israeli spies. We spent many hours in the police station trying to get released. Our American friend confronted them again and again with his diplomatic passport: 'Do you or do you not recognize the validity of this document?' I don't think they could read English. I suppose the difficulty of getting away from curious people is the lot of sketchers in the Middle East ever since Edward Lear.

Asked by his father whether he was finding his work interesting and enjoyable and whether the grandson of an old friend of his should be encouraged to join the Foreign Service, Julian replied :

'The complaint about the increasing shift of responsibility from the hands of diplomats into those of politicians is often heard, but I don't myself think there is much in it. In my five years in the service I have seen three major rounds of negotiations. I would say that the presence of a Minister as one's nominal boss only demands extra qualities of tact, persuasiveness and force of character in the task of keeping him up to the mark, if not indeed on the rails at all.

In general I am delighted with my career and I am sure most of my colleagues would say the same. Of course there are exceptions, but I know more unhappy dons and schoolmasters than foreign servants despite the mathematical odds against this being the case. There is no doubt it is by far the most interesting of all the ill-paid jobs. In what other career would I be master of a large house and garden (rent free) with a car and a gramaphone, an expensive camera and a lot of other nice belongings, giving orders to two servants and still saving at a rate of about £400 a year? I stand a fair

chance of promotion to First Secreary soon when I shall be entitled to a doubled sal-
ary plus a transfer grant, an entertainment allowance and a rent and representation
allowance. If I pass the Arabic examination, I get more again for the next five years.
The recent warnings about superannuation have caused a flutter in the service, but
the services have lived under a similar axe for many decades'.

Since Friday and Sunday were designated non-working days we were sometimes able to take three days off, and we took advantage of this to explore the
West Bank where we grilled chicken outside villages whose names were familiar
from the Bible. Antonia came happily with us on most of our excursions, was
never bored, and even aged two was good company. We visited the building
where Christ came before Pilate, the stable at Bethlehem said to be where
Christ was born, Beit Sahour, where the angel appeared to the shepherds, the
site where Abraham might perhaps have tried to sacrifice Isaac; and perhaps the
most spectacular of all, the Mount of Temptation above Jericho, where Jesus
was tempted by the devil to make a public display of his divinity. We were
lucky to have Canon Every (from the Anglican Cathedral) to guide us round
the church of the Holy Sepulchre in Jerusalem, this time in a dim religious evening light which faded the garish Latin and Greek finery. We were accompanied by the unmusical wailing of the Armenians winding their way round the
labyrinths of chapels. The basic structure of the church is hidden by the iron
girders put up by the Mandate government after an earthquake. There have
been numerous schemes for their removal but all have come to nothing. The
Roman Catholics want to pull the church down and build something modern,
the Anglicans want to pull away the plaster and reveal, they hope, more of the
11th century church, the Armenians, the Greeks and the rest resist all change,
fearing that any change might result in loss of their present rights. Result,
nothing gets done and about an eighth of the church is completely unused,
the subject of a lawsuit between the Abyssinian church and the Copts. When
Jerusalem was part of the Turkish Empire, the Turks, trying to put a stop to
the eternal wrangling of the Christians, decided to give the keys of the Church
of the Holy Sepulchre to an Arab moslem family, the Nusseibehs, with one
of whom we were good friends. After forty years of marriage, the senior male
Nusseibeh decided to take a new and younger wife, but, as he was very fond of
his old wife, the mother of his children, he asked her to choose whatever she
would like in compensation: the farm in Jericho, diamonds, travel? She replied:
'I would like the keys to the Holy Sepulchre' and that is apparently where they
still are, in the care of the current head of the Nusseibeh family.

We forced our poor car up and down rocky tracks to other places with ancient traditions. Two hours away in Kerak was the remains of the only Crusader
castle in Jordan and two hours further one came to the incredible splendour of
Petra. In an easterly direction there were four or five desert Ummayad hunt-

ing lodges and in Jericho an Ummayad palace with fine mosaics. In the desert there was a small lake at Azraq near whichT.E.Laurence holed up one winter. In a westerly direction there were hidden waterfalls and hot springs where our landlord used to go regularly for his rheumatism.

Dick Sanger, the American Minister, was determined to see Khirbet Qumran, the Essene monastery near which was the cave where the Dead Sea Scrolls were found. He suggested we join him, undeterred by knowing that it was closed to visitors without a special permit and that it was heavily guarded. Sanger was confident that he would be able to 'bull his way through' and he was quite right. A letter empowering him to be out after curfew, and the fact that he was large and American got us through. We plunged through scrub intersected by narrow wadis at a speed of about 2 miles per hour until suddenly we found ourselves on the shore of the Dead Sea. As it is 1412 feet below sea level the heat was terrific. The heavily salted water makes swimming impossible, but the potash in its water was used by the Egyptians for mummification, and is sold in modern times for fertiliser. Refreshed by cold beer, we forced our cars up a one in four rise to the Monastery. The surrounding caves which decorate the western side of the Dead Sea like hundreds and thousands, are where the Essenes buried their library of scrolls in about 63 A.D. when they left to escape the maurading Romans. We found a rope and lowered each other down into the cave where the scrolls were written and another nearby where the pots were fired. Most of the scrolls are small fragments of parchment, copies of books in the Old Testament and also Judaic texts not in the Hebrew bible, copied by hand but with various mistakes, which means they could not be used, or kept in a synagogue, but also were not permitted to be destroyed, as they remained sacred.

Many dubious stories circulated after the news about the discovery of the scrolls leaked out. One rumour was that they revealed an Essene Messaiah who instigated baptism and was crucified in Jerusalem in about 50BC and who had also preached most of the Sermon on the Mount. Our Ambassador, Charles Johnston, had beaten us to see the site of the Essene Monastery, and had met Pere de Vaux, a friar and the keeper of the scrolls. Charles was sure that, had there had been the slightest suspicion of a discovery of such facts, the monk would have destroyed all trace of it without scruple.

We were invited to a small party for King Hussain. I was alarmed when Natasha told me that it was customary for me to ask him to dance. Since he came up to my shoulder, I decided on a ten-minute chat instead. Nobody could be more friendly, polite and easy to talk to but I found the most striking thing about him was his complete self-control and dead-pan expression, so I hadn't the faintest idea what he was thinking. Otherwise the chief event of the week was the wedding of the Prime Minister's granddaughter to a wealthy Saudi. I and about 100 other women were invited to eat pistachio-nut ice cream in a room which might comfortably have held 20. After an hour the bride appeared in western style wedding dress and the groom presented her, piece by piece, with sparkling jewellery as all the girls, young enough to jump on chairs to get a good view, shrieked with delight and applauded wildly. Tentative enquiries elicited the fact that not even the bride's father knew whether the groom had a wife already, apparently it is not the done thing to ask. We left with sugared almonds encased in hideous, but clearly expensive, boxes lined with dark red padded silk.

The desert in April was always a glorious sight with fields of waving grass and wild flowers, most striking of which were the wild black tulips and red anemones. One day we were fortunate to see an immense endless winding crocodile of people, animals and baggage streaming north to Syria from their winter quarters. These we learnt were the Bani Hasan, one of the few remaining Beduin tribes. So delightful was the weather, we decided to pay a longer visit to Petra while we had the chance. A new road to the south hardly deviated from the Roman route. Milestones record that M Flavius Marbulo of such and such a legion built this stretch and for several miles you bump along closely packed Roman stones where the only landmarks are the Beau Geste style police stations where one has to persuade a policeman with a red and white headscarf that one is not an Israeli spy. When the road ended, we left our cars, scrambled over rocks until we turned a corner, and we were faced with the much photographed Kasbah.

The mountains did indeed have a curious dribbly look as if chocolate ice cream has been poured over them, as Edward Lear's cook pointed out. The Nabateans who built Petra seemed to be happy to continue to cut their temples and tombs out of the sandstone rock even though they must have been aware that it would crumble. They chose to scatter their buildings over a large area, which makes it hugely satisfying when one finally reaches a temple after scrambling up staircases for about an hour. It was certainly a site like none other, and we enjoyed every minute of our time there.

We slept in caves divided into cubicles by canvas curtains, and we washed in hot water brought by beaming little boys. Breakfast was served in an enormous applique Egyptian tent. There were signs that what we were enjoying must be the remains of a camp once run by Messrs. Thomas Cook. We were being served lunch, when those who understood the news in arabic became alarmed. The Nabulsi government had fallen and there were demonstrations in the main street of Amman. Since we had an eight-hour drive ahead of us and the clouds promised rain, we decided to make for home at once. The Americans had taken over as the No. 1 target for rioters who were declaring voluably that they wanted to cease being an appendage to the West. However their new supporters failed almost before they began. After three months neither the Syrians or the Egyptians had paid a cent.

In May 1957 Julian wrote to his father:

> *The political situation could only be described as very volatile. Jordan has got through seven Prime Ministers in the last three years and King Hussain, impatient with Nabulsi for dismissing everyone in the cabinet who supported the Hashemite rule, started the new year by giving up any attempt at democratic government. Following serious rioting he has dismissed the Prime Minister, purged the legislature of Palestinian nationalists, banned political parties, ordered a curfew and a blackout, and imprisoned several hundred people without trial – in fact setting himself up as a dictator. This action has brought fifty or so journalists hastening up from Beirut to be first with the story of the riots and the imminent fall of the Monarchy. What has been surprising is the ease and completeness with which the population apparently has become swiftly converted from being pro-Syrian and pro-Egyptian and pro-Russian into opponents of all these things. Ernest Bevan, our Foreign Minister, clearly felt he could not do anything but condemn the abolition of democratic government, but there is no doubt that the Nabulsi government was well on the way to ruining the country.'*

The Press Attache took Julian on a round of newspaper offices to meet the editors, most of whom had been known supporters of Nabulsi six weeks earlier. All now decried the old government and applauded what the king had done. The great mass of the people were calmly disputing whether it would not be better for the King to suspend the constitution altogether. They rally to someone who shows that he is in charge and intends to stay there. Anyway, the country seemed calm, the schools have reopened, the curfew has ended, and the check points have been removed from the roads to Damascus and Jerusalem.

The Military Attache asked Julian to go with him to see a hut in the desert which had been used by the RAF and had been offered to the Embassy. He described the day:

> *'It was a glorious day for mirages; the heat not only created what looks like sheets of water but also elongated the tiniest bushes into towering palm trees. The desert is made of everything except sand and we rattled along over grit, gravel and stones. In one place the ground was strewn with shiny black pieces of basalt like lumps of coal, and in another there were vast mud flats several miles long, now bone-dry and gaping with cracks. The police there were unexpectedly welcoming and plied us with tea out of a kettle and arab coffee from a copper pot with a spout like a pelican's beak as we sat on rolled up army blankets and rested our elbows on saddles. The RAF hut turned out to be an unsightly shack of corrugated iron full of broken furniture and useless cooking equipment. We headed for Mafraq, the RAF station half way to Baghdad, where we tried to persuade the RAF to hand over the hut in a habitable state, but I fear our offer came too late; they had already given it to the Arab Legion.'*

To make up for my having missed the desert trip, we set off the following week end for the West Bank. As we were driving down the new road which the American Point Four team have built (shortening the journey to Jerusalem by two hours) we saw what I thought was an immense flock of starlings darkining the sky. No they weren't locusts either, Storks! By the hundreds, on their way north for the summer, I suppose. The sight of them wheeling down to land all together made a stupendous sight. We drove through Nablus and Ramullah, through pure Mediterranean scenery of olive groves and cornfields, to the monastery of Latrun where Trappist monks make a quite agreeable wine. It really brought home to us what the Arabs have lost in Palestine. Latrun is a salient into Israeli territory and just before the border all cultivation stops and there are fields of weeds and thistles beyond which we can see Israeli water sprinklers revolving over ploughed fields.

On June 13th we celebrated the Queen's birthday with an evening party for 500 in the ambassador's splendid garden, which possessed the only lawn in the country. Julian was given the job of whispering into the Ambassador's ear the names of each approaching guest. (Fortunately he had a kind of long stop to help him if he faltered).

A few days later we had an immense party for Antonia's second birthday: all the children we knew between 6 months and 6 years with their parents. We left the children to amuse themselves with four rubber paddling pools, a sandpit and a donkey as well as a swing which was our present to Antonia. I have never been more exhausted in my life – such an enormous mound of refreshment needed, tables and chairs to be borrowed, balloons to be blown up and the temperature of the ice cream and the iced coffee getting hotter every minute. I think everyone had a great time even though some of the children broke into tears as they unwrapped their presents. With a little judicious swapping everyone left more or less contented.

Jordan, in a valiant attempt to cope with her balance of payment position, limited the sale of meat to four days a week. This was not difficult to bear because Jordan is a paradise for vegetarians. Vegetables are incredibly cheap and plentiful. Globe artichokes have been on sale for the last five months, followed by melons, apricots, peaches, enormous succulent plums, figs, grapes, pomegranites and delicious mulberries. Marrows cost twenty for twopence and cucumbers and tomatoes only a little more. We also used to go searching for a kind of wild artichoke, called *a'kub*, which one finds hiding below little bumps in a ploughed field and excavates with a knife. My garden was particuarly magnificent since, wherever there was a space, self-sown hollyhocks would rise up in glorious colours, rising to about 10 feet without a drop of water. Apparently it was the Crusaders who first brought them to England, their name originally pronounced as *Holy Hock*.

The latest American gift to Jordan of £20m, making £30m in all that year, was received with no more gratitude than we used to get for our own subsidies. The doctrine that the poor have a right to be maintained by the rich is well established here, applied to countries, as it is in England applied to individuals. The one concrete and useful result so far has been the granting of permission for the Embassy and the rest of the foreign community, to use the former RAF swimming pool at the airfield. Both we and the Americans have been trying to get this for months, but it was the dollars that did the trick.

For the Fourth of July the Americans have planned a huge aquatic party and hired the largest pool in the country, at the former British Army base at Zerka ten miles away. The 4th of July came round and with it the American party. Next day both Julian and I developed fever, but after about a four or five days in bed, I decided we ought to try getting up. With the greatest difficulty and throwing his weight entirely on me, Julian managed to reach the sitting room. I was seriously worried. The local doctor less so. He said it was flu and some of his patients never walked again after serious bouts. About a day later one of the nurses from the Church Missionary Society, whom Julian had met at the time of the Suez crisis, dropped in. She advised me to get him to the American Hospital in Beirut immediately. This was difficult. The regulations in those days were that medical treatment would be repaid only if taken in the country to which one was posted. A friend in the Beirut Embassy arranged for a doctor from the American hospital to be on hand the minute we reached our hotel. He at once diagnosed polio but said, since the fever had abated, there was nothing now to be done but complete rest and later exercises.

Understandably Julian's parents were devastated by the news, because a polio epidemic had swept England and the newspapers were full of stories of iron lungs and life-long paralysis. It occurred to us that it might be a good idea to consult Jack Yekutiel, a leading Jewish epidemiologist, and married to Julian's cousin Margaret Cairns. This meant going through the Mandelbaum Gate into Israeli Jerusalem, and into the orthodox quarter where Jack and Margaret were living. We had to unscrew our Arab number plates and put back our GB ones. Jack endorsed what we had been told in Beirut. Julian had been extremely lucky and he need not expect that it would affect his career. I was even luckier to have had the fever without the paralysis. Before that 4th July I had known little of Polio. The newspapers had reported the discovery of the Salk vaccine, produced in America, which I think was available at that time, and perhaps accounted for why none of the Americans at the party were affected. In England, because of Polio's relation to infantile paralysis, it was not thought that grown-ups were susceptible. A more alert Medical Officer of Health in the Foreign Office might have thought about vaccinating diplomats posted to the Middle East, especially those posted there for the first time. One wife became a lifetime cripple and one diplomat in Baghdad died. Julian was indeed lucky. So was I —three months pregnant. After three months of rest ,and his iron determination at exercising, movement slowly came back into his legs, but left him with a permanent limp and a curled up left foot. It put a stop to his famous spin bowling and also to being able to deliver a competent tennis serve. Fortunately he regained the use of his fingers and he was delighted with discovering that it was possible to give them practice by taking down the BBC news in Arabic at dictation speed! The Ambassador arranged for all our expenses to be reimbursed, and ordered Julian to take as much leave as he needed. So we packed our things and moved with Antonia for three months into a hotel at Beit Mery, in the hills above Beirut. When Julian began to feel more himself, we would go down to the beach and I would help him to move as much as he could in the water. Julian even managed to enjoy an evening concert in the ruins of the splendid Temple of Jupiter at Baalbek. The music was not particulaly good but any music sounds good when you have heard nothing but gramophone records for the last twelve months. Eventually Julian returned to work, and I returned to painting, but without Julian who told me he was giving it up as I was the better painter. Not, I think true, and he was certainly the more meticulous.

Christmas 1957 came round. The political situation in Jordan remained unchanged: martial law remained in force and from time to time a bomb would explode somewhere not far from Embassy houses. Everyone we knew gave splendid Christmas parties. Julian was making steady progress with walking and I was heavily pregnant with Vicky, but we were both well able to enjoy the Ambassador's magnificent party at the Residence. The table was the most beautifully decorated one I had ever seen. Somehow Natasha acquired boxes and boxes of firework-filled crackers (even though their carriage was forbidden by post or by the diplomatic bag). Encouraged by her, we pulled crackers until we could hardly see across the table, while she sat clapping her hands and calling her beaming Egyptian servant to bring another four boxes. I was somewhat worried about the affect of polio on the foetus of our new baby, but fortunately Victoria Ann showed no signs of being affected when she was born in January1958 in the Italian Hospital, a curious feature of which was that, in common with most of the hotels in Jordan, all the lavatory paper had GOVERNMENT PROPERTY stamped on every sheet.

Lying in bed surrounded by roses, gladioli, stocks and narcissi, I looked out of the window as the light over the green and purple hills changed every second, beginning and ending with spectacular dawns and sunsets. Their splendour may possibly have been due to the terrific storm which in one night had turned all the dry *wadis* into a sea of swirling mud, and caused the smiling waiter to clump in with gum boots on his feet, quite a contrast to his white gloves and the elegant tray of delicious Italian food. On the ground in front of the hospital a large crowd of women made ullulating noises louder and louder every day. I asked a nurse why, had it been a male child perhaps? '*Uno e morto*' she replied in an impassive kind of way as if it were something that happened too often to worry about. We discovered that the religious order to which the nurses belonged allowed them to go home only once every six years, and in between they got very little time off, so we organized a picnic outing to Jerash for as many as we could get into our car.

Now that the political situation was calmer, we seemed to be having an endless stream of visitors. While I was enjoying a rest in hospital after Victoria's birth, Julian was invited to dine at the Residence with the Duke of Rutland, the Duchess of Argyle, and Miss Frances Sweeny (who Julian reported, as well being as stunningly good looking, was able to beat the Prime Minister three times at backgammon). Lady Diana Cooper (friend of the Ambassador of course) also visited with her son John Julius Norwich, at that time a junior member of the Embassy in Beirut.

Some visitors stayed with us: the Queen's Messenger, who arrived weekly with official letters from the Foreign Office, and took our reports back to London, and there were achaeologists, glad to take us to be the first to see the inside of a Middle Bronze Age tomb in return for board and lodging.

4th May 1958 Julian wrote to his father

'Difficult to resist describing our last visit to Jerusalem, this time, with Robert Curzon fresh in our minds, to see the eastern Easter ceremony of the Holy Fire in the Church of the Holy Sepulchre – but nobody was trampled to death this year. They could have been, all the same, and burnt to death too. We had a good position in the first of the galleries round the inside of the dome, and could look straight down on the throng of Armenians, Copts, Greek Orthodox, Russian Orthodox, Syrian Orthodox etc. as they stood jammed against the opening from which, after several hours of waiting, the Holy Fire duly emerged. To while away the time the pilgrims chanted raucous slogans, led by young acolytes or neophytes or proselytes carried on the shoulders of others, while the rival sects set up rival noises in the other parts of the church. A company of police prevented them from actually coming to blows, and kept open a narrow path for the eventual procession round the Tomb of Christ, when the Holy Fire is handed out through the loophole in the tomb, and is received by special runners in tennis shoes, who race off with it through the mob to certain special altars. Each wants to be the first to have their candles lighted, and in an astonishingly brief space of time the whole church is full of flames and smoke. At this stage we discovered that the chapel behind our seats was the headquarters of the Armenians, who set up a tremendous racket with a huge cracked bell and two of the most primitive musical instrument that I have ever seen, not excluding the Arab one stringed fiddle. It was then that the American Consul, who had climbed onto a step to take a photograph, was swept off his feet by the rush for the doors and broke his leg, so there was one casualty after all. We got away quicker than most, thanks to the doorkeeper at the Consulate-General, who had

brought with him a heavy silver-mounted stick, a relic of the mandate if not earlier, which he alternately jabbed into obstructing backs and bounced on the flagged floor to produce a dull booming note. Later that day we went to the Abyssinian Monastery where a stylised search was carried out for the Body of Christ at the end of which, not having found it, they announce:' He has risen.' We were admitted to the emboidered tent where the Abyssinian priests sat. The atmosphere here was much more dignified, but more African than anything else, with strange wailing music and a large tom-tom. They say they are having difficulty in keeping up numbers and that in a few years there may be no one to beat the tom-tom or carry the jewelled umbrella'.

The christening of Victoria was not something we shall easily forget. The Anglican Archbishop in Jerusalem had telephoned earlier to ask the names of the godparents. After I had named them, he replied that he could not accept Natasha as a godparent as she was not a member of the Church of England; the Anglican church being in communion with the Russian Orthodox Church was not good enough This put me in a difficult position as I did not fancy having to explain the situation to Natasha. I asked an old Oxford friend to be godmother *in absentia* instead, but I said nothing to Natasha about having been banned. The Archbishop arrived very late having been held up by a road block and an accident. We whiled away the time by taking photos of Vicky in all her finery – a superb Victorian robe, about three times as long as her, and covered from top to toe in a riot of frills, handed down from my father's mother. Vicky was given several beautiful presents, including a heavy gold chain with a pendant cross in turquoises from Natasha. Eventually the Archbishop swept into the compound with a scrunch of brakes. For about twenty minutes all went smoothly, but just at the moment when the godparents were about to renounce the devil and all his works, Natasha fell back in a most terrifying faint, and had to be carried out by Julian and the Ambassador amid hopeful whispers from the children behind of *'Is she dead?'* Carrying her was made easy by the fact that she had become as rigid as if she were a piece of furniture. Neither of the Johnstons spoke afterwards about this or offered any explanation. We went back to our garden for much needed refreshment. I dipped a finger into my glass and offered it to Vicky. She smacked her lips enthuastically on the champagne and opened her mouth for more.

In February 1958 King Feisal of Iraq persuaded his Hashemite cousin in Jordan to join the the Arab union of Egypt, Syria and Iraq. This was celebrated with a tremendous jamboree in the desert. An enormous marquee was filled with Arab Legion soldiers in their splendid ceremonial dress and both kings made speeches. Feisal's delivery was diffident and did not carry well. Then came Hussain, who surprised all of us speaking with a loud rolling bass, so unexpected in such a small man. I understood not a word, but there was no doubt that he raised the spirits and impressed even those who did not understand. It was a short-lived union. Feisal and his pro-British government were assassinated in July which put paid to the Union. Its collapse caused the political situation once again to became uncertain.

Foreign journalists appeared like flights of starlings occupying every available bed in Amman, eager once more to be in at the kill, or rather to be on hand to report the end of the Hashemite monarchy. Among them came Kim Philby, begging the use of our spare room and claiming the close friendship between his father and Julian's father in Jedda as his justification. There was little truth in this. My father-in-law had despised St John Philby for trying to ingratiate himself with Ibn Saud by taking a local woman into his bed, abandoning his English wife and four children and declaring himself a muslim. However we were always glad to have visitors. Amman society could be monotonous. If Julian knew anything about Philby's dubious career he did not warn me. I was amazed that Philby spoke with such a very pronounced stutter. When I mentioned this after his flight to Moscow, I found no one seemed to have noticed any speech impediment. Years later I chanced on a book by Philby's number two in the Iberian peninsular during the war. He described his boss as being a good mimic who often adopted an accent or a stutter when he chose to. Perhaps it gave him longer to think up a reply, or perhaps he thought it could make his interlocutor sorry for him. Perhaps one was less likely to be suspicious of anyone with an impediment, and less critical of the truth of his words?

The foreign journalists never got the story they came for. The U.S. stepped in and promised more generous monetary support for Jordan. Charles Johnston's personal influence in London managed to get two battalians of British Paras stationed in the Army barracks to show support for the Hashemite King, a clear indication that any rioting would be firmly put down. Not all our Palestinian friends were pleased by the arrival of the Paras, and to show their hostility, the Committee decided not to make the officers guest members of the tennis club. Before Christmas the Paras left and so did the troop of Hussars who had been defending the port of Aquaba in case of incursions from the Israelis.

September 1959 came and James was born in the Italian hospital. The congratulations I received from my Jordanian friends this time were from the heart: 'NOW YOU HAVE A SON!'

In December, after almost four happy years, Julian was told to return to London and would be promoted to First Secretary. We were going to miss greatly those long weekends which we liked to spend based in the Polish hospice in Jerusalem, where the food was delicious. I went to say goodbye and thank the cook for the good meals we had had. I told her that though we had always eaten well in my childhood, my father, being a clergyman, thought plain cooking had a special affinity with Godliness. The Polish cook replied:' *We are taught that though God made all the animals, plants and fruits on earth, it is our duty to bring them to perfection, and make them as good to eat as we know how: It is like making a prayer.'* We were also going to miss driving down on hot summer nights to the Dead Sea and eating spatchcocked pigeons by the light of the moon. Julian would miss being a star in amateur theatricals or in Shakespearean productions organized by the British Council. Most of all we were going to miss exploring Jerusalem and the West Bank, being shown Kathleen Kenyon's new excavations in Jericho, picnicking in Jerash or Ajlun, and those wonderful excursions to Petra and the desert castles.

4

WESTERN DEPARTMENT, FOREIGN OFFICE

1959 – 1963

When diplomacy fails war tends to follow
PRESIDENT WEIZSÄCKER 1985

L OOKING out of the car window in London in the third week of December 1959 Antonia asked why so many cars had the initials GB their bumpers. She thought Julian had replied that it stood for Grey Britain, which seemed an appropriate description. Apart from the weather, the atmosphere in England still echoed Harold Macmillan's election slogan 'You Never had it so Good!'

We were homeless. We left Vicky with my mother and Antonia and James with friends and went house hunting. Anything conveniently accessible to Whitehall that we liked, we could not afford. Clearly the Foreign Office had a vision of their employees having a comfortable family home to which they could always retreat, with parents always ready to welcome children, and of course plentifully supplied with servants. It was no good thinking that either of our families came into this category. My father had died, and my mother no longer lived in the large rectory in which I grew up. Julian's parents had retired to a cottage with roses round the door, but no piped water or electricity and a long way from any shops. If there was food needing to be chilled, a flagstone had to be removed from the floor of the kitchen and the food lowered in a bucket down a well. Julian's younger brother described his mother:

The audience listened in wonder
When Miriam Bullard held forth,
With 'Lightning's much safer than thunder"
And 'South winds blow down from the North'.
She crossed when the lights were at amber
And gave precise dates for the Flood,
Walked slowly when showers descended –
'It's rushing that wets you in rain!'
And, once knowing how the plays ended,
Would never watch Shakespeare again;
To remind her, kept handkerchiefs knotted,
But of what, was unable to say;
And harvested fruit till it rotted,
When she carefully threw it away.

GODFREY BULLARD

Julian's father was the son of a London docker, who, by hard work and driving ambition, had risen from being a Third Dragoman in the British Embassy in Constantinople, to becoming His Majesty's Ambassador in Teheran, where he hosted the Prime Minister for the Teheran Conference, and was rewarded with a KBE. At this point he decided to be known as Sir Reader Bullard, because, he said, 'There would be no shortage of Sir William's but only one Sir Reader.' Nancy Lambton, who had worked under him in the Embassy in Teheran, described him thus:

'He was a man full of wisdom and common sense with gentle, if somewhat ironic, sense of humour. His honesty was unflinching, his hatred of injustice uncompromising. His strictest censure and disapproval was for humbug, hypocrisy, double-dealing and calculated worldliness. His outlook was stern in its demands, but he was always ready to see the best in others. His joy in the simple things of life was unlimited, and his kindliness and compassion, shown in the most unobtrusive of ways, were boundless. He was pre-eminently one in whom self was forgotten'.

To his wife and her family, he was known as Haji, although he had never made the required pilgrimage. I think it was Giles who decided to refer to him as 'The Guv'nor.' And it was Giles and Julian who greeted him at Oxford Station on his return to the UK at the end of the war, doubtful if, after six years absence, they would recognize him.

Fortune was kind to us. One of Julian's colleagues was looking for a tenant for his house in Blackheath – the opposite end of London from where we had decided to buy a house, but our need was so urgent that we accepted with relief. The road to Whitehall ran down the side of Greenwich Park and a For Sale notice hung outside one of the houses. Three months later we signed documents making us the owners of a fine but dilapidated four-bedroom Georgian house. The asking price was £4,500. Even this was more than we had in the bank, and Julian decided to beg the owner for a reduction. Startlingly she replied: '*You're not a Jew are you?*' We were undeterred by the fact that it was semi-derelict, had no heating except one gas fire, and the sanitation was antediluvian. We found we had chosen very well. Half the houses in Crooms Hill had been bought by people like us, not long down from Oxford or Cambridge with children the same ages as ours, all unable to afford a house nearer to the centre of London. Five houses away lived Nick and Claire Tomalin, details of whose on/off marriage we followed with great interest. No. 14 was owned by the unforgettable Ann Broadbent, one year behind me at St Hilda's College, where she was the first girl to wear Christian Dior's New Look. Hers was one of the grandest houses in the road, decorated by her with flamboyant wallpapers, junk picked up for a song at street markets, and portraits of unknown men labelled as family ancestors. She had cards printed: 'Ann Broadbent Interior Decorator', and taught me that the mere presentation of one of these cards was enough to knock 25% off the price of the most expensive paint or wallpaper, and also entitle us to buy our food wholesale. The finest houses were occupied by an older generation of clever and distinguished people: Jill and Cecil Day Lewis, Bert Lloyd, who collected folk music, and a painter called Noel Adeney, 'a member of the Camden Town group'. This was the start of a totally new life, so absorbing, that what Julian did from Monday to Friday became almost a closed book to me.

Julian had the Berlin desk in Western European Department. It was already clear, while he was in Amman, that his job would be no sinecure. Germany had been divided into four zones, each under the control of one of the four Allies. Bonn had been chosen as temporary capital, but Berlin, completely surrounded by the Soviet zone, which had now been given the name of the DDR, remained of vital importance. By 1960 the Russians also had nuclear weapons and the West had abandoned whatever faith they ever had in Soviet goodwill. As Ernest Bevin had earlier written: '*The Russians have decided upon an aggressive policy based upon militant Communism and Russian chauvinism ... and seem determined to stick at nothing, short of war, to obtain their objectives and is clearly directed to challenging this country everywhere*'. The gradual take-over by the Communists of the Czechoslovakian government in 1948, had given the first inkling that wartime alliances were breaking up. The Korean War and later the Vietnam War heralded the Cold War as The Free World versus Communism. Another element of the Cold War was the goal of the Soviets to support and encourage the spread of communism wherever they could, which in England involved supporting strikes and the nuclear disarmament movement.

Greenwich: *left to right:* Vicky, Robert, Antonia and James on the sofa 1963

22 Crooms Hill, Greenwich our first house

Shortly before we returned from Amman, Nikita Khrushchev had issued the Western powers with an ultimatum that their troops must withdraw from Berlin, and announced that within six months the Soviets would delegate to East Germany the control of all lines of communication with the West. The reason for this was the large seepage of East Germans escaping to the West. Walter Ulbricht, the DDR's chief decision maker, had convinced Khrushchev that the country could not survive economically unless the border was closed. Closing the border meant that the western powers would have access to West Berlin only with permission from the East German government. The western allies could not accept this, and were determined to claim their legal right of free access through right of conquest, since a peace treaty had never been signed.

It was Julian's task to deal with the important confrontations of the Cold War, which brought us close to a nuclear war. Throughout 1961 and 1962 there was continual harassment at Check Point Charlie, which marked the border in Berlin between East and West, and where East German Border guards continually refused passage to allied soldiers and diplomats for one new reason after another. The Allies would send several trial probes to uphold our rights, supported by lines of tanks at Templehof airfield, which were countered by 33 Soviet tanks being driven through the Brandenburg Gate, ten of which drove to within fifty metres of the sector boundary. The US tanks then moved to an equal distance on the other side. This was termed Cold War by Proxy, It was extremely stressful for Julian's department never knowing whether it might lead to war as the tanks loaded with live munitions faced each other. He would come home in the evening to find me fully occupied with three small children, scraping paint, painting woodwork, wallpapering, cooking, and going to art classes.

Alec Douglas Home, now Foreign Secretary, wrote to Dean Rusk: '*Berlin is not a vital interest which would warrant determined recourse to force to protect and sustain.*' President Kennedy was also all for avoiding any action that might threaten war, and Kennedy and Khruschev met in Vienna. The West did not have sufficient forces for a conventional fight, and yet did not want to be seen by its Western Allies as too ready to use nuclear weapons in response to the East's rejection of the right of the western allies to travel to Berlin. Kennedy and the Allies tacitly accepted that the wall could remain in place. The Soviets for their part agreed to remove their tanks, provided the US tanks made the first move. Kennedy declared: '*It's not a very nice solution, but a wall is a hell of a lot better than a war.*'

Neither Julian or I had ever before hung wallpaper or used a blow lamp, or stripped old pine furniture, or used a sanding machine, but soon we were both carpentering, painting and plastering in every spare moment. Julian threw

himself into DIY, determined, as in everything he did, to do it as well or better than anyone else. He would do two hours work blow-torching old paint
off the walls, then wash as well as possible under a cold tap, gulp down some
coffee and catch the 8.25 am train to Charing Cross. Soon we learnt that you
did not have to remove all the old paint before putting on a new coat, and the
walls got painted rather more quickly. For some weeks we had no plumbing
and we had to use the huge Slipper baths in the Public Bathhouse. Living in a
working-class part of London had its advantages, such as the generous supply
of parks equipped with swings and roundabouts where at 3pm every Saturday,
we could also take the children to watch live theatrical entertainment. We delivered Antonia every day to the local London County Council infant school
and Vicky to the Robert Owen nursery school. For both these completely free
schools we had nothing but praise (and Antonia's included a hot lunch). Soon
the school run collected other children from Crooms Hill.

My mother was lent a holiday house above Bude in Cornwall for the month
of May. There was room for all of us to join her. The children and I took the
evening train to my mother in Somerset, leaving Julian to put varnish on all
the landings and stairs from top to bottom. He painted himself out, shut the
door, got into the car and arrived about 8.30 a.m. while we were in the middle
of breakfast, having been stopped by the police for speeding on the way. Remembering how cold our French honeymoon had been, I joined The Jigsaw
Puzzle Club of Great Britain, to keep us amused on days when the sun did not
shine. I paid a month's trial subscription and collected the first two puzzles
from what looked like a private house in Pont Street. When we opened the
parcel in Cornwall, we found the puzzles were more than somewhat over the
heads of our small children, so it was the three grown-ups that pieced together
the puzzles in the evening, puzzles with no two interlocking pieces, and no
straight edges. Each puzzle was accompanied by a small book in which previous members had written their comments. Some thirty years later, when Princess Margaret invited us for tea on the island of Mustique, we arrived to find
her hard at work, wearing nothing but a bikini, piecing together a huge jigsaw
puzzle of a familiar style. We had clearly met another member of The Jigsaw
Puzzle Club of Great Britain.

By the end of the summer of 1962 the house improvements were finished
and huge bills started to come in. Although Julian and I were prepared to do
everything in the way of decorating, we could not build on bathrooms and
lavatories, or rewire, or install central heating. We realized that surviving, even
on the increased pay of a First Secretary, was running us into debt. Julian's
Aunt Gertrude invited him to help himself from the pile of pre-Raphaelite pen
and ink drawings stored in her garage, which Julian sold at Colnagi's in Bond
Street, (though doubtless it would have been a better financial investment to

have kept them). Aunt Molly left Julian £100 from which we bought a desk for £40, but something more drastic was needed.

How I thought I had time for a full-time teaching job, I am not sure. It was the only job that would allow me to be at home when the children were not at school. I filled in a form. I found two referees. I had a searching medical examination, and was summoned for an interview at County Hall at which I was given two pieces of advice: *'You can't teach anyone anything unless you love them'*, and *'Never let it be known in the staffroom that you have an Oxford degree.'* I was delighted to find a vacancy teaching at Kidbrooke, the first girls' comprehensive school in London, not far from where we lived. I chose to teach in a comprehensive school because these were a new breed of schools introduced by the Labour government to solve a major difficulty in State Education, caused by streaming children at 11 according to their ability. The core principle was that they took all children aged 11, regardless of their ability, and gave them a chance to develop their talent whether for sewing or ancient Greek. We were also keen to experience the education which the State provided free, but which so many of our friends rejected.

Kidbrooke School had engaged me to teach business studies to girls of 15 and 16, and also to take three classes of 14 year-olds who needed to be occupied until the law allowed them to leave, after which they would look for jobs as hairdressers or tea-trolley girls, earning money to enable them to afford the clothes or the amusements to which they felt as 15 year-olds, they were entitled. These were the least popular classes to teach, since throughout the year the classes continually reduced in numbers. I was told I had a free hand about what I taught provided the girls were kept reasonably quiet. I chose to offer a mixture of topics that I hoped would be useful afterwards in getting a job. We wrote answers to advertisements for employment, weighed letters and parcels, learned to do business on the telephone, putting questions and answers intelligibly; we practiced receiving clients, learnt ways of copying documents and how banks work, how to keep a petty cash book, and enough of P.A.Y.E. to enable them to understand their own pay packets. Sometimes I hesitated as to whether it would not be better for them to be learning to write legibly and to spell, but I decided it was most important to offer a course which aroused their interest.

Most of these girls had less than average ability and an unprepossessing appearance, with jerseys and skirts that were far from clean and often needed mending. Their minds were on other things, be it boyfriends or domestic difficulties. They were often absent when the strain of four days intellectual effort would begin to tell, and they preferred to stay at home and do Mum's shopping. These were the girls who, if a ceremonial visit brought important visitors to see over the school, would find their classes hurriedly shifted to the most unobtrusive part of the building. They never had pens and pencils. Every third lesson they had 'left their notebook at Gran's'. At first I approached their lessons with reluctance and sometimes dread. However, the more difficulties I had with individual girls and the more I learnt about their difficulties at home, the more I enjoyed our lessons even though I felt sometimes it was I who learnt and not they. Then came the Parents' Evening. Two parents settled themselves down beside my desk and said '*We felt we wanted to meet you, Mrs. B. Our daughters enjoy your lessons so much.*' I asked their names. Impossible! I supposed what the daughters must enjoy was the freedom to sit in the back row and have a nice gossip before I spotted them. But no, it seemed, they went straight home and told their mothers what they had learnt.

At a conference in Bath, the Head of Music spoke about the difficulty she had getting girls for the choir and the orchestra because girls with musical talent were the same girls as those working for university entrance. Academic girls also wanted to sign on for cooking and sewing. Others, less gifted could not even thread the sewing machine. Since this was against the whole comprehensive idea, The Headmistress, Miss Green suggested that perhaps the Head of Music should try teaching somewhere else.

A noticeable difference from my own school days was the lack of pressure from examinations and the almost complete lack of competitive spirit. The classes were (secretly) streamed according to ability, known only by the initial of the surname of their form mistress. Reports bore only the simple comment: Good, Fair, Poor, or Disgraceful. It also surprised me to find how comparatively well teaching was paid, even though I had an entirely irrelevant degree in Politics Philosophy and Economics, but like the Foreign Office, I was not paid less because I was a woman. The other side of this penny was that, had I been a man with a wife and ten children I should have been paid exactly the same. The Foreign Office at that time paid married diplomats a one third addition to their salary, which struck me as a fairer deal than ignoring the teacher's domestic situation. On the other hand, women diplomats were made to sign a document promising to retire should they get married, which I thought clearly unfair. Had I been in their shoes I would not have felt bound by an agreement I had been forced to sign so many years earlier. How strange it was that none of them put up a fight against this.

Whatever our view of the British state system, Julian and I would need to send our children to a boarding school when we were posted abroad, the fees for which would be largely paid by Her Majesty's Government. There could not have been a greater contrast between the modern and almost luxurious atmosphere of the comprehensive school and the chipped green and cream paint, the bare boards and the make-shift equipment of the fee-paying boarding schools we visited.

Somewhat to my surprise I found I was again pregnant and my teaching career was brought to an end three months before the expected date of Robert's birth. London County Council regulations considered having an obvious bulge in one's stomach too distracting for the girls. They were also easily distracted by male window cleaners.

On September 11th 1962 Julian flew to Moscow for three weeks. The Embassy was temporarily short of staff. My guess is that Julian suggested that since he had continually to deal with Soviet-backed trials of strength, direct knowledge of the Soviet Union would be a help, while never having been there put him at a disadvantage.

Julian wrote from Moscow:

It is perishingly cold here and pelting with rain. At the airport we were introduced at once to the classless society (diplomats to the front of the queue and having to fill in forms with questions only in Russian or Chinese). Russia has a special smell: equal parts of Russian petrol, Russian tobacco and Russian soap (or lack of it). The Embassy looks like a Viennese palace. I am staying in one of the flats in what was the old stables, with Michael Duncan and another member of the Russian Secretariat. I have a desk in Chancery but not much work. I have been told it would be utterly useless to sit in the Embassy all day but that I should get out and get the feel of Moscow and try to make contacts with some Russians. How? I think my clothes would mark me as a foreigner without a doubt. One suggestion is to try different barbers until you find a talkative one, or encourage your children to start talking or playing with other children.

Julian spent his daytime hours exploring, going by metro to visit the Kremlin, the Tretyakov and Pushkin galleries, stumbling on a film being shot, and deciphering shop notices such as 'There is for sale milk' in a shop labelled 'Milk'. Sadly, the communists had spoilt Moscow with monstrous blocks of flats in dirty grey or pink – Stalin's cathedrals. In the evenings Julian and Michael ate bortsch and kotlyetty (cutlets) at the National hotel. Michael considered that the capital had drifted a long way westward since the barbarism and eccentricity of the Stalin era, and was now spiritually part of Eastern Europe.

Julian wrote:

'For the first 10 days it never occurred to me that I might be followed. Then on Saturday afternoon Michael Duncan and I went out to a group of churches 10 miles from Moscow and were followed all afternoon by two 'tails.' We hopped off trains just in time to catch them exchanging hats or lurking in entrances to an underground Gents. It was the same on Sunday at Zagorsk. In the evening I got off the bus, watched the tail get off, got on again, all of which he copied. I was in the centre of Moscow, not in a sensitive and prohibited area. I visited Tolstoy's town house with places laid for lunch and a half-finished boot on its own lathe, and went to the puppet theatre and saw a take-off of a variety concert. Musically clever as well as technically extraordinary. I saw

nothing better while I was in Moscow. We were lucky to get permission to go to Pskov near the Estonian border at the weekend. It is a former imperial palace on a splendid bluff overlooking a great bend in the Moskva river and the plain beyond. A string of timber barges were rounding the bend on their way upstream when we arrived, and were still rounding it three hours later when we left. When I get back to London I shall be a lot less sympathetic to last minute requests from the Soviet Embassy.' (After Russians banned foreign diplomats from going further than 15 km from the centre of Moscow without special permission, the Foreign Office told the Soviet Embassy in London that they would have the same restriction, but Russian diplomats were always telephoning at the last minute pleading a special case).

Julian returned to London to be greeted with the news of the Cuban missile crisis, a part of the Cold War that did not come under Western Department, though it was the moment when the West and the Soviet Union came closest to nuclear war. Nikita Khruschev had secretly supplied nuclear missiles to be used as a bargaining chip, to 'give the Americans back some of their own medicine'. What he had not reckoned with was the capacity of US aircraft to take high-resolution photographs which meant that President Kennedy had time to plan a naval blockade to prevent Soviet ships coming within 500 miles of Cuba. After a little secret diplomacy, the Russians removed their missiles and in return the US agreed not to attempt to overthrow the Castro regime. This time Julian's role was to persuade Alec Douglas Home to support Kennedy, and in this he was successful. The Foreign Secretary expressed his views in the Lords:

'There has been a good deal of speculation about Russia's motives. To me they are quite clear. Their motive was to test the will of the United States and to see how the President of the United States, in particular, would react against a threat of force. If the President had failed for one moment in a matter which affected the security of the United States, no ally of America would have had confidence in United States protection ever again.'

Christmas approached and inspired by the Russian puppet theatre, Julian set to work making a theatre for the children. I was required to create curtains able to pull apart on request, and to paint ANTONIA'S PUPPET THEATRE in Russian capitals on the front. I put the children to work tearing up copies of *The Times* and mixing flour paste in order to make papier-mâché heads for the puppets, later to be coloured and clothed and given hair cut from Antonia's pigtail. Julian had brought presents for all of us from Moscow. Vicky tore open her parcel but said with disappointment: *'Daddy, I didn't want three Russian dolls that fitted inside each other.'* Julian looked at her coldly. *'Oh! what did you want?'* *'I wanted a box with mouses in it and when you opened the box they would fur your hand'.*

My fourth baby started to arrive two weeks earlier than expected while Julian and I were watching *That Was The Week That Was,* on TV, but fortunately the baby decided to wait until the midwife and her assistant arrived on their bicycles the next morning. Claire Tomalin came round and kindly scooped up the three older children, bringing them back when Robert was tucked up in his cot. James' comment was: *'Mummy those women have left their baby behind.'* I explained it was our baby. He took another look and announced*: 'That baby's going to be my friend'*. When Robert was three months old, we let our house, watched our belongings being packed into a huge van, and piled our children, and anything we found we had forgotten into our new Morris 1100 estate car, and set off for the Embassy in Bonn. Our car came with a manual which said that the drive was so smooth you could thread a needle or drink a cup of tea while the car was being driven. I tried without success to do both of these things. After spending three years being a 'Cold War Warrior' the FO naturally appointed Julian as 'the Berlin Referent' in Bonn. It was March 1963.

5

BONN, GERMANY

1963– 1966

The priceless asset of the diplomat is that he is there
LIVINGSTONE MERCHANT, U.S. Diplomat 1964

I N March 1963 when Julian arrived in Bonn, Germany was seldom off the front pages and it was his role to deal with problems that arose in Berlin. He and his opposite numbers in the U.S and French Embassies and in the German Foreign Office, felt themselves spearheading our defence in the Cold War. Between 1948 and 1949 the Russians had refused the western Allies access to Berlin through the Russian sector of Germany (the GDR), but had been totally defeated by the airlift which brought one and a half thousand tonnes of food and 3,500 tonnes of fuel into Berlin every day. The Allies felt they were fighting for liberty against communism and in surviving the Russian attempt to seize control of Berlin, they had won an important battle which countered the Communist takeover in Czechoslovakia some years earlier.

However, most of the Embassy wanted to talk about nothing but the Profumo Affair. Quite suddenly the atmosphere in Britain seemed to change. George Blake and John Vassal, British citizens, were found to be spying for our enemies. *Lady Chatterley's Lover* was brought out by Penguin and completely sold out the first week. The Sunday papers started to reveal a sordid affair which involved the Soviet Naval Attaché, a 19 year-old call girl, a dubious osteopath, Lord Astor, the swimming pool at Cliveden and the Secretary of State for War. The aristocracy and members of the Cabinet may have done such things before, but no one had told us about them in such detail. The dinner parties in Bad Godesberg, the Bonn suburb where most of us lived, talked about nothing else from the soup to the coffee.

We had been allocated a modest and unattractive house in Bad Godesberg, which held our family of six and a nanny only with difficulty. It had one advantage – our friendly and very agreeable neighbours were the von Hase family. Karl Gunther von Hase was a diplomat, later seconded to head the Second TV Channel, and after that appointed Ambassador in London. When we arrived, they came round with a loaf of German rye bread with little dishes of salt and sugar embedded into the top – an old German custom to welcome people moving into a new house. Renate von Hase advised us to send Antonia to the Robert Koch Schule, a state primary school for children of both sexes with parents from all walks of life, where she stayed until she was nearly 10. She was fortunate in having an exceptionally good teacher of her class. No praise could be high enough for Herr Frings' skill in coping with one child who had not a word of German. When she answered him using the familiar second person singular (as he had used to her), he silenced the giggles in the class, and told all the other children that there was to be no laughter when she made a mistake *'She is clearly intelligent and she will soon learn.'* After 6 months, he said that he would no longer make allowances for her not being German. Antonia told us that on one occasion a guest teacher came to take her class and told stories about his childhood. One began something like *'After the British bombed our apartment building in Hamburg, my family moved to the country'*. Some of the boys started to tease her about this in the playground. This was reported to Herr Frings who became very serious, shut the door and told all the class that the war was the fault of the Germans, not the British, and that the boys should never be proud of Germany's part in it. Antonia spent two years at the Robert Koch Schule and one at the Amos Comenius Gymnasium, doing so well that she was allowed to skip the first year in the Gymnasium, not something that I would have expected in a country so addicted to Order.

Before leaving London, the Head of Personnel Department had asked Julian to do what he could to improve morale at the Bonn Embassy, in particular that of the junior staff. Because nobody expected it would be 44 years before the British Embassy returned to Berlin, the housing arrangements were somewhat haphazard. Higher grade diplomats were fortunate to have inherited spacious villas in a pleasant neighbourhood, but non-diplomatic staff were housed in inferior flats in a working-class area. At school Julian had always played a leading role in theatricals, and even in Amman he had appeared in *Dial M for Murder*. He decided to make the widest use of the available talent by putting on a Christmas cabaret show. He wrote most of the lyrics and skits himself, and luckily there was a Cambridge music scholar, a great ragtime pianist, among the diplomats. The German administrative staff, asked to turn the Embassy cafeteria into a theatre with a stage, curtains and lighting, understood at once what was required, explaining that most of them had been prisoners of war in England, where they had had a good deal of experience in creating stages! Thus began the tradition of the British Embassy annual theatrical production which became an important feature in the calendar, and was still going strong until, after the wall came down, the Embassy moved to Berlin, and ghetto life became a thing of the past.

I fear I did Julian no credit by getting into the bad books of the Head of Chancery, Tony Duff, over several things I did while we were in Bonn. The first was after his daughter (much the same age as Antonia), had come to tea and borrowed *Black Beauty* to take home to read. Her father spoke to Julian severely about the very unacceptable thing I had done – lending to someone else's child a book without asking her parents' permission. They considered *Black Beauty* much too sad for a nine year-old. And then there was the guide book I produced, which he ordered to be destroyed. I had compiled '*What's Where in Bonn*' thinking it would be useful for new arrivals, especially for junior wives not accustomed to living abroad. It was not a very high-class production, in fact there were a good many typing errors. I remember that the stable where one could hire horses told riders that they would be charged double 'If you bring back the horse's hat,' but it also included useful pieces of advice such as suggestions for amusing the children at weekends, swimming pools which offered waves every 15 minutes, and where to find ponds for skating. I did the layout and design myself and had it printed very cheaply but even so it cost me about £25 to have 100 copies printed, so it was a blow when the Head of Chancery ordered all copies to be destroyed. Why? Shopping in Bonn could be baffling: each of the Allies had their own shops, primarily for the troops, but also open to Embassies. At the American Commissary one paid in dollars, in the NAAFI one paid in British Army token money called BAAFS, in the French Economat in francs, while one could also buy things in the German shops measured in kilos and priced in Deutchmarks. My guide book included a handy table showing which shop had the best bargains. Tony Duff wanted my book destroyed on the grounds that if everyone took my advice, the NAAFI (where prices were highest) might be closed down, in which case the Americans and French might refuse to allow us to use their shops.

I was also in hot water on the occasion of the Queen's first state visit to Germany after the war. Our Ambassador, Frank Roberts, was so very keen that everything should go without a hitch he sent round a memo: '*All leave cancelled for the next three months*'. The Bullards were not alone in thinking that this was ridiculous. As is usual on such occasions, the host country gives a grand dinner followed by a return one from the visitors, but since our Ambassador's residence was not large, it was decided that the Queen should host her dinner in a once famous hotel on top of the Petersberg, one of the Seven Mountains across the Rhine from Bonn. The hotel had been occupied during the war by the German Army and needed major refurbishment. This meant that absolutely everything for the Queen's dinner, including the food and drink, had to be flown in. I happened to hear that one plane was entirely full of bottled water and rashly divulged this titbit, with a scornful comment, to a journalist friend. Next day's headline was: *German water not good enough for British Queen.* In England this would not have been worth more than two lines but the Germans are extremely particular about the water they drink, never drinking what comes out of a tap. I was immediately identified as the likely source of this story and the Bullards were told they would be punished by being left off the list for the Queen's dinner party. Senior diplomats were not amused. It was surprising how much space the German press gave to this story, but in the end all was well. The media concluded that the reason why the Queen was not prepared to drink the water of Bad Godesberg (which was after all a spa town), must be because, in order to make the English tea satisfactorily, one must have the proper English water, and not just English, but bottled Malvern water. In the end I was allowed to walk behind the queen carrying the bunch of flowers she was to lay in front of the statue of Beethoven. 'A lady in waiting 'mit angedeuteten Knicks' was how the local paper described my attempt at a curtsey in front of a huge crowd in the Beethoven Platz – most embarrassing.

Bonn was one of the largest embassies, so there were plenty of families with children much the same age as ours. David Cornwell was also a First Secretary, and had already had two crime novels published. Tony Duff asked to see them. Two days passed without comment, and David couldn't refrain from asking if he had enjoyed them. Tony's reply was: '*I returned to them as a cat to its own sick.*' We went on holiday in Brittany in a camping van, taking with us his latest manuscript: '*The Spy Who Came in from the Cold*' on which David had asked for Julian's comments. After the book was published to such success, we went skiing with the Cornwells in Lech in Austria, where David was besieged by journalists wanting to interview the author of the book on the top of the best-seller list. Sometimes at week-ends we took the children to an old mine we had discovered on the top of one of the Seven Mountains. We would take a picnic with several other families and let the children amuse themselves pushing the rusty trams along the narrow railway with the smaller children on board, shouting and singing.

One day invitations reached all diplomats ranked First Secretary and above for free admission at a gala evening in a newly opened casino in Bad Neuenahr, a little further up the Rhine. We accepted out of curiosity. To our surprise we found the Ambassadors of all the poorest nations were very much in evidence at the gaming tables. We wondered if perhaps their salaries were so low that their only chance of surviving would be to try to double them. Not far from Bad Neuenahr was the Nürburgring, a huge motorracing circuit which also attracted gamblers, the Bullards not among them. Julian and I had been taken to a Point-to-Point once where it was clear that we were expected to put money on the horses. This I did reluctantly, and was laughed at by those who knew a lot more about horses than I did. To everyone's amazement my horse won and I was handed a fistful of notes. I was pleased until I found that I was expected to treat everyone to champagne for the rest of the day. This made me dismiss gambling as a fool's game.

During our first week in Bonn I met Lieselotte Vogel, a very keen painter with twin daughters the same age as Antonia and a husband in the Finance Ministry. She and I signed on for courses at the University, sketched in the Eiffel together and remained friends for life. Her husband told us that his bad eyesight had excused him from military service during the war, instead he had been made to write the regulations which would be enforced had the Germans occupied the British Isles. Julian thought we ought to join a choir since we both liked singing, and he asked the advice of a German diplomat, at the time in hospital having his toe-nails removed to prevent infection, in preparation for being posted to Africa. The choir in which he sang was delighted to have a substitute. Conveniently, evangelical churches had choral music only on feast days, so we sang a wide range of non-religious music every Monday evening and were only occasionally required to give up our Sunday mornings to perform in church.

In March 1964 one of the large villas, in a road hitherto reserved for diplomats of the rank of Counsellor, became vacant and finally we had a room and a table big enough to entertain. I can't remember why we had Alan Bullock to dinner. He was Master of St Catherine's College, for which Arne Jacobson had just completed its elegant modern buildings. I treasured and kept the flattering letter he wrote to me afterwards: *'It is a long time since I have enjoyed an evening so much, both for the food and for the company. I have had a good deal of official hospitality in which the objective triumphed over the noun. It was a great pleasure to come into a house where both host and hostess seemed to enjoy entertaining and really made one feel welcome'.*

In December 1958 a terrible story had appeared in the Press: a British diplomat's wife had killed herself and her two children. The only house her husband had been able to afford was a cottage in the depths of Sussex, which meant he had to leave early and would arrive home late. The *Daily Express* said because she was not British, nobody had welcomed her, so finally she had killed herself and her family out of loneliness. None of us felt blameless about this tragedy, and the story had the direct result that soon afterwards the Diplomatic Service Wives Association (DSWA) was founded with a regular newsletter and meetings with talks and refreshments so that we would get to know each other. The DSWA would also act as a kind of trade union. I was elected onto the committee and wives were encouraged to write to us and make their difficulties and suggestions known. We later learned that the media had not given a totally true picture of Diana Bromley's story. Neither her husband nor the Foreign Office nor any diplomatic wives were really to blame. She was 'not British' only in that her grandfather was said to have had an Indian wife. Her husband had known she was mentally unstable and she had three times had to be put into in a mental home. She came from an interesting family. Her uncle, who acted under the name of Boris Karloff, was the mad murderer in the film *Arsenic and Old Lace*, and her grandmother had been a governess to a royal prince in Siam, and an account of her life became the film '*The King and I.*' However the event was the catalyst which caused the Foreign Office to take some responsibility for the treatment of spouses. The Plowden Report of 1964 specifically mentioned the useful contribution to the success of a mission made by the wives through helping with dinner parties and receptions, and proposed that there should be an increase in marriage allowances, and that our children should be allowed two tickets to join their parents each year at government expense instead of one, a proposal which was soon acted on.

We were on mid-tour leave and I was in Oxford collecting James from the Dragon School, when I found Oxfam had taken the end lease of a shop in the High Street, and filled it with fairly shabby books and parts of books. On paying £1 you could take away as many books as would fit inside a plastic bag. This was an offer I thought should not to be missed. I carried away two great finds: one a novel about life in Cambridge written by Margaret Bullard (but not me), the second *Memoir and Correspondence of Caroline Herschel* by her niece, long since out of print, and telling the moving story of an eighteenth-century German woman's utter devotion to her brother, the discoverer of Uranus, who occasionally allowed her to look through his telescope when he was away. Searching the night sky on her own, she discovered no fewer than seven comets. This opened a new interest for me and for a long time I pondered about writing the story of Caroline Herschel. I found that a story of such selfless devotion was not a marketable commodity, and I abandoned the project, but not my interest in Caroline.

Early in 1965 Julian was told by Personnel Department that he was to be posted to the Canadian Defence College in Kingston, Ontario. He was not best pleased. He told me he didn't want to get onto the Defence Circuit. Julian told Personnel Department that he did not think he had the qualities required for the Canadian Defence College, but received the reply that notices of a posting were expected to be regarded not as a suggestion, but as an order. It chanced that those at the Defence College were on a world tour, and at that very moment were in London, so Julian asked them about the course. I asked what the wives did while their husbands were inspecting defence installations.

'*Oh! we have a great time. Mostly we go bowling.*' After turning things over that night, Julian decided to go back to Personnel and agree to be posted to Canada. '*Too late I fear there were many people who were only too delighted to go there!*' Head of Personnel said that all he would now be offered would be the post of Commercial Secretary in Baghdad. The new policy in the Office was that all diplomats should be *au fait* with commercial matters, since this was of great importance in our current financial state.

On the calendar soon after was Encaenia, the Oxford jamboree at which Honorary degrees are awarded. Before the ceremony Rohan Butler used to invite his friends to a silver tumbler of brandy sour in his room in All Souls. After the ceremony the new Honorands and all the good and the great were invited to lunch in the Codrington Library as guests of the Fellows of which Julian was one since 1951 when he was awarded a Prize Fellowship. I found myself talking to Patrick Reilly, a senior diplomat with whom we had lunched at the Paris Embassy on our honeymoon. He asked about Julian's next post. I told him the saga of the Defence College: that Julian was now threatened with Baghdad by way of punishment; that he was not best pleased because he did not want to be labelled as an Arabist, nor was he keen to do commercial work. Patrick said '*Idiots.*'

Most of our leave that year we spent in Castletownshend a town in the south west tip of Ireland where we rented Mall Cottage, which belonged to the Somerville family. We had become friends with Dan Somerville and his wife Celia in Amman, where he worked for the British Council. It was an ideal place for a family holiday. We were advised to appear at the Church of Ireland morning service on Sundays, where we would meet the non-catholic families. We would then be on the approved list to be included in birthday parties, tennis tournaments, treasure hunts and sailing races. If we were regulars at Mary Ann's bar, we would not be included. Sometimes we were ferried about in small dinghies after dark to picnic on an island in the rain, sometimes it was a lovely evening and the tide was high and we fished for whitebait dressed in our swim suits, dragging a net into a little inlet. When we saw it enclosed millions of little fish, we scooped them into an old pillowcase and let the water drip out. We then lit a primus and fried them, washing them down with beer followed by blackberries and cream.

Back in Germany we planned a grand party for Rohan Butler and his wife Lucy who were *en route* for the Historians' Conference in Vienna. We invited the Ambassador and his wife Cella, Professor Max Braubach (author of the Life of Prinz Eugen of Savoy in five volumes) and another Professor with a long line of academic honours: Prof. Dr.h.c. Dr h.c. and I borrowed a very impressive silver candelabrum to make our table look grander. I had been reading Browning's poem *How they brought the Good News from Ghent to Aix*, following the ride on maps, but baffled by what actually the good news must have been, and why it was necessary to carry it so swiftly. I was very disappointed to find that neither of the Great Professors could offer any solution. But later I was told that the entire story was Browning's invention. How extraordinary to write several pages in which nothing much happens about an event that never had happened at all!

At the suggestion of Herr Frings, Antonia joined a four-week summer camp run by the Red Cross in the South Tyrol, taken from Austria and given to Italy in the settlement after the First World War. This would help her fluency in German. Her teacher's daughter Dorothee was also going and would keep an eye on her. The camp was nominally for poor, working-class city children. However, we filled up the forms, concealing neither her rude health or her nationality, and off she went in a long hot crowded, shabby, special train on a journey of many hours in a compartment packed full of girls from the Ruhr. She returned brown and happy, full of stories of climbing up to a high Alp to collect cheese, with a repertoire of comic songs and also a bottle of wine which she proudly told us that she had managed to get more cheaply than the other children. She had seen no signs of anything Italian except for the money, the postage stamps and the policemen guarding the water supply.

Besides the modest castle on top of steep hill from which the mineral water flowed – and after which the town was known as Bad Godesberg – its other proud feature was an elegant 1790 neo-classical building known as La Redoute, where Beethoven had once performed before Joseph Haydn, and which was used by the President for his New Year Reception. It had recently been opened to the public as a restaurant with prices greater than we could afford. The French Minister, Francois de la Gorse, an elegant bachelor, invited us to dine there. We were surprised to find we were his only guests. An expensive wine, chosen with much care was poured into his glass but waved away for some reason and a second bottle brought. As we had yet to taste it, we assumed this was justified, but we were extremely embarrassed when the second bottle met the same fate. Our host explained: '*There was nothing wrong with either bottle, the waiters can enjoy the wine I sent back, and I shall not need to give them a tip.*' I have often wondered if this was acceptable behaviour in France. Soon after, Personnel Department informed Julian that there had been a change of plan and he would be going to Moscow, so we had no time to worry about what kind of return invitation we should issue.

Most Germans were away from Bonn campaigning for the elections in September 1966, the last general election before we left. How different from elections in England! we drove out into the Eiffel where, in a large beer cellar, Fritz Erler, the socialist candidate (and most likely to be foreign minister if the socialists won), spoke for an hour at least, choosing difficult subjects and

handling them in detail. Nobody looked in the least bored, and the few inter-
ruptions were speedily disposed of by Erler amid triumphant cheers. Most of
what Erler said could almost as well have come out of the mouth of the oppos-
ing CDU candidate. Not only had the socialists long since accepted NATO,
German armed forces, etc. but there was nothing as controversial as nationali-
sation in their home programme either, nor any mention of a future re-united
Germany. This made it easier for governments in Germany to be so frequently
a coalition, and for many years, whether the Right or the Left were in power,
everyone seemed content to have Hans-Dietrich Genscher, from the smaller
liberal party, as Foreign Minister. Many years later, perhaps inadvisedly, I tried
to persuade Mrs Thatcher of the benefits of proportional representation. She
silenced me with: '*I don't know what you think is fair about it: it just means
Herr Genscher is always in charge of Foreign Affairs!*' True but it also meant that
general elections did not mean great swings from right to left and vice versa
because neither could form a government without support from the Liberals.

We said goodbye to everyone in Bonn and got ready for Russia. We signed
on for Russian lessons and we started making lists for two years of tinned food
to take with us. The Braithwaites, whose flat in Moscow we were to inherit,
advised us that although one could always buy bread, one could not expect to
find shops selling much else in Moscow.

6

BRITISH EMBASSY,
MOSCOW

COMMERCIAL DEPARTMENT 1966 – 1968

*The great Russian lie was born as an essential instrument of self-preservation;
to tell the truth was likely as not to be fatal, in the most literal sense. But it goes
much beyond that. All those who have dealt with the Russians over the centuries
have commented on their indifference to the truth. The lie in Russia has gone
far beyond its original purpose and has become an art form. Russians lie when
they don't need to, without reason, by some inner compulsion, even when they
know that their listener knows that they are lying. Russians have a word for it
`vranyo.'*

RODRIC BRAITHWAITE

A letter in *The Irish Times* suggested that Intourist should be interpreted
in the light of such words as incoherent, inedible, etc.

J ULIAN was told to arrive in Moscow before the end of September 1966.
Looking at the atlas, we could see we could combine the journey with having a marvellous holiday (which in my opinion Julian had long earned).
We could drive to the south of France, take the car by boat to Athens, drive
round the Peloponnese, take a boat to Istanbul and stay with the Consul General (married to John Addis' sister), then on to Odessa and drive to Moscow
seeing Kiev and *Yasnaya Polyana,* Tolstoy's country house, *en route.* The approved route of travelling to Moscow was for us, our two boys, and Renate, the
German Russian-speaking girl who was coming to help us, to fly business class
and for our Peugeot car to be crated, shipped to Leningrad, and sent by train to
Moscow. The cost of this was so unbelievably expensive that I thought nobody
would object to our plans, which would save the taxpayer money. Our plan
was agreed, but someone, somewhere must have insisted for some reason, that

it must never be done again and everyone in future must go by the approved route. I have heard that common sense has since won. Today you are handed cash covering the approved route, and if you like you may travel by bicycle.

Our first taste of Russia was stepping on board the ms.Litva for an overnight trip to Istanbul from Piraeus, a short trip, but long enough to notice the difference after the Adriatica Line, which had brought us in great style from Venice to Piraeus. Now we were in the land of unsmiling faces, shut offices and long unexplained waits to which we became accustomed under the Soviet system. On the other hand, the purser cheerfully changed our cabin when Julian complained about the noise, and no one minded when we helped ourselves to things out of the car as it stood on the deck of the m.s. Felix Dzerzhinsky in which we made the voyage from Istanbul to Odessa. No notice was taken of our tourist tickets and we were shown into a cabin, clearly first class, and later into the first-class restaurant. Russians have old fashioned attitudes on class, and the Arab students, whose luggage consisted of cardboard boxes and shabby rucksacks, got third class treatment. At Odessa there was a lot of waiting about to get into the harbour, and for various officials to come on board (three hours), and finally for the same officials to stop smoking and stamp our documents. As we loaded the cases into our car, we saw the Turkish melons and oranges with which the Egyptian students were hoping to supplement Russian food, being dumped into the Black Sea, ostensibly to avoid importing foreign germs.

The drive to Moscow was more difficult than we anticipated owing to the absence of signposts and also of filling stations with anything but the lowest grade of petrol. In the end we were grateful to accept something poured out of a watering can. We drove about 300 miles – an endless succession of plains and swamps and Ukrainian villages of mudbrick houses with thatched roofs, until we saw the golden domes of Kiev strung out along a high bluff overlooking the Dnieper. Some of the many churches had become museums, one of which showed Vatican priests shooting on barricades, another the Inquisition and Roman Catholic Nazis. We took a boat trip and talked to three old women, trying, I think unsuccessfully, to convince them that in our country we, too, were given holidays with pay.

It was getting dark when we reached Orel, where I chanced to see a sign saying CAMPING. Intourist in London having told us that all camp sites closed at the beginning of September, we were not at all surprised to find this one open, since accurate information is not what Intourist deals in. It was less of a camp site, just a collection of wooden bungalows. Everyone was perfectly charming to us. This was the first and last bit of camping we were able to do in the Soviet Union, as, once we were officially diplomats and not tourists, they were forbidden to us. Luckily, visiting the country houses of the famous is one of the few things that are actively encouraged, so we had an interesting stop at *Yasnaya Polyana*, and a few hours later bedded ourselves down in our small, empty, stuffy and inconvenient flat, just above the British Embassy's commercial office. Unless the Embassy could find us something better, at Christmas all four children would have to sleep and play in a room about ten-foot square. Perhaps Personnel Department ought to move diplomats with four children only to posts from which diplomats with four children were being transferred!

Julian had spent some of the summer being instructed in the work of Commercial Departments. I had spent the time getting fur-lined boots, sheepskin coats for the girls, padded jackets for the boys, trying to master a little Russian, and working out how many tins of what we would need to buy to keep us from starvation for two years. We moved into the Braithwaite's flat which had been decorated with curtains and covers patterned in orange and black specially selected by the Ministry of Works as nice and cheerful. Next morning the Braithwaite's stout and cheerful cook/housekeeper Masha arrived, supplied by UPDK, a branch of the all powerful Security Service known as the KGB, and required to send regular reports on our activities and visitors.

For the first time we had to leave both girls behind at boarding school. As Vicky was only eight, we were glad that her school was near enough for her to spend the day with my mother at weekends. The boys flew out with Renate to join us. Robert was to go to the Embassy play school in the mornings, and we planned to deliver James, aged 7, to Russian School No.56, crossing our fingers in the hope that he would survive and be happy. We were motivated to do this by our ridiculous distrust of the only alternative, the American school, also by the success of sending Antonia to a German school, and by the fact that James at just seven, would be starting school at exactly the same age as Russian children. I also had a false notion that School 56 might prove to be just right for a cheerful tough boy who liked all kinds of outside activity.

The first problem for us was to get him fitted out with the correct uniform. No one could point us to a Shepherd and Woodward where all one had to do was sign a cheque. When we finally thought he had everything, he said that he still needed to buy a badge for his lapel, but he had seen the one he needed on a street barrow. '*Do you know who that is James?*' '*I think it is Jesus, but I am not quite sure.*' (Lenin of course!) There were other problems. He used to come home having wet his trousers. At his age I thought he ought to be able to manage better. '*If you could just see the lavatories Mummy!*' A few weeks later we were asked to come to meet James' teacher after school had ended. His book was produced alongside the book of one of the Russian boys. '*Griazni!*' she said, tearing James' work through the middle and discarding it into the waste paper basket. But a few weeks later he came home with a huge red star '*For good work and good behaviour,*' he said. He had a 15-minute walk to and from school carrying his books because they had no lockers. Luckily his natural friendliness and good mixability saw him through, and he could soon recite poems about tractors and the beauties of the Moscow underground. I got the impression that the other children were good to him.

Shortly after we arrived the Old Believers celebrated a special holy day. They were a sect of the Russian Orthodox Church who had followed Patriarch Nikon in 1653 in continuing to use three fingers to make the sign of the cross and also continued to write Jesus in Greek. We were taken into the gallery of the church by a German diplomat who knew Renate's family. The aroma given out by the wax candles in the chandeliers was very evocative. By their flickering light we could just about make out the ikons carried round the church by a procession of the most unattractive priests imaginable.

A few days later we were lucky to get tickets for the parade celebrating the anniversary of the October Revolution. Tickets had been sent for a Counsellor who had been transferred, and Julian managed to acquire them although they were stamped 'valid only with personal proof of identity'. We managed to talk our way to Red Square, helped by Julian's boss whose astrakhan collar and cigar must have impressed the guards. He was one of those people who thought that if you behaved as if you were accustomed to the best, you would probably get it. We found the parade distinctly thrilling, especially when the soldiers answered 'Hurrah' to the General's greeting, as they used to do in the time of the Tsars, with the guns and the national anthem sounding off together at the end of the ritual speech. We watched the four tiny Chinese diplomats departing impassively in their Mao Tse-tung caps in protest against the references to their country. After about an hour we noticed that the people marching in the parade seemed more anxious to look at the faces on the platform rather than the other way round, and, our feet by now being blocks of ice, we melted away, but not before recognizing Renate also walking in the parade. She told us she had realised the only chance she had of seeing the parade was by walking in it, and had managed to join a group from a factory. They had all been friendly but none of them made any attempt to prolong their meeting, still less fix another. The ordinary people accepted that contacts with foreigners are best kept superficial if you didn't want trouble.

That evening we were invited to dinner by the Ambassador as Basil and Nicolette Grey, were staying with him. They were neighbours of ours in Greenwich and also friends of Julian's family. Basil was Keeper of oriental antiquities at the British Museum and they were in Moscow for the wedding of their daughter Camilla to the son of the composer Prokofiev. A few months later Camilla got in touch with Julian and asked if he would send a parcel containing the Prokofiev family jewels in the Diplomatic Bag, which was the only way to get them to their English relations. It was no surprise to me that Julian refused, but Camilla was cross. and said the in that case she would not introduce him to the cream of the Russian intelligenzia, all of whom she knew personally. Nicolette told us later that Camilla had been determined to have the baby she was expecting exactly as any ordinary Russian mother would, and without any special priviliges, but that Camilla had unfortunately died after a complicated childbirth. The little boy was brought up in England by his Grey relations.

One day I joined a group of Embassy wives who were being taken to visit a specialist language school where all lessons were in English. They had invited us because they wanted to record our voices (without asking us) so that they could be sure of learning the correct pronunciation. Russia approved group visits, but except for art museums, you were not welcome if you were alone. I asked why there seemed to be three times as many girls as boys learning English? The reply was: ` *That is due to the birth rate.*' Russians who deal with foreigners always seem to have a quick (and unlikely) answer ready on their lips for any questions: just as Rodric Braithwaite described at the head of this chapter.

The Foreign Office can supply a wodge of detail about any post in the world to which you might be sent, but it seems to be no one's business to keep it up to date. The document we were sent on Moscow told us that we needed to bring enough food to last two years, but when we arrived with a van load of tinned sausages and rice pudding, a shop had been opened for some time, open only to foreigners and privileged people in the government, where anything in the world could be bought – for payment in dollars. On the list of availability were lampreys. I don't remember trying them but we could even have met our end dying of a surfeit!

Julian told me he was having to host a delegation from The State Committee for Trade and Industry and would I do the food? I thought, in addition to the usual canapes of prawn and smoked fish, I would have small portions of beefsteak tartar on rye bread. I assumed wrongly that with a name like that, it must be a dish with which they were familiar. Not long before, we had been skiing in Austria and had met a jolly Dutch group who introduced us to the necessity of tucking into a plate of beefsteak tartar when one comes in from skiing at the end of the day. Alas, the members of the Russian Trade Committee were appalled at the idea of eating raw beef and wouldn't touch it!

A letter arrived from Julian's cousin Tommy Hodgkin. He had been in Russia visiting some friends but come home without his anorak. Could Julian send him the address of our Moscow flat, so that his friend could drop the anorak in on us, and Julian could return it next time he was in Oxford? Two weeks later the bell rang and a middle-aged Russian asked if this was where Julian lived, then flung a none too clean anorak at me and fled as fast as he could. I was ashamed that Tommy had asked for it to be returned. Apart from the fact that it looked too old even to be given to a charity shop, it was difficult to believe that Tommy could have failed to know that a Russian citizen would have to give his name and be extensively questioned by the guards at the gate, with heaven knows what result. Tommy's father had been Provost of Queens College, Oxford, his wife was the Nobel prize-winner Dorothy Hodgkin, who shared some if not all of his left-wing views and frequently tried to persuade Julian to intercede with Mrs Thatcher and convert her to support CND (nuclear disarmament movement). Tommy's younger brother Edward was Foreign editor of The Times who explained his brother's communist sympathies thus:

'Tommy's anti feelings were genuine – anti-colonial rule, anti-privilege; his positive ones less so; certainly he had no direct experience of communism and saw it through a friendly pink Maurice Hindus/Haldane/Pitt haze. When things went wrong he felt saddened, like a Catholic convert (eg David Jones) when faced with the vernacular instead of the Latin mass – but equally without his fundamental faith being shaken – and that faith was essentially a conservative one – that the revelation that came to him in 1936 must be unshakable and unshaken – however much outside circumstances change.'

Julian and I discussed this – not of course in our flat because we knew that it was bugged and the conversations of all foreign diplomats listened in to in the fifth floor of the Hotel Moskva opposite. It was impossible to believe that the extent of his faith would have held had he been required to take any unpleasant action for the cause, actions such as Philby took, like sending British soldiers to their death in Albania, but that had probably given Kim no more of a qualm than could be drowned by another few glasses of whisky.

George Brown, then Foreign Secretary, came and visited the Commercial department with a bee in his bonnet about security, and it was Julian who had to receive him. He came to Julian's office, pulled out two drawers of a filing cabinet and chided him for their being unlocked. Julian explained that the drawers only contained addresses and contacts of British firms and a list of products which British business-men would be only too delighted to supply should any Russians show interest in them.

From Julian's letter to his father describing the visit:

'At lunch with some Trade Unionists, George Brown became involved in a furious argument with a Soviet woman unionist who gave as good as she got. After lunch he continued drinking. That evening was the dinner for Gromyko. After dinner Brown and Gromyko sat opposite each other across a coffee table. The subject was Anglo-Soviet bilateral issues. Brown pulled out his brief and began to read in a befuddled voice: 'Brooke? Well, what about Brooke?' Gromyko simply said that this should be discussed at the meeting next morning. 'Cultural Agreement? What about that?' An Under-Secretary seated on Brown's right chipped in to say that there were certain difficulties on this point. Brown banged his fist on the table. 'Shut up! You're always

making difficulties! I want a cultural agreement and I want to sign it now! Bring me a pen!' Gromyko then said icily 'I think the ladies are waiting for us.' Brown started to wag his finger and say 'Oh no you don't!' But at Gromyko's words the room emptied and Brown allowed himself to be raised from his chair and led by the arm into the next room.

A terrible performance. But I am told Brown was excellent with Gromyko and Kosygin at the formal meetings, in spite of having almost no cards to play. And the British Trade Unionists at that same lunch party obviously worshipped him. To his credit I saw that he had declined to endorse the Israel backslapping of almost all MPs except Mayhew and Gilmour who are regarded as pro-Arabs.

One freezing day I set out for a distant part of Moscow having received an invitation to a coffee party. For the first time I climbed into a bus on my own. I looked for the coin which I needed to put into a slot before helping myself to a ticket. Only roubles! No one ever seemed to have the exact change in buses and the most friendly contact I was ever likely to have with a Russian was the to-ing and fro-ing which went on all around the bus, always surprisingly resulting in everyone having a ticket and their proper change. After a bit, people at the back started shouting at the driver about a man lying across the gangway halfway up the bus. At last the driver stopped the bus, got out, picked up two handfuls of snow and brutally rubbed it into the man's ears. Not a flicker of a response. The driver did not seem to be in doubt as to what was the matter. He grabbed the man's collar, dragged him along the floor of the bus and threw him out into the snow. The man's trousers had come off and these he picked up and threw after him. As the temperature must have been about minus twelve degrees, the man might very well have got frost bite. I was assured by the passengers that regular patrols come round picking up drunks and taking them off to a cooler. If he wasn't, he would end up like so many others we saw on the streets with no legs at all, pushing themselves around on little hand-made trolleys. I asked our doctor whether protheses were not available in Russia and he told me that if you had lost your leg in the war, Yes. If through frostbite while drunk, No.

Julian was worried that his job seemed most of the time to be somewhat nonexistent – at least he said it was difficult to see how the improvement he was doing to the country's balance of payments could ever equal what it must cost to keep all of us here. He found that if he ever tried to propose something, Alan Rothnie was inclined to take it as a reflection on him for not having had the idea himself. Julian saw an article in *The Times* about a brickworks in the West Country, where a workforce of 28 make 15 million bricks a year, and he decided to see how difficult it would be to sell the Russians a brickworks or a bus factory. He thought it worth some sort of a try – one of his predecessors got the Russians to buy £30,000 worth of patterned stockings. But even if we could double our exports to Russia it would still only be less than half what we sold to Sweden. I thought that Julian was actually starting to enjoy this new kind of diplomacy. Because Julian found keeping an eye on Soviet production statistics was somewhat repetitive, he managed to get himself invited to join the ten o'clock meeting at the Embassy every morning, where he formed the opinion that nothing could be worse than the work done by those in Chancery, who had far fewer contacts with Russians and could see absolutely no rewards for what they did.

We waited in great excitement at Sheremetevo airport for the plane bringing the children for the Christmas holidays. We heard the plane circling overheard which was also bringing the Ambassador's wife with a repaired broken wrist. But then came the announcement that conditions for landing were not good enough, and the plane would now be landing in Copenhagen. I gathered the children had a marvellous time playing games all over the Hotel de l'Angleterre – whizzing lifts up and down and eating themselves silly at the buffet. Next day the plane managed to land. I saw Mimi Harrison (the ambassador's wife) and commiserated with her about having to see that the British children behaved themselves in the smart Danish hotel and she replied: '*Most certainly not! I went to my room and ordered a light supper and read my book. Not my job to nanny other people's children!*' When her husband greeted her, I very much doubt he would have confessed what had been happening in her absence. He had been enticed into having an affair with one of the maids supplied by UPDK (with exactly that situation in view). He was nearing 60 at the time and this affair was picked up in the Press only after he had retired. I was told she sent him a begging letter, and his reply and money was intercepted when he sent it by Royal Mail.

There were a great many children of all ages from Embassies of all countries in our block of flats, and during the holidays it wasn't a question of keeping the children amused, but rather of trying to keep track of where they were, and of getting them into bed at a reasonable hour. In the winter holidays the older children took charge of turning part of the car park into an ice rink, which involved a considerable amount of hard manual labour. When the snow melted the children made fortresses and houses out of the huge empty packing cases lying about, or staging raids on the houses of others. We took the children to the circus, Puss in Boots at the Puppet Theatre and Cinderella at the ballet, which ended spectacularly with the Prince running across the width of the Hall of Congresses (seats for 2,000 people) bearing Cinderella in the palm of one upstretched hand. We were extraordinarily fortunate that we had very good friends in the Danish Minister and wife who lived directly above us and very kindly offered their spare bedroom to Antonia and Vicky for the holidays. We weren't at the Thune Andersons' dinner party when the waitress tipped a serving dish at a rather too steep angle in order to reveal the elegantly decorated fish, which then slipped gently to the floor. The two waitresses hastily scooped up the remains and cleaned the carpet while the guests, including the hostess, wondered what was happening in the kitchen. I think Mrs Thune Anderson must have received some kind of sign to stop her worrying during the very long wait during which the Minister recounted various past embarrassing diplomatic occasions. Eventually the doors opened and a similar dish was presented to the guests, not scooped up fish, but a perfectly baked roast beef wellington. As the guests left, one asked the hostess '*How on earth did you manage it?*' to which she replied that she always told the chef to have a reserve dish in case of accidents. The story went the rounds of Moscow's diplomats who all wondered whether they could possibly match Mrs Thune Anderson in rising so brilliantly to the occasion. The real story I learned later. All our domestic staff were supplied by a department of the UPDK. They were part spies, part servants, had all trained together, and were often good friends. The servants knew that the Australian diplomats upstairs were also having a party and knew exactly what their planned menu was, only on that particular evening the Australian guests got scooped up fish covered with a hastily defrosted sauce and garnished with fresh shrimp. I imagine the Australian diplomat was of lower rank than the Danish Minister.

When winter arrived in Moscow it arrived in earnest. The Canadian diplomats in the flat nearby took one look at the boys' padded jackets from Marks and Spencer, and insisted in ordering winter kit for them from a store in Canada immediately. Most days we would be woken at about 6 am by old women shovelling snow off the pavement and out of the gutters, by the grinding of starter motors that wouldn't start, and the roaring engines of the luckier ones who managed to get their motors going. Julian went down about nine a.m. and, with the aid of a red and a black cable which sucked juice out of the battery of a car that had managed to start already, he would join squadrons of snow ploughs moving in a slow echalon down the middle of the road. Roadside drifts were scooped up on moving belts into lorries which dumped the snow into the frozen river Moskva. Unfortunately this rather spoiled skating except on the public rinks and the Ambassador's tennis court which were kept clear and flooded every evening with hose pipes of hot water.

The diplomatic shop sold everything but bread, which we bought from the bread shop directly opposite our block on the other side of Kutuzovski Prospekt, but to cross the road we had to walk a third of a mile to the south to an underpass and a third of a mile back to the bread shop, queue to select bread and get a bill, queue at a till to pay, take stamped paper to the counter, queue to collect bread, and then walk the two thirds of a mile back to the entrance of our block of flats. On a freezing day this was enough exercise for one day. The children were apt to get suddenly slapped on the cheeks by a Muscovite should they notice a child's cheeks starting to go white in the middle, which is a sign of frostbite. My granddaughter Sophie, who spent a year at Moscow University, had butter spread all over her face by her landlady to help her survive the Moscow climate. If the weather was warm and I was not wearing my fur hat, I might be stopped and told that the points of my silk scarf folded in half round my neck were not exactly together, and should be adjusted. They did not do any of these things with a smile. No one smiled. People looked at us usually as if they were thinking what their own government might do to them if they were found speaking to us. Curiously the papers never mentioned Stalin or Kruschchev or even printed pictures of those past eras. They were indignant about the Chinese cultural revolution – how the classics are banned, while every word of Mao's is extolled etc. and it did not seem to strike them that it was they that started it all! On the way back from the Air Show where James and Robert had been allowed to climb into the cockpits and touch the joysticks, we stopped and asked the way to the river only to receive the answer 'The question is, are you allowed to go to the river?'

When his boss was on leave, Julian got to go to interesting meetings with top people from the CBI and ICI. He also went with the Ambassador to call on the State Committee for Science and Technology.

Julian wrote to his father:

> 'Academician Kirillin is a charming old buffer – stooping shoulders and golden tooth. Thoroughly bourgeois office – no picture of Lenin, but a nice old engraving of Marx in a maple frame. I could see it was an important occasion because, on the green baize table there was lemonade to mix with the water, and a line-up of five or six people on the other side of the table: Kosygin's son-in-law Ovishiani, one or two others I didn't know, and right at the bottom the Russians whom I consider too senior for me to call on myself. They could not have been more agreeable or helpful, which I suppose is to be expected from an organization which exists partly to pick the brains of the outside world at least cost to the Soviet Union.'

Julian tried to explain to me about the problems that faced him in his job. The Russians wanted Britain to take part in the exhibitions they were planning: food-handling equipment, mining machinery, fishing and clothing. Even though the Soviet policy was that self-sufficiency was the ideal, to be departed from only in case of absolute need and then at minimum cost, Britain was pressed to take part because the French were taking part, and the French were pressed for the same reason. The Russians were hoping to buy the goods on the stands at knockdown prices at the end of the exhibition. Nine out of ten of the exhibitors would sell cheap just because it was not worthwhile to take them home. Some firms say it was worth selling cheaply abroad just to keep the factory functioning at home. There were many articles in the press about the poor supply of clothing in the shops, and I imagine the main purpose of having a fashion show was to give their clothing manufacturers a chance to copy what the west was wearing. Courtaulds refused to take part in any exhibitions anywhere, but most firms don't feel strong enough to take that line. It might be to our advantage to ban all sales with the USSR. We might lose £50 million of exports a year but we would save the hundreds of thousands spent every year by the Government and businessmen on visits and exhibitions. The crux of the matter was that the Soviet Union forced us to buy goods from them that we could easily get elsewhere, as a condition of their buying from us half as much as we buy from them.

Lucky Julian went to England for three weeks to escort a group of Russians being shown round twenty factories in England – Ford, Perkins, Girling, Leyland, Glacier Metal,etc – travelling from Liverpool to Birmingham and Peterborough to Southend and Hendon sipping gin and tonics in coaches with large plateglass windows. The Russians kept commenting on the quality of everything – easy to see why after Moscow, but what struck Julian were the enormous differences between the various companies: some glossy and modest, friendly and distant, dirty and cheerful and clean but soulless. He hoped that we would be able to accept the invitations he was given to drop in on them in Kharkov or Yaroslavl, as he enjoyed their company.

Julian no longer complained about having too little to do as he did at the beginning. He had to look after an endless stream of visitors e.g. 17 members of the Northampton Chamber of Commerce, all of whom had to be escorted to the Soviet Trade offices. Even if the administration was exhausting and the visible results few, it provided him with a welcome opportunity for otherwise impossible contacts with Russians, though Robert thought otherwise. After getting the wishbone in a chicken he said gloomily: 'I wish there could be no more businessmen coming to lunch' and explained '*Because when THEY come we don't have Shepherd's Pie.*'

We had been invited to stay with a friend in Helsinki and Julian thought we should accept as this would make a welcome change. We could have a sauna and visit the local Harrods; and I could try on a few dresses at Marimekko. We had a good time but the most memorable experience was on our journey home. At the frontier the train was boarded by a group of business-like looking females. One came into our compartment which we were sharing with three German students, took out a syringe and indicated that the Germans should bare their arms. Understandably the Germans tried all the arguments they could think of not to submit. None of us understood what we were to be injected with or for. It was made clear that either we consented or we must leave the train. They gave way, were injected, and left the train at Leningrad without looking any the worse. Julian however, showed our passports and said in a firm and negative way that we were diplomats and therefore exempt. This was accepted, amazing us as much as the students!

In May 1967 I organized a fete to provide cash for a facelift for the Embassy dacha, a charming traditional green wooden one-storey house on the edge of a wood with a pond where in the winter old men used to sit patiently fishing through holes in the ice. It needed decent washing up facilities, cheerful bed-spreads and some garden furniture, none of which were available in Moscow. I managed to rent an old grey horse and cart to give rides to the children while their parents spent their money on games, sideshows and raffle tickets. I went round the Embassy begging items for sale, for the raffle or for prizes Asked for suggestions about what kind of things people would buy, I suggested toys to one wife, but she misheard and gave me about twenty of her husband's old ties. Of these, surprisingly, the embassy staff seemed to be greatly in need, and their sale made a major contribution to our total take of over two hundred pounds which covered the cost of all we needed to buy in Oxford. Rather conveniently I had been sent home to have a minor operation and I managed to get the air-line to accept my bulky luggage.

Julian passed his intermediate Russian exam with 160 out of 200. Alan com-mented '*I remember I got 188 in the Advanced Arabic exam.*' To a businessman who excused his lack of Russian, saying that even the alphabet was more than he could master, Alan replied: '*I mastered the Russian alphabet in one evening, I remember it was in the Northern Atlantic and we were chasing a German destroyer at the time*' . . .

We woke up on 5th June 1967 to hear that the Israelis had beaten the armies of Egypt, Syria and Jordan, captured Gaza, taken Sinai, the Golan Heights, East Jordan and large portions of the West Bank. He wrote to his father:

'*What a world my children are growing up into! I see nothing good in the present situation except that the great powers are determined not to be drawn in. The Soviet government's statement seems to me as conciliatory as it could possibly have been. At a party yesterday I found myself alone in seeing any justice in the Arab's cause and the general tone was 'gallant little Israel' It is painful to think of Israel emerging this time with bits of the West Bank – even of Jerusalem.*'

14 June.

'*I hadn't realised until last week how deeply I cared about the Middle East – in par-ticular about Jordan and the Arabs. Hearing the recital of Israeli conquests every day on the news was a physical pain, and having to picture Jewish soldiers in the places we were so fond of: Jericho, where the car broke down and was mended one night by an Arab mechanic with a Lancashire accent, Hebron, where Muslim fanaticism hung about in the air like the background noise of the traffic, Ramallah, leafy and green and peopled with Palestinian boys strolling along with their textbooks in the evening, the twisting road from Jerusalem to Bethlehem where we were 'moved on' by an Arab soldier in a manner which we thought rude at the time, but not now we have had experience of the Russian equivalent, and Jerusalem, breathing the last enchantment of the Mandate. These feelings make us very conspicuous among our colleagues, whose attitude seems to be: 'The Arabs won't let Israel live in peace, so they have only themselves to blame, and anyway the Russians were backing them. So we are glad they lost'. Questions like whether Balfour had any right to issue his Declaration, or how many Jews were there in Palestine when he did so (65,000 or about 9% I find) are dismissed as Arab sentimentalising. Even the question of who attacked who on 5 June doesn't seem to trouble people here, they are too busy marvelling at the incompetence of the Arabs at not dispersing their aircraft. Perhaps the Russians will now have a Middle East policy more in line with what they are really prepared and willing to do when it comes to the point.'*

Julian joined the Financial Times correspondent mingling with the students demonstrating outside our Embassy. The road had been blocked at both ends with watercarts and mounted police. They were allowed to demonstrate for an hour, after which a loudspeaker announced 'the demonstration is now over' and the demonstration obediently dispersed.

As the summer approached Moscow filled with white fluff from the kapok trees and long columns of shabby buses decorated with red flags bore children on their way to summer camps. We were not very surprised when we were told that James could not go to a camp because they are not arranged by the schools but by the 'enterprises' to which all the parents belong. There seemed to be an 'international' camp for foreigners only, run by UPDK, but we could not go there because it was beyond the restricted limit of 50 km. On Sunday we took our inflatable boat to a local beach. A police car immediately appeared bellowing at us through a loud speaker that such boats were forbidden. I drove out to inspect the camping site in some woods to the south where I thought I might take the children. We were given a great welcome and told us just to give them a ring when we wanted to come, so I applied to stay at a site at Kalinin on the road to Leningrad, only to be told by Intourist that 'all beds in all camping sites were fully booked for the whole of the summer'– indeed for the foreseeable future! I later heard that our Canadian friends upstairs got round this by sending telegrams to the mayors of the towns where they hoped to camp, bringing their own tents. These kinds of frustrations were so frequent and irritating that I hoped Julian tells business men in London about them when they talk about the wonderful friendliness and frankness with which they are received. Of course it was part of a deliberate policy not to allow diplomats to fraternize with any Russians except on business and to remind us that we were here on sufferance.

The Clothing Exhibition came and went and amazingly was a tremendous success – 250 British exhibitors including 32 models and a dozen fashion editors. Other countries took part but all Moscow seemed to wanted to see were the French and the British shows. The French accompanied their mannequins with stately classical orchestral music, the British boys and girls danced wildly to pop. The Russians bought 12m pounds worth of clothing from us this year but they drove such a hard bargain that there was seldom much profit for the firms. However, firms seemed to find a special kudos in a Russian order – it means nothing to them that our exports to Finland are greater.

It was a great moment for me when the young man to whom I was chatting at the farewell reception at the end of the show, told me he was the accompanying hairdresser. 'Oh!' I said, '*How I would like to have a hair-cut!*' '*Come with me – I always carry my scissors,*' and he boldly opened several doors until we found a broom cupboard and he got to work. Presently we were of course discovered and told to go away in no uncertain terms. '*Just finishing! Just finishing!*' More Russians were brought in and expressed their anger. '*Nearly finished! Nearly finished!*' Twenty minutes passed while staff waved their arms threateningly at us. Happily they weren't actually prepared to take physical action!

The Ambassador decided to invite the various British business – men and engineers living and working in Russia to a party, and all British diplomats living in our block were told to provide the food – 150 people! I thought the engineers from the polystyrene factories at Kazan, Ufa, Polotsk and Baku must have a really pleasant life in their spare time going down the Volga and the Don to Rostov, but although such trips are advertised all over the world, and yes foreign tourists may take them – they are closed for foreigners living in Russia!

If the Embassy doctor needed equipment or medicines he dealt with the local Polyklinik, and he asked us if we would to like to join him and the doctors he knew for a picnic, nominally to celebrate International Doctor's Day – '*and bring the boys.*' We were told we were to meet at the Polyklinik one Sunday morning at 8 am. Our doctor apologized for the time but said it had not been his choice. Forty minutes later, just as we were about to give up, they arrived. '*Where are we going?*' The Russians did not think much of the doctor's proposal – a small lake a few miles from Moscow – and suggested we go to a place they knew on the Volga. We explained that as it was further from Moscow than we were allowed to drive, the police would turn us back. The Russian doctors were amazed. We were guests in their country and of course we could go anywhere we wanted. '*I know! We'll get an ambulance and you can sit inside.*' So we spent the day in an prohibited area driven in a Russian ambulance. The doctors played with the children, and pretended that it was James who had caught the huge fish. They knocked back a lot of Armenian cognac and proposed countless toasts. The ambulance driver described how his elder brother died of hunger in the siege of Leningrad and he himself only escaped in 1943 across the ice with a crowd of children. When we left, they wanted to present the fish to me. Knowing that fish did not seem to be on sale anywhere except at the diplomatic shop, I wanted them to have it, but they would not accept it. I had been presented with the very latest in cigarette lighters at the fashion show, so I gave them the lighter, and promised to send them a cartridge of gas for refuelling. Later I delivered the gas to the *klinik* but the inevitable stout fierce woman at the entrance desk made me hand it over to her.' *I will see that he receives it* As I parted with it, I realised my mistake, and tried, unsuccessfully to take it back. I still feel very guilty about this whenever I think about it, because I later learned that the doctor to whom I gave the lighter was moved to another *klinik* where he will not be tempted to take dangerous gifts from foreigners. I can't bear to think that the punishment might possibly have been something terrible like banishment to Siberia, nor could I think of anything I could do about it.

Julian's letter to his father described a visit to Leningrad escorting Professor Kaldor:

'Professor Kaldor came here on a visit. I had to share a compartment in the train with him and also a bed in Leningrad, as an alternative to me sleeping on the floor. At the bottom of an immense moving staircase in the underground we found an old man behind a counter selling not Playboy and the Evening Standard, but the Life of Einstein and Simple Problems in Higher Mathematics for Schools. This pleased Kaldor very much. In the picture gallery he merely read out of the guidebook: 'The viewer cannot fail to recognize the something something of the chiaroscuro' and then asked whether the chiaroscuro was that chap on the left. He was however good at putting up with the delays and frustrations of travelling by public transport, instead of demanding an In-tourist car, because as a result we got into conversation in the train with an aggressive engineer and a charming sailor from the Crimea. As we parted the engineer, rather drunk, gripped my hand and said: 'I have a message for Mr Wilson from the Soviet people. In 50 years we have acquired education, culture, armed forces, technology etc and we are not going to let anyone take these things away from us. You are a diplomat: please give him this message'. As so often in these encounters, one is left with a feeling of doubt whether some authority was not behind it, as when an odd boy picked us up at a church outside Moscow, accepted a lift in the car, ducked out of sight when we passed policemen, told me he wanted to emigrate to Britain, got my telephone number out of me and did actually ring up twice before fading out of our lives.

It was difficult to keep cheerful all the time with the continual pinpricks of Moscow life. Julian had fits of gloom – whether on account of approaching middle age or general worries about the Chinese hydrogen bomb or the pitiful figure cut by Britain on the world stage. Fighting a losing battle can't be agreeable. This fit of depression must have been influenced, I think, by learning about the collapse of sterling and the prevalence of wildcat strikes in the newspapers.

I found some discarded antique furniture in the ambassador's attic and after a good many fights with authority, a very elegant eighteenth-century marble-topped chest made the journey to our flat in Kutosovski Prospect. This led to delays in moving in, so on the spur of the moment we decided to go to Vladimir and Suzdal, harmless tourist attractions, so there would be no problem getting permission to go there. The largest church in Vladimir is a 'working church' and we saw a procession of old ladies crossing themselves every second step. At one empty church standing in the middle of water meadows we met a charming Russian girl who had rented a room for a month's holiday from her job as a tourist guide in Leningrad. Her room was a mile across the fields from the nearest buses, trains, shops, restaurant and drinking water, but she gave us a glass of lake water (boiled) and Julian promised to send her some books. Two days escape from Moscow meeting nothing but friendly faces and scarcely seeing a policeman did us a lot of good.

The Russians charged extortionate rates for all tickets and hotels for diplomats, so only if we were making a business trip, and could call the trip duty and charge the cost to expenses, did we get to travel far. I was therefore delighted when Julian was told to visit Kazan, capital of the Tartar republic, and Ufa, the Bashkoristan capital, where Simon Carves and ICI were building factories to make polyethylene. The British engineers had run into one or two problems, one being that letters from home were arriving in envelopes addressed to engineers other than the man to whom the letter was written. At Kazan we had some strange experiences. For an unexplained reason the Russian in charge of the Kazan plant said it was not permitted for us to be shown over the plant, even though it was of exactly the same construction as the one we had been shown over at Ufa the day before. To be shown once more over a similar plant was not high on our interest list. Julian asked Intourist if we could perhaps call on a member of the government or see the editor of the Tartar newspaper. '*Nyet. All occupied.*' We walked round the town and were accosted by a strange figure in a cloak who asked us not to take photographs. Julian said: '*If you are a policeman, you have the right to say that, otherwise not*' He answered '*You are right*' and slunk off into the bushes but reappeared from time to time. He ignored other tourists. Who was he? Our old Baedeker described a beautiful monastery nearby at Sviazhsk, and so we suggested to Intourist that we might hire a car and visit it. Intourist never give one excuse when they can think of six. We could not go because there were no boats. The trains did not stop there. The monastery was destroyed at the time of the revolution. It hadn't been destroyed but was now occupied by psychiatric patients and nobody was allowed '*Not even we may go there!*' The level of the Volga had now risen eleven metres on account of the barrage.. . . ..

A stout English deaconess escorting thirty teenagers round Russia was told, when she arrived on a Friday morning and asked when and where the next church service was: '*In Russia services in churches are on Thursday evenings.*' She found out the time and place from a taxi driver but up to the last minute they tried to prevent her from going to church. Meanwhile the weather had turned bitterly cold and wet and we were shivering in our Moscow clothing so we asked to be put on an earlier plane back to Moscow. Intourist seemed very relieved to see us go. Once inside the plane we were made to sit on a sofa at the back, from which the protesting occupants were ousted. The sofa was not fixed very firmly to the floor and had no seat belts. Just before take-off an old *babushka* entered and we were told to make room for her on the sofa. She told Julian she was the wife of a teacher at the University and her husband, on holiday in Riga, had been taken ill and she was hurrying to join him. It was her first flight and she thought each moment might be her last. Could she hold Julian's arm? She closed her eyes and held tightly to Julian for about ten minutes while we sat on the tarmac. Then she opened her eyes and asked Julian if we had arrived in Moscow yet! Two hours later when we reached Moscow his arm was quite sore. The only reason we could see for our being made to sit on the sofa was to stop us looking out of the windows at the ground below, but through them we could see just the same (and just as little) as from the rest of the seats.

From a letter from Julian to his father:

'*The girls are here for the summer holidays Both the girls are so good and intelligent and responsive, quite unlike our mischievous and often quarrelsome boys, who play endless card games passing one card at a time under a shut door as neither trusts the other not to cheat. The daughter of our Ambassador in Amman, Lucy Adams, wrote to Antonia describing lying on the floor in the Residence for three hours while Israeli planes attacked the king's palace next door. James excused his work on the grounds of not being able to see the blackboard even when he was not in the back row for misbehaviour. The eye specialist at the Polyklinik has diagnosed astigmatism and myopia and says it is not possible to have a pair of spectacles that will deal with both problems. Poor James. There never was a child less suited to specs and we hate having to accept only Russian advice*'.

Autumn is almost here and we went with all the children on their first mushrooming excursion. I gave them all baskets and told them to pick any they thought were good and we would take them home and compare them with our mushroom encyclopaedia and learn which are good and which bad. Their baskets were so full that we decided to leave them in our hatchback car and go for a walk in the woods. We returned to find our car surrounded by Russians all loudly trying to prevent us from poisoning ourselves! This turns out to be a much better way of meeting Russians than any other. After learning the names of the mushrooms and throwing away the baddies we were invited to join in their vodka and balalaika parties.

Having enjoyed our walk in the woods so much, I decided to take the chil-

The Meyer Landrut family visiting the Bullards at the Embassy Dacha. Andreas later served as German Ambassador 1980–83 and 1987–89.

The annual parade commemorating the October Revolution in 1917, looking towards the GUM department store.

dren to try the diplomatic dacha on the Volga, a hundred miles to the north. It is a long way to go for the day, but the cost of an overnight stay is exorbitant. We did not take James because he refused to leave his friends, preferring to play destructive and unsuitable games in the yard. But he was very happy to come with us when our turn to use the Embassy *dacha* for a week came along. James, who turns out to be a wonderful mixer, made the acquaintance of the family next door and ended spending the night with them. When we called next day to pick him up, we found the children all in high spirits, the grown-ups all slightly tipsy, it being someone's birthday. The father clapped James on the back and said '*A fine strong boy. He's going to fight with us against the Americans.*'

At the beginning of the autumn term, after James had been at School 56 for a year, he developed a high temperature. The doctor had no suggestion as to what was the matter, and I jokingly said to James: '*Is it going back to school that is making you ill*'? He sat up sharply. '*Yes*' he said. After a day of indecision, we transferred him to the American school. It helped us to make this change when we found that this year he would be in the second shift at School 56, which would mean being at school from 1.15 to 5.30, most inconvenient for us as a family. The standard of the work at the American school was low, but James was clearly much happier. James' birthday came on 20th September. It was difficult to find presents for him. I thought he might like some puppets but he said he would prefer an ice hockey stick. The trouble was that he would certainly lend it to somebody who would lose it, as had happened the previous summer with his bicycle.

Julian came home for lunch and said: 'Did we bring at atlas with us? See if you can find a place called D U B A I? He had earlier been told he would be returning to London in April. But everything had changed. He was to do a course to brush up his Arabic in the Lebanon and then be Political Agent in the Trucial States for two years – about the last thing he was expecting. But being promoted to Counsellor at the age of 40 was good going.

We had been finding every moment since the Israeli attacks on 5 June unbearable, except when the girls were here to take our minds off the Middle East situation, and so we decided to divert our journey home to stay *en route* with Archbishop and Joy Mckinnis in Jerusalem. We wanted to see how things seemed on the ground, and hear how it was that the Jordanian army didn't stay in barracks and instead, by joining in the fighting, gave the Israelis their chance to seize the West Bank. It was insufferable to hear the Israeli's claim that right as well as might was on their side. We flew to Turkey and thence to Tel Aviv.

Sitting in the outer office of the Israeli Military Governor of Jerusalem hoping to get a permit to cross the Allenby bridge and visit Amman (refused), Julian jotted down the things that most struck him:

The Jews have achieved the most astonishing fait accompli. If you want to telephone to someone on the West Bank not under Israeli governorship, just dial 8 first.

A No, 27 bus takes you from Sion Square on the Israeli side to the Damascus gate on the Arab side.

Three out of four people in the Arab restaurants are Israeli tourists.

Arab resistance is invisible except in the refusal to re-open the government schools – from which the children rather than the Israelis are the victims.

There is no great show of military force: no soldiers in the streets or outside public buildings and only a casual customs check on the road to Jerusalem. 'Ashkenazies' in broad hats and ringlets walk boldly though the suq on their way to the Wailing Wall, and so far from lifting a finger against them, the Arab shopkeepers sing out 'Shalom'! as they pass.

The main complaints we heard were material: high Jewish taxes, poor quality Jewish goods in place of the imported goods people are used to. At first the troops behaved well but after a few days, lorries arrived with foraging parties to seize anything portable they fancied and round up any cars that looked abandoned and so on. The Israeli authorities, while cracking down on any attempts at resistance, seemed outwardly to be on their best behaviour. On first sight things weren't as bad as we feared, and perhaps being under Israeli rule might be no bad thing – a better solution than union with Jordan, but it took only half an hour with Amos Elon, an Israeli journalist for the newspaper Ha'arez, whom we knew in Bonn, to put us back on our habitual pro-Arab point of balance. He showed self-righteous ruthlessness which we found disagreeable. The plan seemed to be that west Bank Arabs would have to suffer Israeli rule without qualifying for social benefits or medical care, or supply of public utilities etc. He was indignant about Arab terrorism in Israel, which I thought disproportionate in a people that produced the Stern Gang, and was also indignant that 'no Arab country had accepted Israel's offer of 'negotiations'. Joy Mckinnis had terrible stories of the Palestinian camps near Bethlehem. Early after the fighting, soldiers entered the camp and locked up all the men in the school. They then went into the huts, emptied the flour, rice and sugar on the floor and poured the oil and vinegar on top. The women by this time were screaming and weeping. Loudspeakers then announced that buses were waiting outside to take them to Jordan, where they would be given nice houses to live in. There was no alternative. On the way home, we spoke to some Jews from Eastern Europe who had tried living in Israel for nine years but had decided to leave, and were hoping to start a new life in Frankfurt! They explained: '*We are used to living in a Christian community*' and '*Friends? In Israel one has only acquaintances. No one has time for friendship*'.

On 20 November, our brief leave over, we were back in Moscow. Most of the Christmas holidays were spent skiing and tobogganing. We pulled sledges and watched an almost purple winter sunset over Moscow with great pillars of coloured smoke ascending into an enormous sky. In Gorky Park a loudspeaker intoned the healthful and beneficial effect of skating and the need to wrap up well when you do it. I thought there must be something basically good about the multitudes of Russians setting off into the pine forests with their rucksacks and children of all ages, and something basically bad in the way Sunday is mostly spent in England, wearing dressing gown and bedroom slippers, reading rubbishy newspapers or roaring down the M40. There was plenty not so good in Soviet life of course. You had only to read about the latest writers' trial, or try to buy an oboe reed (for Antonia) in a city of 6 million people and the capital of a country with 235 million. After many false trails we discovered oboe reeds were only available if you are a member of the Musicians Union.

I had thought we would be leaving Russia without ever having been invited to a Russian home, but in our last week we were invited to dinner by Victor Louis, a Soviet journalist with an ambiguous status and an English wife. Together they had produced an invaluable A to Z of the City of Moscow. His splendid dacha (not in any way typical), has colour TV, Potterton oil-fired central heating system, three or four servants and a house full of trophies from his foreign trips, but also serious books and antiques. When Julian had been in EESD he had become aware of Victor Louis as a factor in British-Soviet relations. His name would appear in some of the more interesting files. He seemed to embody all the ambiguities of the East-West intelligence scene. There could be no doubt about his receiving a salary from the KGB. He was used by the Soviet machine as a channel for the emission of carefully constructed leaks – they could turn out to be wild geese, red herrings or genuine trial balloons – but he had journalistic talent in his own right. He deserved a footnote, in the history of the Cold War even if only to disentangle the threads of relative truth and falsehood.

After this interesting evening our lives became full of farewell parties. So goodbye Moscow. But what a pity that we hadn't been able to do as much travelling as we expected. Looking back on his time in Moscow I could see Julian was glad to have had commercial experience, and thereby acquired a good deal more fluency in Russian and more self-confidence than he had before. He was very pleased to be promoted to Counsellor and looking forward to becoming Head of Mission in Dubai. It looked like a challenging job – preserving British influence but without the aid of British military strength.

7

H.M. POLITICAL AGENT
DUBAI

1968 –1970

Next year we are to bring the soldiers home
For lack of money, and it is all right.
Places they guarded, or kept orderly,
Must guard themselves, and keep themselves orderly,
We want the money for ourselves at home
Instead of working. And this is all right.

It's hard to say who wanted this to happen,
But now it's been decided nobody minds.
The places are a long way off, not here
Which is all right, and from what we hear
The soldiers there only made trouble happen
Next year we shall be easier in our minds.

Next year we shall be living in a country
That brought its soldiers home for lack of money,
The statues will still be standing in the same
Tree muffled squares, and look nearly the same.
Our children will not know it's a different country
All we can hope to leave them now is money.

PHILIP LARKIN

I N Dubai Julian's official title to expatriates was Political Agent, PA for short, but to everyone else he was the '*Mu'atamad*' (the accredited one) and treated with much respect. He was also the Political Agent representing the Queen in five of the other Trucial States: Sharjah, Ajman, Umm al Qaiwain and Ras al Khaimah along the Gulf coast, and Fujairah, on the Indian Ocean. In January 1968, soon after the devaluation of the pound, Harold Wilson and Denis Healey announced that British troops would be withdrawn in 1971 from major military bases 'east of Aden', including the Persian Gulf. Julian thought the government had blundered into committing Britain to withdrawal. It could not really have been that we couldn't afford to stay, (as if Britain couldn't afford £20 million a year in a region worth £200 million to us). It was not like withdrawal from India, which we felt ought to be independent. It could not have been just cash, because the richest of the Trucial States, Abu Dhabi, had offered to pay the cost if we would remain, and was refused. Harold Wilson was chiefly interested in being rid of relics of our imperial past, and was also influenced by the unhappy situation of sterling. Julian had been given the difficult task of seeing that the many treaties of the nineteenth and twentieth centuries were still complied with, but at the same time laying the foundation of the federation that became the United Arab Emirates (UAE), but which the rulers themselves at that time showed no sign of wanting.

After he retired Julian was asked which had been his favourite post. His choice of Dubai surprised his audience. *'Because, you see, nothing beats the first post when you are in charge.'* Apart from that, the attraction of being Political Agent in Dubai was that it was totally unlike almost any other Foreign Office posting. The closest thing might be an assignment in the Indian Civil service to one of the princely states. On early maps the present UAE was sometimes called the Pirate Coast, since once it had been a base from which Arab dhows attacked British ships on their way to India. To put an end to piracy, a detachment of British ships sacked the town of Ras al Khaimah, and on 8 January 1829 four Sheikhs of the region were persuaded to sign a treaty with Britain by which they agreed never to attack British ships, and not fight each other or anyone else during the pearl diving season (at that time the sale of pearls was the only source of income for the region). Thereafter the region was named the Trucial Coast, put under British protection, and offered free access to all British controlled ports. In return Britain promised to defend the rulers against aggression by any foreign power.

For the first 130 years there were no British officials based in the sheikhdoms to see that the Treaties were enforced. The collapse of the pearl industry brought poverty to an area whose wealth Milton had once said compared only with the richness of Satan's throne in Hell. It was some years before oil was discovered, 1960 in Abu Dhabi and 1966 in Dubai, but oil changed everything. It created an urgent need for agreed boundaries in the desert, for the establishment of the rule of law, and an end to the continual internecine skirmishes among the sheikhdoms. I could see trouble ahead when I heard that the Shah of Iran had renewed his claim for the islands of Abu Musa and the Greater and

Lesser Tunbs in the Gulf, but I thought he would most probably wait to claim them until no British troops remained to defend them.

As the Queen's representative in the Trucial States, and a trusted advisor to its six rulers, Julian would need to have a better command of Arabic, and in particular Gulf Arabic. Written Arabic does not vary between regions, but Julian would need to be able to speak the local dialect of the Gulf, so he was told to spend the summer improving his Arabic at the Middle East Centre for Arab Studies (MECAS), the Foreign Office school in the village of Shemlan in the Lebanon. This may not have helped much because most of the teachers there were Palestinian, and did not speak Gulf Arabic, but a summer in the hills above Beirut could only be looked forward to with delight. MECAS was locally known in the area as a school for spies, because the sound of explosions seemed to come from one of the buildings. (I don't think the villagers had ever heard of the game of squash). Shemlan was a charming village. Julian worked at his Arabic under an Iraqi teacher and studied the Gulf rules of etiquette; that is to say, he tried to learn the many ways of being very polite and complimentary and learning to avoid the many ways of being rude by mistake. I was advised to try to master enough Arabic to be able to talk to the wives of the rulers.

We rented a small stone house in Shemlan from where we could look down on the distant shimmering Mediterranean. Every morning Julian walked over to the school and after leaving four-year old Robert at a nursery, I would follow him. At the end of July, the older three children joined us for their summer holidays. Antonia brought the news that she had won the prize of a four-day sailing course in Cheltenham for a story she had written for a Puffin Books competition, and was angry that she had to ask for a cash prize instead because she would be away in Lebanon.

An idyllic summer followed. When we had had enough of the beach, we would explore crusader castles, have a picnic by a deep pool in a shady stream, visit the ruins of Baalbek, or go to watch the potter at Jisr el Khadi (the bridge of the judge) and stock up with earthenware pots to take back to England. Our car had been delivered to Dubai, so we had bought an old banger just for use in Lebanon. Coming home from Byblos after bathing in the Dog River, our aging VW beetle failed again. Julian managed to find a teenage Armenian mechanic who diagnosed dirt in the fuel (again), and rigged up a device which involved Julian driving slowly to the garage with him sitting sideways on the back bumper, and hanging on with the fingers of one hand, while feeding petrol into the engine with the other.

Julian left for Dubai on 30th August, telephoning after he arrived to warn me that the shade temperature was usually about 105 degrees and very humid. It would not be until October that we would have 'Director's weather.' Warned to expect guards of honour and bands playing the national anthem, Julian had bought three hats before leaving Beirut: one for taking salutes, one for every-day in hot weather, and a five shilling one for picnics. It was just as well he did because he needed No. 1 as soon as he landed.

He wrote describing his arrival:

> 'My predecessor warned me that I would always feel I was just _acting_ the part of Political Agent. The signal is given for you to leave the plane, the heat biffs you in the face, sweating and clutching your hat firmly, you step out. Flash bulbs pop and there is a flicker of salutes led by a Lieutenant Colonel of the Grenadier Guards. You doff your hat while a band plays the national anthem on pipes and drums. Inside the airport building the local notables and the British agency staff greet you. In a flagged Humber we have priority over all other vehicles and we draw up in the Agency where another guard of honour is waiting inspection beneath the flagstaff – mostly Indian or Pakistani, all of whom seem to be persuaded that you are indeed the new Political Agent. So that appears to be that.'

He also described his first impression of the rulers, five of whom came to call on him next day (the other being away shooting bustard in Iran).

> They each came with armed retainers and in a Mercedes. Sheikh Rashid of Dubai, strong, decisive, energetic and quick, Ras al Khaimah, wall-eyed but shrewd, Umm al Qaiwain, sickly but courteous and invites me to lunch next week, Ajman, like the elder Steptoe, with much the same sense of humour, Sharjah, suave and fond of Blackpool and Lytham St Anne's.

Julian had to return their calls the following day. He had orders to chide Ajman for allowing illegal immigrants to land on his shores. The Ruler knew this, but feigned incredulity, and next day 42 immigrants were delivered to the Agency, posing quite a problem. Rashid asked Julian to come to call at his office on the creek, from where he keeps an eye on newly arrived boats, from each of which he takes 4.625% of the value of their contents. Julian had two requests – automatic visas for certain approved journalists and agreement that foreigners committing traffic offences would in future be tried by local courts instead of by our judge in the Agency. Each subject took one minute to explain and half a minute for Rashid to agree to. Rashid then took out an aspirin bottle and filled his long white clay pipe with the dry locally grown tobacco.

Julian's call on Mohammed of Fujairah was rather different. The rules for so-cial behaviour taught at MECAS included: _If you want to insult anyone, display the soles of your feet._ Mohammed had obviously not been taught this because the first thing he did was show Julian the soles of his feet, so that Julian could see how dry the earth had been in Iran, where he had been shooting bustard. From his expression Julian guessed that the Ruler meant no insult and that his action showed only that he had not had a nursemaid to teach him polite behaviour! After the Ruler had outlined his schemes for setting up Fujairah International Airways and a kind of Radio Caroline, he broke into a long speech: how Arabs were children without the British, that we were their best and oldest friends, that he would never take any step without consulting Julian, and ended by asking if we would like to give him two Land Rovers! He kept his tobacco in an aluminium cassette for 35mm films which he thought better than an aspirin bottle.

I stayed behind in Shemlan because, as a result of cooling myself in a dirty pond on a mountain walk, I had huge and horrible boils on my legs which refused to heal in spite of injections and prolonged soaking in salt water. The Lebanese opinion of health standards in the Gulf was such that it was thought that on no account should I take my boils to such a dangerous climate. However, as I was keen to join Julian, as soon as I had seen our three older children into the plane for England, I flew to Dubai with Robert and an ex-Dragon School matron called Janet, whom we had engaged to keep an eye on him. As soon as I had the opportunity, I swam in the very salty Gulf water and the boils instantly disappeared.

Dubai struck me as a delightful place. We had inherited a splendid major domo, Ghulam, who on special occasions wore a turban fastened with a military badge in the front, and had proudly showed Julian a sheaf of references from the British officers he had worked for on the North West Frontier. He recruited other servants as needed, but for the first year we had a continual problem with the cook. Ghulam would say he knew a famous cook with much experience. He would be given a visa to come from Pakistan. He would arrive and turn out to be a relation of Ghulam who had no idea of cooking anything except basic Indian food. This made entertaining a nightmare because I could never rely on anything being produced that was edible. Eventually, with the help of the owner of one of the hotels, we got a delightful cook from Goa, called Dominique. Dominique's reputation must have spread, because one day I found three Arabs with hawks on their wrists and rifles across their chests squatting in the sand outside the kitchen door, sent by Sheikh Rashid 'to learn how to make roast potatoes'.

When I was taken to meet Sheikha Sanna, Rashid's cousin, I asked her whether she thought there were too many Pakistanis in Dubai. She replied: *'Pakistanis very good, want work night and day. If Rashid allow more people from Egypt or Jordan they only want to make trouble, trouble, trouble'*. Sheikha Sanna was the most modern and intelligent seeming sheikha, and her daughter was shortly to marry Rashid's eldest son. I tried in vain to persuade her that when she moved into the new house she was building, she should not pull down her mud-block square house with gun emplacements round the top. Julian said I would have had more success had I told her that in a few years people would pay good money to be shown round it. Outside her house were a line of dusty old trucks with 'Sanna al Maktoum' written in a shaky hand across the front. She owned nearly all the passenger boats on the creek including the ones that ferried passengers from ocean-going ships and managed them personally. She promised to get her sewing girl to make me a beautiful gold mask, and allowed me to try one on. Since they were impregnated with indigo, even wearing the mask for a few seconds made me look as if I had a heavy cold.

Dubai in those days had dusty winding streets with no names, and houses with no numbers. There was a single (very new) bridge and just one single track paved road leading to Sharjah. The creek wound through the city like the Grand Canal through Venice, its banks lined with elegant wooden dhows. We soon learned the names for the different types: the main ones were either *boums* with a high bow and stern, or *sambuks* with masts raked forward. In those days, Dubai had no deep-water harbour, so goods had to be unloaded onto lighters operated by the British firm of Gray Mackenzie and ferried up the creek. I remember a perpetual stream of men (usually immigrants from Iran, Pakistan or Baluchistan) chanting endlessly some strange mantra as they unloaded bags of cement. If I wanted to buy fish, the Agency boatman would ferry me across the creek in the Agency *abra,* a traditional wooden boat. I would walk down to the beach where, squatting beside their boats, women in *abayas* (like black dressing gowns) wearing face masks dyed with indigo, would sell the fish their husbands had caught. The varied faces in the Dubai *suq* seemed to belong to every one of the many races in that part of the world, so it was impossible to know who was a true native of Dubai. As well as the local version of Arabic, some spoke northern arabic, others urdu, farsi or belouchi. In the *suq* gloomy looking Arabs sucked on 7UP lemonade, watching hawk-eyed as boxes of gold bars were humped into their strong rooms.

We were the first occupants of a splendid air-conditioned house (finished just in time for the announcement of withdrawal from the Gulf – exactly as happened for the Governor's house in Aden). The interior designers, we decided, must have had blank cheques to spend at Heals and Casa Pupo. The house of Julian's predecessor as Political Agent had been passed on to his Assistant, and beyond that was the house of the Archivist, Fred Pett. The Petts' daughter Sarah was about a year older than Robert but that did not stop him finding his way across the sand to the Petts house as soon as he was awake, often at about 5 o'clock in the morning. Her father, with some embarrassment, had to ask his boss politely to keep his son indoors before breakfast.

I gradually learnt about the history of the Trucial States, how we came to be there, what we were doing, how it was changing, and to appreciate what a big job Julian had in front of him. Since 1951, all the Rulers had met regularly as the Council of the Trucial States, to discuss problems and solve differences. The meeting was always chaired by the Political Agent. To enforce their decisions there was a small local army, the Trucial Oman Scouts (TOS), with headquarters in Sharjah, most of whose officers were seconded from British regiments. I had no difficulty in believing that in the not-too-distant past, life here had been nasty, brutish and short. There were impressive Beau Geste style forts everywhere, which were now serving as local headquarters for the Scouts. Even in 1969 some tribes preferred to settle old scores by gun battles. Coming home in the dark one weekend from Dibba on the Batinah Coast through the mountains near the Musandam Peninsula, Julian and I rounded a corner to find the track ahead blockaded, with 12 or so rifles pointing directly at us. With help from our driver Gamba, we learnt that the blockade had been set up by men from Fujairah who had some on-going dispute with a group of the Shihuh tribe from Ras al Khaimah, but they proved quite willing to let us pass. We drove at once to the nearest Scout fort at Masafi, and Julian ordered a patrol out to deal with them.

Because oil companies needed to know the exact limits of the areas on which they were buying concessions, boundaries had to be established, which involved many disputes. A junior British diplomat had spent several winters trudging and riding over the interior asking who owned which tree and who had dug which well. I remember quite soon after I arrived Julian got a message to say that men from a certain tribe had taken away women found drawing water at a well which the men claimed did not belong to them. Julian ordered out the Scouts, who saw to the return of the women to their families, and then visited the two Rulers in question to reach a permanent agreement on the disputed boundary.

In 1959, long before we arrived, the Gulf states had reason to be very grateful for the terms of that 1829 Treaty. A Saudi force had overnight occupied part of the Buraimi Oasis, in the sheikhdom of Abu Dhabi, where the Saudis had been advised that an oil strike was probable. Under the Treaty of 1829 Britain was bound to defend all the Trucial States against marauders, and Julian's father, who had recently retired as British Ambassador to Iran, had been appointed the British representative on the arbitration commission. He resigned after discovering evidence that the delegates from Pakistan and Cuba had been bribed to settle in the Saudi's favour. One of Julian's predecessors organized the TOS, reinforced by the forces of the Sultan of Muscat (also with British Officers) to occupy the oasis and expel the Saudis. Whether the Saudis ceased to pursue their claim on account of the adverse publicity they had received over their bribery, I cannot be sure, but had it not been for the 1829 Treaty which specifically gave the British Government the duty to protect the integrity of the Trucial States, a satisfactory result might not have been achieved or not without bloodshed —nor would Abu Dhabi have become as rich as it is today.

Julian had only been in Dubai a short time when a telegram came from

London, sent to all posts world-wide: Heads of Government to be approached and asked to support a boycott of trade with Rhodesia. Julian sat up most of the night with a dictionary thinking how best to explain the idea of a boycott to his six rulers. Shortly before 4 am he left in a Land Rover making first for Fujairah, the most distant sheikhdom, and then driving west along the northern coast of the Gulf to see the other sheikhs in turn. Finally, just before the heat became intolerable, he reached Sheikh Rashid of Dubai. Over lunch he told me how intently Sheikh Rashid had listened while he did his best to explain that the British Government hoped that mounting world pressure and cutting off imports to Rhodesia would cause Ian Smith to set a timetable to transition Rhodesia to majority rule. The Sheikh looked at Julian with his penetrating eyes and said: '*And you think that sanctions will achieve this?*' He obviously had his doubts, but said: '*If Her Majesty wants to have my support, please tell her that I am very happy to give it.*' Julian was very pleased that he was able so quickly to cable back to London his 100% success in obtaining support from all the sheikhs for Britain's policy of boycotting Rhodesia.

Some time after this, instructions arrived from the Foreign Office proposing that countries who held sterling should undertake to keep a fixed proportion of their reserves in London and in return we would undertake not to devalue our currency. Julian made an appointment to see Rashid asking if his oil advisor could be present in case his Arabic should fail, and in fifteen minutes was back in his car with Rashid's signature to the agreement in his pocket.

On one of our early evenings in Dubai we were on the way to dinner with the Commander of the TOS, when, reaching the point where the road to Sharjah diverged, it was clear that something odd was happening in front of us. Julian ordered the driver to stop and got out to investigate. It was quite dark. Dubai had yet to have street lights. He found a truck being driven by Eric Tulloch, the Scottish road and water engineer, with Sheikh Rashid on board and the back filled with empty oil barrels. The Ruler himself was positioning the barrels in the road to mark out the perimeter of Dubai's first roundabout.

It was an exciting time to be in Dubai. Everything was changing, new enterprises popped up overnight; the deep-water port was built and then grew bigger and bigger. Then there was a new hospital, an English church, and whatever was done was done by British firms, British engineers, and British architects, and it seemed that nothing happened without Julian being in some way involved.

When July and August came round, I immediately saw that Dubai had one major imperfection: the summer climate, which was unbearable, not only for the heat but also from the curtain of humidity which made it impossible to see the other side of the creek. Fortunately it was the custom for senior expatriates to fly home for the summer and leave the country to their assistants.

We thought the place that offered the greatest contrast to Dubai was Ireland and we decided to spend our leave once again in Castletownshend, where we rented Mall Cottage, which belonged to a relation of Dan Somerville. It was an ideal place for a family holiday. This time we rented two small sailing boats, which all the children but Robert learnt to manage.

Although the Prime Minister's 1968 statement had referred only to removing troops, Julian thought it clear that the special British position and the Treaties would have to go at the same time. Three years was a dauntingly short time to dismantle British protection and put something workable in its place. Poor Julian. The Rulers still trusted Britain to a remarkable degree and most of them wanted more advice about how to set up a union of the emirates than we felt able to give them. The main obstacle was the rivalry between Abu Dhabi and Dubai, each of which thought there was not much advantage in the union for them, and were therefore reluctant to make concessions. Abu Dhabi was very small and unbelievably rich. Its Ruler, Sheikh Zaid, wanted to build a bridge over a creek as Rashid had done, only he had no creek. So he ordered a bridge to be dug and water made to flow underneath at a cost of about £8m.

After one meeting of the Trucial States Council, Julian found himself sitting on the ground eating rice with his fingers with rich Sheikh Zaid on one side and on the other, the ruler of Ajman, who had many wives, slightly fewer camels, and no oil. Since the announcement that the British were leaving, the rulers had been prepared to take decisions in principle, but preferred leaving the details to others. Eventually they reached the stage when the details too required decisions, and Julian was afraid that if things did not go well, the two big states might go their own way and the smaller states would sell out to the highest bidder. However, thanks to Rashid's charm and tact, and Zaid providing £1.7 million to balance the budget, everyone parted in good humour.

Besides trying to prevent disputes between the sheikhs, Political Agents were sometimes called upon to give advice. Julian was involved in a decision about the size of the new deep-water port. When the old harbour became silted up by the action of the sea, Rashid had been advised by a previous PA to take advice from the English engineering firm of Sir William Halcrow. At a meeting to consider their recommendations, Halcrow's local representative, Neville Allen, explained that, considering the prospects for future trade, his firm recommended that a deep-water port be built with berths for four ships. '*Four berths!*' said Sheikh Rashid. '*You British think too small – eight berths*'. The British consultants were amazed: '*Where will these ships come from*'? '*Not eight, Sixteen*' Sheikh Rashid replied. Nobody could have been more surprised than Julian when Rashid was proved right. The very first month the port was open, every berth was occupied, not by boats carrying cement or loading oil, but long distance freighters and tankers calling to replenish their water tanks, because at that time Dubai was the only gulf port with sweet water – a permanent piped water supply from Al Awir (discovered by the Scottish water engineer Eric Tulloch) having been available in Dubai since 1963. Dubai sold water before it earned a penny from oil.

We had a house with piped water and central air conditioning, but Government money did not run to landscaping, so soft pale sand surrounded our house on all sides. Our new house had been designed and furnished to a high standard by the Ministry of Works – but had the kind of faults that might be expected, since I doubt if those making the house plan had ever visited Dubai. Rain was infrequent, but not unknown, and when it rained the flat roof leaked. One room was lined with shelves, but I seem to remember the post report said 'Don't bring books if you value their bindings'. We had obeyed instructions and so the shelves were unnecessarily bare. Upstairs we had a purdah room, with ceramic screening on the windows. But since no Arab ladies in purdah ever visited me, the only use we found for this room was for monopoly and other long-running games played by the children in the holidays. The Agency compound included a hard tennis court and a swimming pool shaded by bamboo slats. Further away was simple accommodation for our servants, that in British India might have been referred to as 'native quarters'. In front of the Agency offices the Union Jack fluttered. A high wire fence shut out intruders. In theory any slave wanting to be freed, was, when he touched the flagpole, entitled to the protection of the British Government and a ceremony of manumission would follow. In fact, no one tried to avail themselves of this while we were there, although I was told that some time previously a group of men from the Ruler's palace had arrived, but changed their minds when they found that there was no monetary reward on offer. Slavery had of course long since been abolished, but I believe some of the servants in the entourage of the rulers might technically have been slaves, since I doubted they were paid, or that they had any prospect of leaving the family they worked for. One day about a year later, the ruler of Ajman asked Julian if he could help him with a debt owed by the Saudi royal family. Julian said he would be very pleased to help if he could have the details. It turned out that it was payment for 'girls' supplied at the request of the Saudis. I think, so far as Julian's help was concerned, the matter of payment was dropped.

Everyone knew that the old order was about to change, and what was so exciting was that there was an enormous feeling of optimism. To me Dubai seemed like Paradise. In the *suq* you could buy gold and real pearls. The alleyways, the sandy *sabkha,* stamped smooth by generations of sandals, were crowded with people in exotic dress buying spices and incense and brightly patterned Indian materials. I used to poke about in the *suq* and take an old dress to be copied by one of the Indian tailors, who would often have the gar-

Women drawing water from a well 1968

Meeting of Trucial States Rulers 1968

Margaret Bullard beside the creek in white MG (first open top car in Dubai)

Sheikh Rashid Bin Saeed Al Maktum, ruler of Dubia with Julian 1970

ment ready for collection the next morning. Goats fed on rubbish in the vacant lots between the shops. There was considerable laughter when our white MG was unloaded, the first convertible car most people had seen, but, on hardened *sabkha*, where we did not need a Land Rover, it was much admired, especially with a Union Jack fluttering from the bonnet when Julian was at the steering wheel.

For long journeys over uncertain terrain we used the Agency Land Rovers which were driven by one of three local drivers, the most notable being Gamba, a former pearl diver, a huge man and a great character. Gamba knew everyone and everyone knew Gamba. One weekend, when the children were with us, we drove to the beach beyond Ras el Khaimah to the point where the mountains came down to the sea, set up our tents, cooked an evening meal and lay in sleeping bags round a fire while Gamba told stories in Arabic about the stars, which Julian translated for us as we dropped asleep. If there had recently been an unaccustomed storm, we would pick up broken bits of Chinese blue and white porcelain (some shards were later identified by the British Museum as being 16th and 17th century), evident traces of the route by which in years past Chinese products had reached Europe. Antonia, Vicky and James spent most of the mornings during the Christmas holidays taking swimming lessons from the RAF sports instructor and went proudly back to school with Bronze, Silver and Gold Life Saving badges to show their friends.

After the children had returned to school, we drove down the Batinah Coast on the Gulf of Oman to Muscat, which took two days. There was no road. We drove with two wheels on the wet sand and two wheels in the water, stopping at the two villages we came to. At Sohar all the men of the village were engaged in fishing by slowly hauling long ropes at the ends of a net the size of two tennis nets to the accompaniment of much chanting, until, as they neared the shore, the central part was one boiling mass of very small fish, which were eaten or laid out in the sun and sold for fertiliser. The first sight one got of Muscat was stunning. Clamped in a ring of mountains and cringing under the two forts which commanded the harbour, were several elegant palaces all but one belonging to the family of the Sultan, but none so fine as that of the British Consul General, its ironwork and balconies the signature of the British army sappers who had designed it. The town itself was mostly made up of wretched dwellings of reeds, sacking, cardboard and beaten out tin cans. Everything in life was regulated by the Sultan 300 miles away in Salalah, who forbade not only drinking and smoking, but also dancing, singing and all kinds of music. At 8 pm a gun would boom, the gates of the town would be shut and no one might stir in the streets without a lantern, or, if in a vehicle, without a written permit. Muscat's climate had a terrible reputation, many British Consuls General having met early deaths, which made one glad to be living in Dubai.

We went home with a bag of shells and a silver model of a ship with six move-able guns and a pair of flags flying in opposite directions, which later looked splendid in the centre of our dinner table in Bonn.

Even with money coming in from oil, the Sultan of Oman was very reluc-tant to spend any of it on improving infrastructure and the lives of his citizens. There were other complaints against him: one was his refusal to take British advice on rules of the road. Bill Cardon, the British Consul General, had been instructed to tell the Sultan that now he was no longer the only car driver, it was necessary to have a rule on whether cars should drive on the left or the right and to suggest that it would be best to adopt the right, the same side as the neighbouring territories. He immediately asked: *'Which side do you drive on in England'* The Consul was forced to admit the truth, which I suspect the cun-ning ruler knew already, *'But you see when the traffic routes have been the same for a hundred years or so, it would be very costly to change'*. *'I will change when you change'* was his reply.

It was the Arab tradition of hospitality that filled our social life, because there was always a visitor who must be entertained and of course at every large party given by one of the more permanent residents of Dubai, the *Mu'atamad* had to be included. If it was an Arab feast, the food would be served early. After coffee one could leave and still have a couple of hours before bed. If the hosts were Asian or expatriate, their habit was not to serve the food until the very end, in order to keep their guests as long as possible. After some weary evenings, Julian got into the habit of saying to his host on arrival *'I am expect-ing visitors on the plane from England* (which arrived about 11.30pm*) whom I have to meet, so I shall have to leave in time to get to the airport'*. We had end-less visitors from London and from Bahrain, and we had to arrange the right ambience for them to meet whoever they needed to see. There were parties to greet new arrivals or to say farewell to those leaving, new bank managers, new managers for Costains, Schlumberger, and the other oilfield supply companies, and colleagues from other posts who wanted to be shown the most exciting city in the Gulf, and of course to call on Sheikh Rashid. We had a visit from Mrs Neame, a left-wing Oxford intellectual who asked about the strength of the opposition to the rulers, at which Julian laughed and said *'There isn't any'* and was immediately rebuked by her that alas that was the typical Foreign Of-fice view – to notice nothing until it was too late. Julian replied that in Dubai everyone with any brains was making money as fast as they could, and that was all they had time for.

A Conservative delegation led by Ted Heath, accompanied by Douglas Hurd, came to decide whether the Labour Party policy to withdraw from the Gulf should be reversed by the Conservatives should they win the next election, provided the rulers were to say publicly that they wanted us to stay.

We invited most of the influential locals to discuss the matter with our visitors from London. After they had left, we gathered round the pool with cold drinks. Ted Heath turned to Julian and asked for his advice. I remember Julian answered that since Harold Wilson's statement had become so widely known, it was not realistic to suppose that a future government had any option but to carry out the policy. Ted Heath tilted back his chair and replied: '*Yes, but if we were in power you would be paid to say the opposite, wouldn't you?*' I was stunned. Julian's advice was surely of little use if he was expected only to support the view of his questioner. Surely objective trenchant advice would be what Ministers would want to hear? I did not like to think that Heath would prefer to hear support for his own party's policy trotted out. I wondered if the Conservatives knew that Sheikh Zaid had offered to cover whatever it cost to keep the British presence in the Trucial States? The Ruler of Sharjah only wanted us to stay because he looked to Britain to throw the Iranians out should they try to take Abu Musa. Julian explained to the visitors that the discovery of oil in offshore Dubai had already inevitably changed our outdated Treaty relationship with the sheikhdoms, and that the happy framework of life in the Gulf before 1968 when British paramountcy was accepted almost without any troops needing to be here, had been disturbed for ever, and could not be restored either by taking the troops out or by leaving them where they were. If Wilson were to lose the election and Heath became Prime Minister, we might have to unscramble the omelette, but Heath seemed to be under the delusion that we could stay without a collision with Iran, and that what the Rulers wanted was of secondary importance. In a subsequent article in the *Sunday Times* Heath wrote that we would remain as 'a presence in some form'.

Later, as we retired for the night, I was amazed to hear Ghulam saying to Mr Heath: '*What time you like Betty, Sir?*' I could not believe what I was hearing. But Julian's hearing was better. He heard: '*What time you like bed tea, Sir?*' Heath was not a man who tried to make himself widely loved. I met him not long after at a London reception and mentioned his visit to Dubai, and he said: '*Oh yes! I remember visiting you in Dubai. Your bathroom was very uncomfortable, it was impossible to avoid hitting one's head on the taps.*' Rude and also baffling because the guest bathroom was an exact replica of ours in which it was quite impossible to get hit by the taps.

At MECAS we had got to know Bill and Diana Peyton. They were now occupying the only beautiful traditional old house in Muscat, (now the museum). Bill's job was to liaise between the government and Petroleum Development (Oman), which in effect meant its operating partner, Shell. They kindly invited us to stay and sent a company plane for us so that we could avoid the long drive down the coast. Julian had received orders after our last visit that I would only be allowed to visit Muscat again provided my legs and arms and head were covered at all times. Nourah, the wife of the ruler of Sharjah, obligingly lent me a turquoise satin tunic with trousers to match. The Peytons invited an elderly relation of the Ruler to lunch. He brought an ancient camera and took many pictures of Diana and me inside their house. Naturally, with an inside temperature of well over 100 degrees, we were wearing cotton dresses and flip flops. Like the rat I should have guessed him to be, he showed his snaps to the Sultan, who demanded that Julian never bring his wife with her bare legs into his Sultanate again! There was hardly time for me to get this news, before, with connivance from the British Government, the Sultan was removed from Oman and his son put in his place. The Sultan ended his days in the Dorchester Hotel.

Looking at my photograph albums, I can no longer give names to the many Arabs, Iranians, Indians, Pakistanis and Europeans we knew in Dubai. There are photographs of excursions to Easa Gurg's farm and staying at the Agricultural research station, fancy-dress parties, a team event with hockey sticks, pictures of local girls getting married, staying in TOS camps in the desert, and taking a group of children on a camel ride to a swimming pool in an oasis belonging to Sheikh Rashid. I remember sailing with the Allen family to camp for a weekend on Abu Musa, where the fine red sand, coloured by iron oxide, was once exported as a basic ingredient of jeweller's rouge. There was no cinema and we had no TV – just the BBC World Service to keep us abreast of what was happening. However, we were able to borrow films and a projector from the RAF, and sometimes we put on a film show in the garden under the stars in a small enclosed courtyard off the dining room.

Sometimes on Fridays we went out fishing in a dhow belonging to one of the gold smugglers. At that time, smuggling gold to India was the main source of income in Dubai. The airport was very small and informal. One walked a few steps across the tarmac to board the plane, often seeing gold ingots in boxes labelled Johnson Matthey piled on unguarded carts. It was not illegal to buy gold in London and ship it to the willing buyers in Dubai, but the Indian government exacted a high duty on the import of gold, since they did not want its citizens to spend their money on something as useless to the economy as gold, but that did not stop wives and daughters liking to be given gold bracelets and necklaces to wear. The Indian navy did their best to board Arab ships and confiscate the gold. When a ship left Dubai, the sailors wore padded jackets with many pockets stuffed with gold ingots, the cost of which was spread widely around the whole community in Dubai. Sometimes the Indian navy caught the smugglers, and then there were long faces in the *suq*. Sometimes when an Indian patrol boat was sighted, they lowered their gold below the surface, marked the place with a buoy, and retrieved it after the Indian authorities had conducted their search.

During one of the children's holidays we took them on a fishing trip on a boom – or was it a sambuk? But certainly it was in one of the boats used to carry gold to India. The day dawned calm and still, with a forecast of light showers from the west, so we set off. After about two hours, we hove to, and began to fish, (actually we just held the lines, leaving the sailors to put on the bait and pull the hooks out of the creatures' mouths and so on). I had just caught two on one line, when we felt a sudden puff of wind from the northeast. It was obvious at once that there was a storm coming towards us. Five minutes later the crew were frantically putting up canvas screens to protect us from the rain and spray. I found a place where I could wedge my back against the wheelhouse and anticipate the worst waves. I didn't move for three hours. It took us much longer to return home because we couldn't go at full speed. At first I wondered how many people would be sick, then if anyone would not be sick, then whether one of the children would be washed overboard, and then whether the boat had radio in case the single engine stopped. The owner of the boat, in a beige summer suit, just laughed and said we ought to see some of the storms off Bombay. The only other person who was laughing and not saying their prayers was Janet, the former matron who looked after Robert. She had tied herself to a mast with her scarf and was leading the children in singing sea chanties.

The owner of the boat was a charming chap who had arrived in Dubai 20 years before with one small boat and now had eleven *boums*. He was illiterate but gold smuggling had made him a great deal of money, so much that he seemed to think it rather a joke that he had lost a boat laden with gold worth two million rupees not long before. The day ended with him handing presentation gold watches to everyone. Julian's and mine had of course to be sent to the *Toshakhana* in Bahrain. This was a small strong room where all gifts to British civil servants were stored, each one clearly labelled by whom they were given and when. Then, when a civil servant was invited to a wedding by someone eminent, he could ask to be supplied with a suitable present from the store in Bahrain.

When local women invited me to their houses, there would be a lavish spread often accompanied by Victorian children's games and even dancing. I remember at the house of the Galadari sisters, members of a Dubai merchant family, playing pass the parcel with the variation that when the music stopped, the person on whom the parcel landed, had to open the string and read aloud a task she had to do, and to whom she had to pass the parcel afterwards. '*To the most beautiful girl in the room*'. How could a local girl do that without arousing lifelong enemies? This was often solved by passing the parcel to me so that no one was slighted. Sometimes I entertained them at the Agency, offering a swim in the pool, or a game of ping pong, which they enjoyed. Once one of them took us out in one of her husband's dhows 'for a picnic' at which they passed round betel nut stuff that we had to chew. It was rather nasty and turned my mouth purple.

I had spent two months trying to learn Arabic at MECAS with a view to being able to talk to the wives of the rulers when I made the obligatory calls on days of religious celebration: the birthday of the Prophet, or Eid at the end of Ramadan, I can't say I was very fluent. I used to take a Palestinian lady, Mrs Bitar, with me when I visited Sheikha Latifa, wife of the ruler of Dubai, and all I can say is that sometimes, and only sometimes, did I understand her answers to my questions! On one visit Sheikha Latifa had just returned from her first visit to London. She told me that her husband had told her to stay inside her hotel room until he returned when he would show her some of the sights. He was away a long time and she was impatient, so she and some of her ladies took a taxi and asked to be taken to Harrods, the fame of which had spread to Dubai. *'What did you buy'* I asked. *'Material' 'Patterned or plain?'* I asked (which was about the extent of my Arabic vocabulary). She looked at me with some scorn and replied *'Patterned of course.'* I gathered she had selected four whole rolls of patterned silk material and expected Harrods to deliver them to her hotel after which she would send a man with payment. I believe she made quite a scene when she discovered that without payment, they were not prepared to let her purchases leave the store!

All the Political Agents, the Consul General in Oman and their wives were invited every year for a two-day conference in Bahrain, hosted by the Resident, at that time Sir Stewart Crawford. Julian's comment was that all the others had much duller jobs than he: one state, one set of problems, one ruler. Julian's job had endless variety: dining with the Chairman of Costains, adjudicating the ownership of date palms, dealing with bank guarantees (at which he felt quite at home after Moscow), and once even conducting a marriage ceremony for a Dutch businessman. He may have been less experienced in tribal matters, but he told me he got round this by persuading the parties to settle at the lowest level and only as a last resort appeal to him.

In December, just as we were greeting Antonia, Victoria and James for their second Christmas in Dubai, (and I remember I had had a boy's sized TOS uniform made for James, which he wore for the rest of the holidays), and just as we were considering whether the children would mind very much if we had no Christmas tree, because real ones were impossible to come by, a FOR YOUR EYES ONLY telegram arrived for Julian. It was a command that he should present himself to the Prime Minister at 10 Downing Street on 23 December at 3 o'clock. I imagine Julian guessed what it must be about, though the telegram was not explicit.

At No. 10 he found Tony Parsons (who had been at the Embassy in Amman at the same time as we were) waiting outside Harold Wilson's office. He realised that they were both going to be interviewed as a replacement for the departing private secretary. Julian thought to himself: '*He will be a fool if he doesn't choose Tony.*' But the Prime Minister chose the third candidate, Mr. Moon of the Treasury. The Permanent Under Secretary (the senior civil servant in the Foreign Office), and Sir Stewart Crawford, the Resident in Bahrain, both sent him consoling letters which, however nice, did not prevent his disappointment. He told me that Wilson's choice of Moon rather than Tony Parsons made it clear that merit and capacity were not the selection criteria. Had he been chosen, he might have been ringing up Washington on the hot-line, instead he had to spend the day dealing with a man from Ras al Khaimah who killed a woman and wounded two men in Fujairah, in retaliation for a murder committed two years earlier which was in turn a reprisal for another murder eight or nine years before that. And when he had dealt with that, he would have to turn his mind to the stamp concessions for Umm al Qaiwain and the problem of the Ajman electricity supply. In other words, small beer. However, at least there were always variations.

Many years later, at a reception in Buckingham Palace, Julian and I chanced to run into Harold Wilson and his wife. We talked, and after a bit Julian said: 'I have always wondered why you didn't choose Tony Parsons as your secretary as it seemed obvious to me that he would be far the best choice.' '*Oh, it was out of the question to choose you or Parsons – both Arabists. The Jews would never have stood for it*'. We assumed he was referring to influential party members in his constituency, not the Israelis.

There has recently been a serious struggle about anti-Semitism in the Labour party, and Jeremy Corbyn, the previous leader was suspended. I believe No. 10 is traditionally of the opinion that Foreign Office advice is bound to be prejudiced in favour of the Arab view, perhaps because many more diplomats have served in Arab countries than in Israel. After all there are 26 Arab cities with British diplomatic and consular posts and only four posts in Israel. In my opinion it is not acceptable that, on the grounds of having being sent to learn Arabic by the Foreign Office, and once or twice been posted to an Arab country, Tony Parsons and Julian should have been refused consideration for an extremely interesting post. Both he and Julian had spent many more years hundreds of miles away from the Middle East than working there.

I found that running a sizeable house with servants took not much less time than doing the housework and cooking oneself! In my spare time when the weather was right, there was tennis, swimming and sailing at the Army sailing club in the creek. But there were three things which were my main interest outside the family: The garden, the Women's Society and the Library. Jean Kendall, the wife of the head of the Development Office, had some time earlier started monthly meetings with local women for coffee and chat, meeting at everyone's houses in turn. Soon after I arrived, the Kendalls left, and I took over as organizer of the group. The young English doctor at the local hospital told me that TB was endemic among the Arabs who lived in the villages scattered about the peninsula, and also in the wretched camps made of paper and cardboard where the poorest foreign workers lived. I thought it would be a good charity project for the Women's Group. So, when I was in London, I went to see Lady Metcalfe, Chairman of the Save the Children Fund, to ask whether they would consider sending one or two nurses to carry out a vaccination programme. My proposal was that we should pay expenses and accommodation but that they would find a suitable team. Very soon afterwards I got the happy news that they could send one experienced middle-aged nurse and we thought Janet would like be her assistant, while Robert was at school.

To pay the expenses of the nurse we held raffles and sales of home-made food, and one year we even put on a fashion show. This was with the assistance of Sarah Miller, wife of our judge, who was a friend of the women who had started a fashionable shop in Kensington called Biba. She persuaded them to send out a large suitcase of Biba designed clothes, which we had copied in material we bought in the *suq*. We asked the most elegant women to be models, after which we auctioned the dresses. I wish I could say how effective the vaccination programme was, and whether TB was effectively reduced or eliminated through our efforts, but alas I have no figures. All I can say is that TB is now a thing of the past in the UAE, and I hope our efforts contributed to this. On my last two visits to the Emirates, in 2009 and 2019, I saw nobody who did not look adequately fed and clothed and housed. Robert sometimes accompanied Janet when she assisted the Save The Children nurse, and he later told me that being moved by the conditions of life in the villages and camps was the main reason why he decided to work in overseas aid when he left university.

I was never bored and I had no difficulty in filling my days. In addition to raising money for the Save the Children nurse and attending all the women's parties, I was sometimes asked to entertain a group of Bahraini ladies, who wanted to visit Dubai for the day. Sheikha Latifa would provide lunch and my smuggler friend would give them a boat trip on the creek. I also spent a great deal of time turning my patch of rough sand into a garden. I would send the gardener and one of the drivers down to the cattle market and get some unemployed boys to fill bags with droppings from the floor. We spread this on the sand, lawn, flower beds, flowering shrubs and even trees and watered, (provided one watered it the sand was amazingly fertile because sand is full of nutrients, it just does not retain moisture). Soon we had tomatoes from the seeds which been through the stomachs of the goats and camels and ended in the manure. I went to the botanic garden in Bahrain and returned with an aeroplane full of plants and handfuls of a creeping grass that flourished in the

Dubai climate. I went to the agricultural research station at Digdaga in Ras al Khaimah and got cuttings. I was given tree saplings, and by the time we left it had become quite park-like and eminently suitable for the Queen's birthday garden party. I did any hard work in the garden before breakfast, often on days when Julian had set off at 4 or 5 am to go to see one of the distant rulers and return before the heat became unbearable. The afternoon heat was enervating and office hours ended at 1.00 pm. After lunch one lay naked under a sheet and dozed until about 3.30pm before going for a sail or a swim.

Ann Coles, the wife of the Assistant Political Agent, spent much of her time making a serious study of how effective the traditional wind towers of Dubai's Bastaki Quarter were in reducing the temperature. How did the wind towers compare with the efficiency of modern air conditioning? She published an impressive study of her work entitled 'Windtowers,' a marvellous reference book of the architecture of old Dubai. The Bastaki Quarter houses were built on the same model as in some parts of southern Iran. Each house had a tower with slatted openings on all four sides, so from whichever compass point the wind blew, it was syphoned down into the main room of the house. I think she regretfully found that the traditional method of cooling a house was less effective than twentieth century air-conditioning.

My other interest was the Dubai Library. The story began in Sharjah where there was a battalion of Grenadier Guards, and later Scots Guards, training in desert warfare. One officer writing home to his grandmother, complained of the boredom of his life in Sharjah, which led Lady Verney to send out a parcel of twelve yo-yos, which, not being appreciated by the Guards officers, were handed on to the English school where Robert was being taught to read and write. Thank-you letters were written to Lady Verney in Eaton Square, who then sent out a huge parcel of books explaining that her husband had died, she was going blind, so she thought that the parents of the children who had written her such nice letters, might like some reading matter. The books were of excellent quality and the only possible place for them seemed to be the empty shelves in our study. When the word got round that we were opening a small library, we received a crate of books of a rather different type from the men working on the oil rig.

When I was home on leave in the summer, I went round church fetes and second-hand book shops and bought classics in reasonable condition – anything that I fancied actually – which I persuaded the RAF to fly out to us. Soon the books overflowed our shelves and there were questions about whether the Agency compound was suitable for housing a library used by the public, in view of its lack of security. Julian suggested we take over two rooms in the *suq* that had been designated as the commercial offices, but were more or less unused because business in Dubai was done in a rather different way. I think

I helped to make the first shelves, which were planks of wood held up by concrete blocks with sand bags at the ends of the rows. Then an ex-Adeni with a British passport asked if he might present us with proper shelves. Every reader was served with a cup of coffee by two tall young Arabs who were probably still on the Agency payroll. Soon we were in the business of reading reviews and ordering the latest new books from Blackwells.

In 1994 I visited a friend in Dubai, and was delighted and amazed to find that the Library was still a going concern in spite of having had to find new quarters many times. When I visited Dubai again in 2009, I found the Library was celebrating its fortieth birthday in the grounds of the British Consulate General, as it had by then become. In November 2019 the librarian wrote to tell me that The New Library had had to move (the eighteenth time!) to a site in the 'Gold and Diamond Park' and invited me to be guest of honour at its fiftieth anniversary celebration. I enjoyed very much being treated like a queen for five days, and got quite accustomed to giving interviews, making speeches and having my photograph taken a hundred times. I was very proud to be feted and to see the Library so well looked after, with more than 2,000 members and 26,000 books. They presented me with a book of photographs of the visit and also letters of thanks and appreciation of the Library, which were unbelievably touching.

It was during our last summer in Dubai that Antonia wrote to tell us that she had become increasingly critical of the math teaching at St Mary's, and that Marlborough College, which had exceptionally good math teachers, were now taking girls in the sixth form. She had written to the Headmaster asking if she could be considered and giving her exam results, and the mother of another girl who had also applied from St Mary's, could drive them over for an interview. I don't suppose the headmaster was accustomed to being approached by a pupil rather than a parent, and he wrote to Julian asking if he was in favour of his daughter's arrangements. We were bowled over by Antonia's competence in arranging her future for herself, a mention of poor teaching at St Mary's was a sure-fire way of getting total agreement from Julian, and in no time at all she was living with three other girls in the Headmaster's attic, and was so clearly flourishing and enjoying herself, that we decided to ask if the three younger Bullards could also come to Marlborough.

It was in the same summer that the Americans landed on the moon. Phillip Hurr, a newly arrived member of the Political Agency in Doha, capital of neighboring Qatar, sent us an amusing description of the arrival of news of the moon-landing there. The Agency had received a copy of its film, and decided to organize a public showing in the largest hotel. His letter ran:

'Rather to our surprise, the Ruler, Shaikh Ahmed, turned up and plonked himself down between Edward Henderson and myself. When we got to the famous 'One small

step for man' bit, the Ruler growled and said in a very loud voice, 'That's not the moon, is it?' Edward assured him that it was indeed the moon that Neil Armstrong had stepped on, to which the Ruler replied, to loud guffaws around the room, 'Huh, it looks more like Wakrah to me' (Wakrah being in those days an empty patch of desert ten miles or so south of Doha). The show over, the Ruler turned to me and asked 'How much did that lot cost then?' I said that I wasn't sure, but it must have been millions if not billions of dollars. The Ruler scratched his chin thoughtfully before growling 'Tell the Americans that next time they can land in Wakrah for nothing'.'

In May we made a short trip to Iran, flying to Shiraz, where smiling officials at the airport accepted bribes from those who had forgotten their cholera or smallpox certificates, and behind them a less smiling official accepted much bigger bribes from those with heavier weights on their consciences, like a couple of pounds of Indian tea or a packet of English cigarettes. Mahdi Tajir, once a lowly clerk and now Sheikh Rashid's right-hand man, begged us to make use of his house in Shiraz for a couple of nights, an offer which we were happy to accept. My fancy was taken by the beautiful colour and design of a locally made carpet in the *suq* in Shiraz. Julian's father had given us the name of an old friend of his who had begged us not to buy any carpets without asking his advice as we were bound to be cheated. This distinguished elderly gentleman came with us to look at the carpet the next day. Persian taste is for fineness and detail of the work. The carpet that had taken my fancy was coarse, bright and in my opinion beautiful. When we told him the asking price (the equivalent of about £25) he looked at us in amazement that we should expect his advice on anything so cheap. We apologised, I bought it, and it remains in the place of honour in the largest room in the house where I live now.

We drove on to Persepolis and Isfahan, delighted to see everyone in the *suq* at work hammering, printing, and stitching, whereas on the Arab side of the Gulf manual work was despised and left to Indians and Pakistanis. We did not have time to visit more than 26 of the 84 scheduled monuments, but we did call on a tea merchant, and ended up buying seven carpets. Julian put a stop to my buying any of the dozen more by which I was tempted, because he did not see how we could get them back to Dubai. We were staying on the shore of the Caspian Sea when a bevy of police cars arrived to tell Julian that he was urgently needed in Dubai. He was taken back to Teheran and put on a plane together with all the carpets. How I regretted that I had not bought more and just crossed my fingers that some way of getting them home would turn up!

We were back in Dubai having breakfast on the terrace of our house when Mehdi Tajir appeared with some papers in his hand asking for Julian's signature. Suddenly Julian realised that this was the *quid pro quo* for having been lent his house in Shiraz for two nights. He wanted Julian's signature to authorize the document on a date earlier than it should have been. Julian never had liked Mehdi and I don't think he found it difficult to refuse. Later I asked Julian if he was often offered a bribe. He told me that he was once receiving a representative of a German company who suddenly started showing him what seemed to be his collection of holiday snaps, until Julian realized that the he was being bribed to take him to see the Ruler. This was of course something which Julian did all the time, if he thought it would be in Rashid's interest to hear about the business proposal on offer. Payment didn't come into it. I could see that Julian found it unpleasant when he met eminent people like Julian Amery and Sir Kennedy Trevaskis trying to get the purchasing agency for Sheikh Zaid's army, although he could see the temptation when Zaid was spending so liberally – £24 m for a port, £4.2 m for the airport and £6.5 m for a new hospital. Julian was saddened to find Sir George Middleton's signature on the agreement for the stamp concession for Umm al Qaiwain.

In August 1969 we flew to Heathrow, hired a car, picked up my mother and the children, took the ferry from Swansea to Cork and returned to Castletown-shend. There, refreshed by the damp greenness of Ireland, and invigorated by the fishing and our friends, we spent a very happy month. During this time Sheikh Rashid had been having a small operation in the London Clinic, after which he was invited to lunch with the Queen at Buckingham Palace, and we were invited to accompany him. All I can remember of that occasion was the particularly delicious pudding made chiefly of mangoes. My neighbour (whose place card showed him to be Controller of the Household) refused to take any, whereupon I told him he was making a big mistake as it was so delicious. His reply, which I thought rather worrying, was *'Had a bad mango once. Never touch them now.'*

Looking back on our time in Dubai, it seems to have been an endless series of enjoyable trips. My favourites were to the tip of the Musandam peninsular, where we watched porpoises jumping, our two trips to Muscat, and our Persian holiday. I remember particularly the pleasure of staying in the house in Tehran where Julian's father, then the Ambassador, had spent most of the war, and being taken to the basement of the National Bank where we watched a wrestling match between huge, near-naked men, after which we were taken to see the Imperial Treasure: mounds of uncut emeralds and rubies displayed inside glass cases.

I was upset when Julian told me that the British government had been asked to approve the Shah of Iran's claim to the Tunb islands, which hitherto had been considered to belong to Ras el Khaimah. I suppose that for commercial reasons, it seemed to London less trouble to arouse the wrath of a small sheikh-dom than to oppose the Shah. The Iranian claim to Bahrain had been settled the previous year by a plebiscite at which the Bahrainis had voted against becoming part of Iran. It seemed to me that handing over two populated islands to another country was an action from a previous century. I was very keen to visit the islands, but the Resident in Bahrain had told Julian that were he to set foot on the Tunbs, the Shah might take it to be an Act of Aggression, but nobody would object if I chose to go. Julian did not think the Shah need know if two ladies visited the islands, and he arranged for us to be escorted by the local British chief of police.

Sarah Miller and I set out on our exploratory inspection of Greater Tunbs. If they were to be handed over to the Shah I wanted to find out whether those who lived there thought themselves Arab or Irani and to learn their views on the islands becoming Iranian. According to the census, only 200 Arabic speaking people lived on Greater Tunbs, which contained the lighthouse and the keeper's house, the largest building on the island. We received a terrific welcome from all the male islanders as we stepped out of our helicopter, but that may have been due to the fact that their last visitor was Sheikh Saqr of Ras al Khaimah, who had distributed 20 riyals to each of the children and two or three hundred to the grown-ups. As we sipped coffee under a shelter of palm fronds, we gathered that a goat had been slaughtered for us. Knowing that the cooking of a goat took at least four hours and that our pilot had to be back by 3 pm, we declined politely. We toured the island and saw concrete blocks being made for a house for the ruler's son, and were shown the power station, the school, and the irrigation pump. We met men making fish traps and a donkey being loaded up with tins of water. Every day someone would take the boat on a five-hour journey to the fish market in Dubai together with anyone who needed to go to hospital. They said they went less frequently to Ras al Khaimah and had never set foot in Iran. I felt that my findings justified me in my disgust at what became British Government policy. I don't believe the Shah hoped oil might be found in the surrounding waters. His claim to the little islands was based on nothing but their alleged strategic importance to a hostile Arab power, and therefore 'pre-emptively' to Iran. I consulted the only Admiral and General I knew in the Gulf about this, and found they considered that any power strong enough to contemplate action against Iran would certainly not have needed those waterless and harbourless islands to mount it from. Sheikh Saqr was still talking about getting his islands back when Julian visited him in 2009. Sadly, later, when Julian was Head of East European and Soviet Department, he learnt that Iranian forces had forcibly collected the entire population of the Tunb islands and removed them to Ras al Khaimah.

If I asked Julian what he had been doing all the morning, he usually replied something like: issuing an arms licence and a liquor permit, talking to the hospital about smallpox vaccination, listening to the woes of the son of one of the rulers whose father does not want him to go to Sandhurst, and receiving a local hotel manager bearing the gift of a silver jug and six mugs in hideous

The Political Agent at home in summer uniform in front of Residence

Fort at Buraimi with TOS Officer

Bombay taste. This, with small daily variations, was what his life was like most of the time. As we neared the end of our time in Dubai, he wanted to leave some improvement behind for his successor. But London turned down his request for a new car with air conditioning and demanded justification for the expenditure of £440 annually for the small motor boat that took me shopping, carried local staff across the creek and did other errands for the Agency. But they did promise to send a piano, even though there was no one in Dubai to tune it, nor anyone who knew how to play it. They did not reply to Julian's suggestion that instead of renting houses for junior staff they should build four or five in a corner of our large compound, which, if not needed after 1971, could be sold off at a profit.

It was during our last hot summer before we returned to England that the representative of Buttes Gas and Oil, which held the oil concession for the state of Umm el Qaiwain, tried to persuade Sheikh Ahmed to extend his offshore limits from 3 to 12 miles (the standard limit for all countries except Britain). This would also have meant encroaching on Sharjah's rights to the island of Abu Musa, which Julian was by the Treaty obliged to protect, as he was also bound to prevent conflicts between the rulers. Julian drove to the old mud fort at Umm al Qaiwain in sweltering heat to persuade Sheikh Ahmed to sign the letter to Buttes Gas and Oil forbidding them to drill offshore in Umm al Qaiwain water for three months. According to our Treaties we had the right to require such action whenever Britain judged that operations in any area might result in a dispute with an adjoining state. Julian said that this justification did not make it any less disagreeable, particularly as it would lead Occidental (which held the concession for Sharjah's drilling rights) to withhold the $1 million due in November. Julian spent four hours sitting on a sofa with broken springs repeating to the diabetic old ruler that he could not leave without Sheikh Ahmed's signature, trying to persuade him that to drill in disputed waters would not be in his long-term best interest, and proposing that perhaps, if the ownership of the sea-bed were to be extended, the money from the expected oil could be shared.

In the meantime, the American oil representative was interrupting and telling the Sheikh loudly and firmly that the British had no right to interfere, that their days of colonial rule were over, that the Sheikh was now his own master and so on. Julian repeatedly said: 'As the representative of Her Majesty's Government I advise you against taking unilateral action but to settle this...' The ruler, who could not read or write, had a thumb pad of purple ink, and his trembling fingers hovered over it. Should he order the drilling to stop or not? At this moment there was a tremendous roar, as if the *majlis*, his audience chamber, was about to be razed to the ground. Several planes seemed about to land on the roof of the room where they sat. The Ruler stopped hesitating and pressed his thumb to the paper. Julian thanked him for his confidence and promised him that he would personally see that he did not suffer in any way for accepting Britain's advice. The Buttes Gas and Oil man was clearly furious and threatened Julian with inappropriate use of force and a law suit.

Julian wrote to his father:

> 'All this placed a severe strain on our relations with Umm al Qaiwain – relations which in the last resort depend on the fact that the Rulers recognize the Agency Land Rover and the flag on the bonnet, connect it vaguely with what they know of British power, and have grown accustomed to doing what we ask, but in the future there will be other sources of influence, Ambassadors from all over the Middle East, messengers from the Shah, bankers with black leather briefcases and above all the oil companies exhaling the irresistible perfume of money'.

Julian remained as calm as he could with the sweat running down his forehead, and drove off to the RAF camp. '*What in the world did you think you were doing?*' Group Captain Max Scanlon looked disappointed. '*Didn't you like it? For the first time we had all our planes operational, so I asked where you were and we thought we'd come and buzz you.*'

The next time Julian came to see Sheikh Ahmed of Umm al Qaiwain he found that the best landing site already taken by a smaller, newer and faster helicopter belonging to Occidental Petroleum.

The threat of the lawsuit was real, but it came to nothing by a fortunate coincidence. The highly distinguished legal expert on the Law of the Sea, Sir John Foster, happened also to be a Fellow of All Souls College, where, after the usual excellent dinner with fine wines from the college cellar, Julian managed to convince him of his total lack of involvement in the buzzing operation, and that therefore there had been no improper pressure put on the Sheikh. Sir John was able to tell Buttes Gas and Oil that he judged that they had no case. Julian received a telegram of congratulations from the Foreign Secretary.

In November 2019, just before everything changed with the spread of the coronavirus, I was invited to visit Dubai and celebrate the fiftieth anniversary of the library whose founding they so kindly attributed to me. I was delighted to find that some parts of Dubai had remained unchanged, particularly the Bastaki Quarter and much of the old *suq*. Even the architecture of the new two storey houses on the tree-lined roads was most attractive and best of all the romantic creek remained, although there was no denying that some parts of Dubai were unrecognisable. The streets were sparklingly clean and tidy, which must be due to Dubai having the most efficient municipality in the Middle East. Thanks to Eric Tulloch, a secondary water system using waste water was feeding the canna lilies planted under the palm trees along the main roads, while the waterfront had been hugely improved without damaging the old buildings. A boat ride on the creek remained almost as pleasant as a vaporetto trip on the Grand Canal in Venice. Perhaps I should have ended this chapter by printing Julian's annual review for 1970 but at 12 pages it is almost as long as the whole chapter. I will just include one paragraph of it:

> 'For all the time we have been here the underlying problem has been: leaving or not? If leaving, what is the solid foundation we are leaving going to look like? With the Bahrain problem solved, the brake has been taken off but the train refuses to move, the difficulty being the lack of steam in the boiler. The last three years has offered the Rulers a satisfactory objective during a perplexing period and discouraged local rivalries, but they need strength and efficient administrators to bear the weight of the responsibilities which we propose to unload on them.'

Julian, Robert and I walked across the tarmac in Dubai and boarded a BOAC plane for London on 12 December 1970.

8

FOREIGN OFFICE

HEAD OF EAST EUROPEAN & SOVIET DEPT
1971–75

I should like to be Head of the Northern Department one day and play a Vansittartish role in the face of all the nonsense that people in high places are prepared to believe about Russia'
JULIAN BULLARD to Personnel Department, Jan. 1971

JULIAN got his wish. Harold Wilson lost the election and had been replaced by Edward Heath in June 1970. Julian returned to the Foreign Office to be a 'Cold War Warrior' once again.

Nicko Henderson wrote to Julian from Warsaw where he was Ambassador:

'We are suffering badly from the total inadequacy of the Northern department at the moment; and I don't think I'm just reflecting the inevitable conflict between home and abroad. As you say the policy of contacts and slow penetration, rather than ostracism of the communist world was decided upon some 10 years ago. HMG were the pioneers, the French and Germans were highly sceptical. But in the last few years the official policy towards that part of the world has been paralysed by panic. The government got it into their heads that as a result of Czecho 1968 we must be more careful, with the result that we've had a tough fight even getting back to the cautious policy of 10 years ago. Partly it's the result of a very weak Northern Department. Partly Tom Brimalow, but I respect him a great deal, more than any of the other Mandarins in the office who are hardly of Ming quality. Anyway all that only makes me long for the day when you take over the Northern seat.'

I went back to London with Robert earlier than Julian, as getting the house back in order after tenants takes a lot of time, particularly as Julian had warned me that both Sheikh Rashid and Khalid, the Sheikh of Sharjah and his family had promised to pay us a visit! Robert had started at the local school and came home saying: '*I wish there was only one holiday, not Saturday AND Sunday. I LOVE school.*' He was improving enormously and everyone commented continually on his good sense, intelligence and reliability.

It was January 1971 when Julian took over the Soviet Desk in what had been Northern Department, now renamed East European and Soviet Department (EESD). He said his seven Ambassadors instead of his former six Sheikhs don't make any less work, because they are all proposing visits and suggesting initiatives of various kinds designed to strengthen any tendency to independence that existed in Eastern Europe, while the government definitely don't want to run after the Russians as Wilson used to do, and anyway they don't want any entanglements until we are inside the Common Market. So Julian has been spending a good deal of time explaining to eager Ambassadors in Prague and Budapest that there is no money or interest at the London end for their splendid proposals.

George Walden, the senior diplomat working for Julian in his new department, greeted Julian with much the same view of the unhappy state of Anglo-Soviet relations as Nicko Henderson had written about. What disturbed Julian was the sheer number of the spies. There were so many that the security services were unable to keep an eye on all of them. In spite of the fact that the Russians had five spies for every one of ours, it was a common attitude to say: '*My dear chap, everyone knows that MI5 and MI6, not to speak of the FO, are stuffed with Russian agents – spying is just a game of cat and mouse.*' The trouble was that they were the cat and we the mouse, and we did not dare to say 'boo' to them. We had endeavoured to limit the numbers in the Soviet Embassy, but the numbers had continually grown as the Russians claimed that they were 'only increasing the Trade Delegation' and when a ceiling was put on that, they countered by saying that they were only increasing the number of 'working wives'. Known KGB personnel had been let into Britain under diplomatic cover on the assumption that MI5 would keep an eye on them, but the truth was that we had no serious means of keeping track of them, and no idea of whether they were doing serious damage or not. It was a choice of doing nothing very much or doing something radical. The prevailing ethos in the department could be described as one of unrelenting hostility, wariness and scepticism towards the entire communist bloc, fear of its creep in Asia and Europe, especially Italy, coupled with a certain negativity as to what the West could actually do. While Labour had been in power, Harold Wilson, who saw himself as being particularly good at wheeling and dealing, had agreed with the Russians to exchange the Krugers, who had passed on valuable information from Portland Naval Base, for Gerald Brooke, imprisoned for a petty misdemeanor

On 13 March the Secretary of State, Alec Douglas Home, spoke at the 50th anniversary of the Soviet Trade Agreement. Julian thought he delivered his suggested text well and got our message across: that it was not our fault that Anglo/Soviet relations lately had been nothing but spies, defectors and skullduggery. Soon after this a Russian Second Secretary was expelled having been caught with a government document actually in his hand. In return the Russians expelled David Miller, a British diplomat. This caused Julian to write to his father:

> 'If I could bring about one improvement in our relations with Moscow, I should regard this as a sufficient monument for this part of my career. But it's a question of who is the stronger the KGB or the MFA. It would be nice to have an excuse to do something really disagreeable to them, and for once we have a Prime Minister who would see no objection'.

George Waldon's previous post had been Peking, which had radicalized him, and given him grounds for thinking the Russians should be treated with suspicion. He certainly did not support the views of Reginald Maudling, (the Home Secretary in charge of MI5), who thought it was a mistake to let espionage interfere with more important things such as good cultural relations between our two countries, a view also held by our Ambassador in Moscow, Sir Duncan Wilson. Julian spent the best part of the year in discussion with George Walden and Brian Fall about exactly how the spy situation should be dealt with, and trying to convince others that if we took strong action, we would not end up the losers. I believe it was George who coined the phrase Operation Boot (because the Russians were to be receiving it). Julian's task was to persuade a rather nervous Foreign Secretary (Alex Douglas Hume) that we should not allow the Russians to have a hundred and five members of the KGB masquerading as bona fide members of the Embassy, and that provided we could devise terms by which it would be possible to gain more than we would suffer by their inevitable retaliation, we would get the best result by expelling all of them at once in a blaze of publicity.

Though most people in England thought of the KGB as spies, in Russia their primary responsibility was maintaining the stability of the communist system, and their main concern the maintenance of a vast machine of internal repression. This meant that any blow to the prestige of the KGB would be a blow against the system. At Julian's insistence everything about the BOOT plan had to be kept deadly secret in order that not a word of the plan should get into Russians hand, otherwise they might, by taking hostages, make Julian's careful plan to prevent strong retaliation, unworkable. In case there should be any undiscovered moles in the Foreign Office, everybody who had no need to know, had to be kept completely in the dark.

The first step of the plan was triggered on 3 September when Oleg Lyalin, a KGB officer, was arrested for drunken driving. His Soviet boss ordered him home, but he chose to defect, bringing with him the names of a large number of spies. A confidential letter was sent to Gromyko listing all the spies and asking for them to be removed. It was part of the plan that we should be able to demonstrate that the Russians had been offered the chance to make a serious reduction in the number of their spies without publicity. This had the expected result: no answer. The next step was a second letter reminding him that we were not prepared to let the matter lie. Again, no reply. At this moment Sir Alec started having gentlemanly doubts, but his cold feet were forgotten after Heath, now Prime Minister, gave BOOT a clear and resolute go-ahead.

On Friday 24th September 1971 the Soviet Chargé was called to the Foreign Office and the text of the notice of expulsion was read to him by Sir Dennis Greenhill, the Permanent Under Secretary. Martin Nicholson, who was present on this occasion, in case a translation should be needed, recalled that Ivan Ippolitov, the Soviet Chargé, commented: '*All is clear. Very drastic measures, Sir Greenhill, very drastic!*' Of the 105 spies expelled, ninety were KGB officials currently in the UK and 15 suspected employees of the KGB at present in Moscow, but who held valid re-entry visas. The number was raised to 105 in order to make a greater impact and to prevent those on MI5's suspect list from being sent to London in place of those evicted. Telegram traffic between London and Moscow that evening was very busy. A press conference broke the news to a flabbergasted press, and everyone involved had a lot to drink.

I discovered that both George Walden and Brian Fall had told their wives about Boot beforehand, and I was very hurt that Julian had told me nothing. I suppose he felt that having sternly warned his department that not a breath of this plan was to escape, even to family or friends in the service, he must keep his own mouth firmly shut, or was it that he remembered how I had told a journalist about the bottled Malvern water being brought from England for the Queen's visit to Bonn? I felt too wounded to challenge Julian about this. It seemed better not to tell him that I knew Brian and George had had more confidence in their wives than Julian had in me.

All those involved in expelling the spies held their breath as to what the Russian response would be after the delivery of the eviction notice. It had been Julian's suggestion that after the expulsions, a ceiling should be set on the number of Russians in Soviet organisations in the UK, after which, for every retaliatory expulsion from our Embassy in Moscow, the ceiling on Soviet numbers in London would be cut by two, with the warning that we would follow any reduction in the Moscow Embassy down to zero if necessary. This bold action had a sobering effect on the Russians, and was much admired by our allies as well as being welcomed in the media. Despite misgivings by the cabinet before the event, Moscow only blustered, but finally backed off. They had been put in a spot. They could not retaliate with head-for-head expulsions as there were not 105 members of the British Embassy, and they did not want to break off relations, from which they gained more than we did in the closed society of Moscow. They expelled four members of the Embassy and one resident business-man. and cancelled Julian's planned visit to Moscow. Relations with the Soviet Union did not seriously suffer, and the chapter was given a symbolic end after Heath was succeeded as Prime Minister by James Callaghan, and Julian and Michael Weir were despatched to Moscow bearing an olive branch from Labour to expiate the expulsion of the 105 spies. At the farewell lunch at the Moscow Embassy, the head of the Russian Delegation rose to propose a toast to Julian as 'The Head of the anti-Soviet Department'. David Miller later told me how much the junior members of EESD appreciated Julian's ability to apply Occam's razor to some of the more problematic situations that had to be dealt with, and to explain the likely outcome in the clearest and simplest terms.

Antonia went for a week of intensive Russian at the Goldsmith's college organized by the Society for Cultural Relations with the USSR. She said that although some of the older students were obvious sympathisers, the 104 pupils on the course had no interest except in the language. A lecture on 'The Soviet System' during the course turned into an argument about Solzhenitsyn. The (Soviet) lecturer maintained that if his latest works hadn't been published it was because they were of no literary merit. How did she know, if they weren't available in print? And what about the Nobel Prize? Antonia asked her teacher to tea at our house. She accepted with obvious pleasure, then asked if she could bring a colleague. The 'colleague' turned out to be 20 years older, speaking faultless English. Her first question was to ask Julian about his job, and it wasn't long before she looked at her watch and dragged the younger woman away. But how to convince anybody who hadn't seen it before that this was the hand of the Party?

No sooner had the publicity for the expulsion of the spies died down than Julian discovered a lump inside his lip and his cheek and in November a 'malignant well-differentiated squameous carcinoma' was diagnosed. Because Julian's eldest brother Matthew had died of a tumour on the brain only about two weeks after the first symptoms were noticed, his family feared the same fate was going to strike Julian. I visited Julian in his ward in the Westminster Hospital, which still had nurses with starched headdresses and silver buckled belts. Julian's neighbour, some years younger than him, said to Julian: '*I wish to God I had never seen a cigarette.*' Beside him sat his weeping wife. This caused me to stop smoking instantly and totally. For the next seven days radioactive needles bombarded the lump. The front of his lip looked as if it had been badly burned. The surgeon assured him that his growth had been completely removed and although his face might go on looking wounded for some weeks to come, he need have no fear, the hideous yellow scabs would fall off and all trace of it would be gone. Radioactive needles had unfortunately also removed his sense of taste and smell. Did his neighbours at All Souls dinners realise that he was unable to appreciate the delights of the college cellars? He always asked to see the bottle and carefully studied what was printed on it, trying, I think, to imagine the taste.

Very shortly afterwards Richard Doll published his findings about the connection of smoking with cancer. Unbelievable now that in those days having ashtrays and cigarettes on the table at a dinner party was normal. How strange it seems watching elegant actors on the TV *Talking Pictures* Channel waving cigarettes in the air. How strange to remember war time when railway carriages and cinemas were usually so thick with smoke that it was difficult to see or breathe. My view was that the cause of his growth was unlikely to be other people's cigarette smoke, but more the tremendous amount of stress and hard work Julian had to get through in his last days in Dubai, the pressure of the BOOT operation, and starting work in a new department at the same time as house improvements at home. The surgeon's view was that the cause was over-exposure to the scorching sun of the Trucial States.

I have already mentioned that I have a bad reputation for rushing into action on the spur of the moment, and, seeing the cold, wet, grey weather outside the window, I bought tickets for ten days in Marrakesh, only to be told by the hospital that sunshine was the very last thing that was advisable after radioactive treatment. Cecil Day Lewis, a Greenwich neighbour, lent Julian a marvellous huge white felt hat from Locks to wear whenever he went outside, and we had a very pleasant idle few days sitting in the garden of the hotel where Churchill took a holiday during the war. We wandered through the *suq* and watched the jugglers in the *Jemma el Fna*, and we explored the foothills of the Atlas mountains. Once home again, Julian said he felt normal for three quarters of the day but then suddenly wanted to lie down and go to sleep, sometimes even before eight o'clock, but every day he seemed to be making progress.

One Saturday morning, the phone rang in Greenwich. Mr Ippolitov wanting to speak to Julian. He was the Russian Chargé who had received the demand that the spies be expelled. The conversation was long and Julian was clearly very moved. Julian told me that Mr Ippolitov had phoned from a public phone at Heathrow so that no one could listen in to the call. He was being recalled to Moscow and did not want to leave without telling Julian how glad he was to have had the experience of working with him, how much he had learnt from him, and how sorry he was that they were unlikely ever to meet again. He also told Julian in confidence that the Russian Foreign Office did not mind the expulsion of the 105 spies as much as we had feared, because the numbers of KGB at the Embassy were so great that very little space had been left for ordinary diplomats at one of the most coveted of foreign postings.

In January 1972 the usual post preference form arrived on Julian's desk. He filled in the form saying that since he would have to find a good part of the fees for four children at boarding school or university until about 1976, he did not want to go far afield until diplomats posted abroad were allowed to have their children flown out at government expense for three holidays instead of two. He suggested that he would like to go as Britain's first Ambassador to East Berlin if diplomatic relations should be re-opened there when he was of the right seniority. I imagine that must have been the reason why he seemed to have been reading a lot of East German newspaper articles lately, even if they were, as he said, dogmatic, unyielding and inspired by hatred and selfishness even more than the Russian ones.

Julian went to the Westminster Hospital for a final check and saw the Head of the ENT Department who had nothing but congratulations, for themselves as much as for him. He was asked his advice about a puzzling case, bureaucratic rather than medical. A Turkish Cypriot with throat cancer had appeared without either papers or money, and with only a letter of recommendation from his doctor in Cyprus. There was no doubt that he was not entitled to treatment under the NHS, but the fact was that he could be cured in six weeks in London by radiotherapy – whereas in Cyprus he would be lucky even to find a surgeon who could cut the cancer out without killing him. Julian suggested that, since he said he had worked for the British Army for 15 years, they should write to the Ministry of Defence setting out the facts and ending '*We hope you will agree that this man is eligible for treatment under the NHS.*' confident that by the time the MOD sent a reply he would have been cured. This did indeed mean that the British taxpayer would foot the bill, but Julian thought that the Cypriot's confidence in Britain should be rewarded, and he should not be sent home without help. Though it is easy to say that all such cases should be decided only according to the rules, Julian felt that when the patient is sitting on a bench in front of you with an expression of complete trust on his face, there was a strong case for acting with humanity.

That summer we took the children on a Scottish holiday. First, we drove to Glenisla to stay with the Neills. (Patrick was now Warden of All Souls). We picked a basket of *boletus edulis* mushrooms in the woods, which, in spite of much trepidation, the Neills were persuaded to eat. They were still alive when we left to drive to Auchlunkart to stay with the Croles, neighbours from Greenwich. I remember allowing the children to sit in our blown-up paddling pool on the roof of the car while I drove slowly along the unfenced roads. The Croles had made up a party for a Highland Ball, and we spent happy days in anticipation teaching the children how to do an Eightsome without disgracing our hosts, and fitting the boys out with borrowed kilts. We travelled back to London on a train from Perth to Kensington with our car in the rear end of the train while we slept at the front end. We were unable to stop thinking about how much we had enjoyed our holiday. Gerry Crole's father, when he retired from the Sudan in the thirties, had bought a huge house with a farm and several acres of woodland. The staircase was lined with pictures of stags at bay, in the garden there was croquet and young pheasants, in the spare bedrooms, Dornford Yates. Somewhere there was a special shoe-polishing place complete with bootjack and buttonhook. We looked out of our bedroom window across Forestry Commission pinewoods and distillery warehouses to a splendid slope of heather where grouse spun out their precarious lives. Were it ours, it would be a nice place to dream about on hot evenings abroad. Julian made each of us write down what our ideal country house should include. The answers varied from Total quiet (Julian) to Big enough to have lots of visitors to stay. (Vicky)

It was this very happy holiday which played some part in making us decide to leave Greenwich. We were in love with the pleasures of rural life, and with the children at boarding schools there was no longer any need to live near suitable schools. We saw a picture of Hymerford House on the borders of Somerset and Dorset in a magazine, and drove down to see it. At first sight on a beautiful Sunday in September it seemed to have everything, including a sailing club on a nearby reservoir. It was mentioned in the court rolls of Henry II, had a great air of antiquity and was the birthplace of Captain Dampier, the privateer who first landed on the west coast of Australia. Its serious disadvantages sank in only later: a 4 ½ hour drive from London and the drains all emptying into a pool underneath the Great Hall. We had also not noticed that on one side of the house was a yard where old motor vehicles were broken up, and on the other a charming cottage which blocked the south sun from coming in through our windows. This was occupied by a tenant paying a controlled rent of 2/6 a week, who could not be evicted. We were fools to have bought a house so far from London and with so many problems. I had to admit the executive arm had been mine. I fell into a state of deep depression. We should never have left Greenwich, and never have said goodbye to the walls we had papered ourselves, and the room where Robert was born.

At first the mistaken buying of Hymerford House did not seem a great problem. We could just tell Jackson Stopps to advertise it again. But they told us that houses put on the market for a second time rarely got the same price. We had only paid £25,000 for it, and it was after all a listed historic building, so I did not have total belief in their views. I decided to live there by myself throughout the winter of 1972, plastering and painting, seeing to the installation of central heating, repairs to the roof and modernisation of the drains, so that the house would be more attractive to buyers. I spent a lot of time hacking away the plaster in the wall between the dining room and the hall in search of the mediaeval arches, which the architect assured us were there. I found one round arch and one gothic, which gave style to the entrance hall. I had new lighting installed. At the back of the house a stone wall blocked the view to a field full of sheep, not ours, under trees of cider apples, which were. After I had demolished a bit of the wall and Julian had helped me install a beautiful old wrought iron gate I had found, we had a fine view into the distance. But I remained very depressed about finding a buyer.

During this period of my life I was dependant on letters from Julian for what his office life was like. The higher your rank in the Foreign Office the less time you seemed to have to spend at your desk, and more time on interesting trips abroad. Julian went to Brussels to be taught the ways of the Community. He found that except for the French, everyone spoke excellent English, but there were too many of them. His second trip was to New York where he was taken to dinner with the rich and clever lawyer whose advice was responsible for Sharjah defeating Umm al Qaiwain over the rights for oil exploration off Abu Mousa, where oil has now been found. Sheikh Khalid, the ruler of Sharjah, had done a deal with the Shah and now giant oil storage tanks are to be built on Abu Musa, the island where we had camped with the Allens, and which for many years had been accepted by everyone as utterly barren and useless. While Julian was living it up at the Chevy Chase Country Club (qualifications for membership according to his hostess: a white face, no connection with trade, and 25 years on the waiting list), I was in Somerset installing new kitchen furniture and a big bookcase and looking after James who had fallen off his bike and broken his right arm.

The East German Embassy was opened in Belgrave Square and Harold Wilson summoned Julian to keep him abreast of our relations with the Czechs. Julian was dubious of why Harold Wilson was so suspiciously nice to him, and wondered if he and the Czechs are cooking something up, but decided perhaps he was trying to make up for having summoned him back from half across the world just before Christmas and then not selecting him as his private secretary!

In March 1973 our 19th wedding anniversary came round. Julian was at his desk. I was alone in East Coker. This is from a letter Julian wrote me in between taking papers examining his fluency in advanced Arabic (the incentive for taking the examination was financial):

'I am as much certain of this as I am of anything that with our reserves, in the shape of assets and prospects and talents and connections, this present phase of our lives cannot last for long, will blow over and will be forgotten except as having given us the kind of compulsory jolt which middle age so badly needs. All we need to do is keep calm, treat East Coker as a rather demanding sort of country cottage and await the day when something unexpected and good will happen, as it undoubtedly will. So re-read my first page, drive carefully and stay happy until we meet again on Friday and meanwhile here is my love just before I go into Dicteé'.

I replied:

'I don't think so far we have ever been got down together, and thank goodness you are up at the moment – or if not up – refusing to give way and are on an indomitable even keel. You are right about the compulsory jolt. My life has never before reduced me to tears. Dearest Julian, I have already said it, but let me say it again, that this nasty jolt has, among other things, led me to value you much more highly than I ever had before. I did not realise how much I needed you, and how wonderful it is to have you to depend on'.

Relations with Moscow had become a little better: but Sir Alec continued to have a healthy detestation and suspicion of everything they did. Julian reported that Gromyko had proposed that it should be made legal for our two states to jam each other's TV broadcasts, and interfere with its relay satellites if they don't like the programmes!

In April I went to stay with my sister-in-law Patricia, in Lewes. She took me for a walk on the Downs with a friend and I told them my problem about selling Hymerford House. The friend's husband held an important position on *The Times* and she suggested that I write an article about the house, its interesting history and situation in the beautiful village of East Coker, after which T.S.Eliot had named one of his Four Quartets, and send it with a good picture to *The Times* Architectural Correspondent, who was a bit lazy and would be delighted to get his week's work done for him. He did not answer my letter, but my article appeared in the paper and it did the trick. You have after all, only to find ONE buyer. A string of people poured in to look over the house and we thought we had managed to sell it to a man who has a factory that makes lifts. We were both sad to leave our ancient house after so short a stay, even if a troubled one. It had been a place of great unhappiness but also of very happy times, particularly when the children were with us, and on the warm evenings when we had driven down to a Dorset beach and cooked supper. Now that we had decided to leave, we found what a good place it was to entertain friends , (and even the Minister at the Polish Embassy) at weekends . Much as the whole family enjoyed the holidays we spent there, we realized that it made more sense to have a week-end house nearer to Marlborough and Oxford.

From a letter to Julian's father 21 June 1973

'A new Soviet Ambassador, Lunkov, has arrived. I think that he is going to be easier to deal with than his predecessor. In fact, I have the sensation that without any conscious decision on either side, we and the Russians have turned a corner and set up a rather different course from the very sour one that we have been following for the last two years.

Perhaps the Russians had decided their attempt to neutralise Britain as a political and diplomatic force was getting nowhere, and our voice struck a jarring note in the choir of détente at Helsinki. A year earlier there would have been a violent protest from Moscow at the arrest of an important Yugoslav for shoplifting in Oxford Street, and two Russian seamen doing the same thing in Aberdeen. The Duke of Edinburgh, as chairman of some equestrian organisation, was in Kiev for a three-day-event, which no doubt played a part in warming the relationship. It was even announced that Brezhnev was to go on a visit to Washington, though Julian wondered what good that could do, Russia would starve without American wheat and America was paralyzed by the Watergate scandal.

Julian always wrote well and fluently and I have been much in his debit for deft improvements in articles or difficult letters that I have written. In a few minutes with a few small changes, he would transform my humdrum, or ill expressed prose, into something more elegant. People who worked under him told me that he would produce draft conclusions at the end of an office meeting before others had put pen to paper. I heard that he had introduced a new custom of making everyone stand for the morning meeting, including of course himself, so that the meetings should be over as soon as possible. After Julian died, I received an enormous number of letters from people who had worked for him praising him for the trouble he took to improve the work of those under him. He also had a deft hand with odes and sonnets. I remember him daring to compose a delightful tribute in verse for Sir Bernard Fergusson, then Head of the British Council, and himself something of a poet. Years later his rhymed farewell speech at Birmingham University was a triumph. I can remember few of the lyrics from his annual Christmas cabarets, but to give you a taste of his talent here is something which he jotted down on the back of an envelope while driving Vicky back to St Mary's, Calne, one Sunday evening. The annual Shakespeare competition required each form to perform a thirty minute extract from one of his plays. She told him her form had chosen a rather dull scene from Macbeth and that she had been chosen to introduce it, and had no idea what to say. Julian suggested a Prologue:

> *Ladies and Gentlemen, this presentation*
> *Requires an effort of imagination:*
> *A span of half an hour, a cast of ten*
> *With girls as girls, but also girls as men;*
> *Such handicaps as these, we'll not gainsay,*
> *A single scene shall represent our play.*
> *We'll skip the witches, skip the embattled thanes*
> *Skip Burnham wood, en route for Dunsinane,*
> *And choose the day when Duncan comes to spend,*
> *Not quite as he expects, a long weekend.*

Vicky wrote in her diary '*I was the envy of the school*'.

When Julian decided on something, he stuck to his decision with unbudge-able determination. He was in fact the rock and final arbiter for all of us. He was also wonderfully staunch when trouble came along. There were several occasions when my foolhardiness – or habit of dashing ahead with more en-thusiasm than sense – landed us in trouble. Buying that Grade I house four hours from London was one. Another was when I persuaded Julian and Robert that one could easily walk down the *Diavolezza* glacier in Switzerland without a guide (for whose services there was a long queue). Obviously one only had to follow the moraine and keep going downhill. None of us had ever been on a glacier before. By amazing luck, we got home without injury. We could so easily have slipped into a crevasse or come to grief at its foot where the glacier from time to time calved off its end, leaving a sheer 30 foot icy cliff. Nothing could be more terrifying than taking that first step over the edge. And there was also that boundary dispute with a rich neighbour, whose lawyer sent endlessly demanding letters which reduced me to despair.

Julian went to Helsinki in July 1973 for the start of the Conference on Se-curity and Co-operation in Europe, the worst part of which he said was trying to sleep in the short summer night with the thermometer in the 80's, no fans and the red summer sun coming up at 2.45a.m. The best parts were the private meetings with the communist Foreign Ministers from Gromyko downwards, which had been the reason for his going. It was a convenient week for observ-ing their differences. Julian wrote to his father:

> 'We now have an agreed line with No. 10 for handling our relations with Russia over the next few months. Gromyko may be coming in October. The difficulty is that though the Russians love to extemporise at short notice, it is not so easy in London. It is rather painful having to be polite to the Soviet embassy most of whom are slimy, thuggish or a bit of both. The Counsellor (Smirnov) is a particularly sharp and shady creature, who very nearly talked the Home Office into agreeing to receive their Min-ister of the Interior. Smirnov naturally mentioned fire services and traffic accident prevention rather than the Minister's other responsibilities. Luckily we heard about it just in time to remind the Home Office about the prison camps and exit visa office which he also controls.

Soviet Prime Minister Alexei Kosygin went to Cairo to try to talk the Arabs into a more reasonable attitude. Julian understood that the Russians did not want to get physically involved, just to preserve their relations with both Wash-ington and the Arab world, and to avoid another crushing defeat for the Arabs. It seemed the Americans were thinking of sacrificing détente for the sake of Israel, and asking the rest of us to do the same. Julian drafted a speech pointing out that to convert the Arab/Israeli conflict into an East/West conflict would help no one but Israel and the Russians.

Letter from Julian at Hymerford House to his father:

> *Antonia wrestles with an unreadable reading list of works that have as many symbols as words, all steadily supplied by the local library. With Vicky it is just a question of keeping a book or two ahead. When she is out of reading matter she pegs away at the cello. James gets up at 6.15 to go milking or haymaking and makes it clear that to see a calf born means more to him than listening to whatever anyone else is talking about. In his last days here, he was not only bringing the cows in and lending a hand with the milking, but acting as midwife. Robert is the one who always remembers to order the milk, switch off the central heating, water the tomatoes, pick the courgettes and change the library books today because tomorrow is early-closing. We think these qualities can't fail to make him succeed in life, whatever may be his place in Latin.*

Julian accompanied Julian Amery (Junior Foreign Office Minister) on a visit to Warsaw in early October. He got on well with Amery after he found he was deeply interested in foreign countries, well-read in their histories and able to conduct substantial conversations in either French or German. He understood that the Polish officials he met in Warsaw and Cracow, who regarded solidarity with Moscow as inescapable, but also beneficial for Poland, were just as representative of their country as the right-wing emigres in London and their British friends on the Katyn Memorial Committee who he met in London. The visit concluded with a boar hunt during which the Minister shot a boar and a buck and the rest of the party got nothing.

We thought we had managed to sell Hymerford House to Mr Duley, but alas he sent a letter saying that he could not produce the purchase price on the date agreed. We had his deposit and the right to charge him interest until he paid, but it left us in a very difficult position. Interest rates were such that it could even be more advantageous for him not to pay the remainder of the purchase price, but to go on paying us the penalty for as long as he chose. To our relief in November Mr Duley came up with his cheque, and we spent some part of his money on a cottage overlooking the bowling green in a small Cotswold village called Filkins, equidistant from Oxford, where Antonia was at St Hilda's, and Marlborough, where Vicky was in the sixth form, and where James would join her in January. It was really two cottages and a barn, which the previous owner had tried to pretend was a Great Hall – spacious, but difficult to get warm in winter. Someone knocked at the door and told us that our cottage came with a strip of land to grow vegetables. Neither we nor our parents had ever planted a row of radishes. Julian took up horticulture with the same determination that won him prizes for Greek verse and with which he attacked rolls of wallpaper. He could not have been more pleased in August when he was awarded the second prize for runner beans in the annual flower show.

It was a grim time for the British economy. The value of the pound had sunk to DM 5.95 from DM 11.10 when we lived in Bonn. I wrote: '*What a Christmas!*

I wish we knew some way of helping the economy. Not switching on lights, not driving the car and cleaning my teeth in the dark seems a small contribution'.

In February another disastrous coal strike was threatened. We watched the fights between the miners and the police on our TV and wondered what methods were open to a democrat who does not approve of militancy, or who does not want what the militants want. I was moved to tears by the so-called Students Demonstration in London. The posters have nothing much to do with students, and the sad worn faces of those carrying them were horrifying.

The Spring of that year saw a great many diplomatic dinners ending in celebrations of the 50th anniversary of the establishment of our Embassy in Moscow and the Russian Embassy in London. Harold Wilson and Heath both came, though Harold Wilson only came to be photographed shaking hands with Mr Gormley, with the Russian Ambassador grinning in the background. Julian said he was going to ring M. Simeonov and ask him why the Soviet miners were interfering in our domestic affairs by telegraphing their solidarity to Mr Gormley. Heath's trouble with the miners cost him the election.

In February 1974 Wilson was back at No.10 with Jim Callaghan as Foreign Secretary. Julian said he felt like taking his pen and making a black edge round the paper, either that or asking for a sabbatical. The Russian Deputy Assistant Acting Minister of Foreign Trade wanted to come on a visit and Jim Callaghan said sorry, he was too busy receiving the Freedom of the City of Cardiff to see M. Cyrek. M. Cyrek then said that in that case he wouldn't come, because M. Brezhnev would be unlikely to be convinced by such an unlikely explanation of why he had not been able to see the Foreign Secretary!

That same month Solzhenitsyn was expelled from the Soviet Union. We learnt from Andreas Meyer-Landrut, Head of the Soviet Department in the German Foreign Ministry, that it had come as a total surprise, although looking back there had been clues that it was going to happen, had they drawn the right conclusions. The German Chancellor, Willy Brandt, had made a speech criticising the lack of freedom in the Soviet Union, in which he mentioned that in Germany Solzhenitsyn would have been free to live freely and write what he liked. Whereupon the Soviet Embassy telephoned and asked for a transcript of the speech. No one recognized any significance in this. Then eight visas were asked for Russians with brand new passports. It was assumed these were workmen coming to do repairs. Shortly afterwards, Andreas Meyer-Landrut was giving lunch to someone from the Soviet Institute for International Affairs, who said that he wondered how much longer Solzhenitsyn would be tolerated by the Politburo. Nobody put these events together, not even when the Soviet Ambassador asked for an appointment at 8.30a.m. on 13th February with the Head of the Foreign Ministry. Asked why it needed to be so early the reply was: '*We want to give you a present.*' When the Soviet Ambassador arrived he said: *'Solzhenitsyn will be arriving at Frankfurt Airport at 11.45am without pass-port or paper. He is being expelled for having broken several articles of the Soviet penal code. In view of the good relations between the Soviet Union and West Ger-many, I hope there will be no trouble'* On the way out Andreas asked: '*Why pick on us?'* To which he replied: '*Because you are the only people who said you would take him.*' Because of fog in Frankfurt they had enough time to arrange for him to be taken to stay with Heinrich Böll, the Grand old Man of German Lit-erature at the moment, who had recently received a Nobel prize. He is a man of astonishing ugliness with a large red circular nose, but has a very friendly manner. It had been decided this would be better than smuggling him away to a Safe House, which might have looked like collusion between the Soviet and German governments.

In May there was an Anglo Soviet conference in Lancaster House, the ceil-ings newly gilded and with fine views in the sun over St James' Palace and the Mall. I was only invited to one of the dinners, the one at which Mrs Kirillin wore a newly bought silver latex trouser suit. But Julian told me about the rest of the week. '*The Russians had arrived looking a bit pale, perhaps because they reached London Airport shortly after a bomb went off, so their welcoming party never arrived, and they had to sit in the waiting room with nothing to read except the front page of The Sunday Times with its special exclusive shock horror mystery tale report about Soviet Red Nazi Stormtrooper Truth Drug Squads Grill Harm-less, innocent Peace-loving Israeli Pilots. On their last day the Russians were given lunch at the East India and Sports Club which they thought was `ochen' traditsion-nyj' especially not being allowed to light a cigarette until the ancient marble clock said 1.45pm exactly. The visit ended with lunch in the Russian Embassy's Palm Court – caviar and vodka to the sound of a dripping fountain – even M. Suslov (the Party's chief idealogue) stopped scowling.*'

In the autumn we were invited to a box in the Royal Festival Hall for a Cho-pin anniversary concert by the Royal Philharmonic Orchestra. All the East Eu-ropean Ambassadors were there and our former neighbour Karl Günther von Hase, now the German Ambassador. We were each given a glass of something and the Ambassadors were welcomed in turn in their own language – more or less. All this made the evening go on so late that many of the guests missed their trains. The review of the occasion in The Times praised the music but asked what business had the government giving such entertainment in a time of financial stringency?

Julian made it clear that he couldn't think how I spent the day, so I told him what passed for one day's work for me:

'I clean the flat. I telephone the gas board and ask for the gas heater to be repaired. (this takes half an hour waiting for someone to pick up phone). I de-cide we ought to have a working TV to watch the coming general election. TV shop sells me a new aerial, still no picture. I decide to hire another TV. Wait two hours for promised delivery. Phone. It will come tomorrow. Trail round shops looking for curtain material for little sitting room. Pass a skip entirely full of coat hangers. Alas can only manage to carry three while bicycling. Look for present for Julian's birthday. All umbrellas very expensive considering he has lost the very expensive one I gave him two years ago. Put off decision. Have battle with librarian about joining library. She says I have already joined twice and must find four tickets or pay fine. I know this is not true. Hung about reading until she went for tea, then consult more sympathetic librarian, who provides new tickets. Took home book on German, Austrian and Swiss painted furniture. On way home passed a rather lovely black fur coat which I could not resist trying on. It comes right down to the ground, made in Hong Kong with a zip somewhere near the knee which shortens the coat to day length, and another zip higher up and you have a cape. I walked on thinking rather dreamily whether to buy it when my eye lit on a notice 'Ladders for sale' I have been wanting a ladder so that I can paint the sitting room. I hastily went in and found a charming old man just retiring to Worthing after a lifetime in the decorating business and beat him down to £3 for a fine extending ladder – that is a saving of at least £30 so perhaps what with the savings on food by nightly entertainment from East European Ambassadors, I might be able to afford that fur coat after all'.

The second general election that year returned Labour with a larger majority. Julian had a certain pleasure in watching as the Labour Ministers, who used to maintain that the Russians couldn't possibly be as bad as the Foreign Office made out, started losing their patience with them, one by one. Jack Straw was made to attend a pointless 'emergency' session called by the Russians on a Sunday and Mr Hattersley did not like being told that *the statements of the British Government have been on the whole not bad, but there is an inconsistency between these and British actions.* Julian was getting on better with Callaghan until the day he had to confess that the Warsaw Embassy had failed to bring the Anglo-Polish Trade Agreement to an end by the date it expired (which meant it automatically renewed itself.) Why not? Partly because the Ambassador is an incompetent nincompoop, but his story is that Princess Alexandra's lady-in-waiting picked up the Treaty and walked off with it and didn't discover it till a couple of weeks later. The Ambassador was summoned to London to explain to Callaghan what had happened. By the following month Julian had managed to coax Callaghan into agreeing to make a speech on east-west relations, and ask their journalists in for a chat and visit all seven countries and talk to their Ambassadors more often.

When Julian was introducing himself to the new Greek Ambassador, he added that he had been born in Athens. Whereupon the Ambassador almost burst into tears and invited us to visit him there. I urged Julian to accept, not entirely in jest, as there was not a single packet of sugar left in Sainsbury's. The following Monday he went to Athens and afterwards Hungary, He had no difficulty in finding as much as he had room for in his case.

In February 1975 Julian accompanied Harold Wilson and James Callaghan on an official visit to the Soviet Union, with Christopher Meyer as Julian's 'bag carrier'. Before they left, the Russian Ambassador gave a 'Send Off party,' and a lunch to meet the Russian Deputy Minister for Foreign Trade, and a dinner for the Speaker of the Romanian Parliament. Julian was also summoned to No.10 for a discussion on Anglo-Soviet Trade. He grumbled that more money is wasted on these visits than on anything else he had to do with. In spite of all this, the Russians were extremely trying about arrangements for the visit: the dates, the announcements, and the wording of the six documents to be signed. They refused to comment on any of our proposals for the visit except that there must be no meetings on Saturday or Sunday because this would interfere with Soviet legislation on the 5-day week. The continuous small difficulties in the preparation led Julian to expect little from the visit, but as soon as they arrived it was clear that the talks were designed to go well. The Press and the Media gave the British visitors much coverage and showed exceptional warmth, announcing that Mr Brezhnev, who had not been seen in public for seven weeks, intended to come to three sessions. The Prime Minister and Foreign Secretary set off for a week-end's sightseeing in Leningrad while the officials worked on agreeing the wording of the documents.

The Russians had invited Julian and Christopher to lunch at the Rossiya hotel after which, they said, 'we will finish the communique'. Julian smelt a rat and told Christopher to put some sandwiches in his briefcase. His suspicions were justified, as the Russians announced that they had decided to reverse the order, *'we will do the documents and the communique first and have lunch when we have finished at the Rossiya Hotel'*. Since the draft communique still had many points of contention which would take most of the whole weekend to resolve, this was clearly a crude attempt to starve us into submission. The faces of the Soviet diplomats were a marvel to behold when, as the afternoon wore on, Julian triumphantly produced the sandwiches on which the British team happily munched. The arguments about the wording of the six documents continued until late in the visit.

The next day Julian and Christopher were rather late coming out of the Embassy to drive to the Rossiya Hotel for Wilson's final Press Conference. As they took their seats in the last remaining car, two burly gentlemen in fur hats and thick coats joined them, slamming the door in a purposeful manner. Julian said: *'One of them put his arm round my shoulders. The car sped off in the direction of the hotel (also the direction of the Lubyanka, headquarters of the KGB). We looked at each other nervously, and I said: 'Vy s nami?' (are you with us?), to which the answer was a significant 'My vsye veemya s Vami' (We are always with you) Three minutes later we got to the Rossiya and they vanished'.*

On the whole Julian felt we made more gains than the Russians over the wording of the documents, even though the Russians also seemed to be sure that the agreement was a great success. The initiative of the Foreign Office in tabling the first drafts of the Joint Statement so well in advance – the Protocol on Consultations and the Nuclear Non-Proliferation Declaration – had been responsible for Brezhnev feeling the meeting was important enough for him to attend, which he did in full vigour after an illness of seven weeks. This meant that the Russians had every reason for the meeting to be recorded as a triumph. They showed themselves particularly keen to give impetus to détente and publicly to encourage France and the Federal Republic to do likewise. It was agreed that there would be annual meetings of the Foreign Ministers, and the wording of 'peaceful coexistence' (words chosen by Brezhnev and written on the back of the menu), was to describe our future relationship. On the trade front they agreed on the words: *Significant expansion and an improved balance and structure of trade,* which was intended to mean a better balance instead of the long-standing Soviet surplus, and in general there seemed to be less scope for trouble between Britain and the USSR. Kosygin's closing speech ended: '*The Soviet side will do all it can to ensure the complete implementation of the documents we have signed, to see to it that relations between our two countries strengthen and develop from year to year*'

The journalists showed surprise that Britain seemed to be held in such high esteem. and asked why the agreement had been considered such a success, and what was the point of sweating to get contracts in Russia on 7.55% credit terms when the oil sheikhs are clamouring to pay cash for our goods if only we could produce them? The answer, Julian said, was because Wilson has a soft spot for trade with Russia.

Julian was sure that this distinct improvement in our relations was proof that firmness with the Russians does pay, and we should make the best of our new opportunity to see whether Britain could influence the Soviets on international issues through frequent contacts, and make sure that our relationship does not return to the doldrums. Mr Brezhnev made it clear that he did not want to delve into the past, but work towards a larger official presence in Britain in the future.

It looked as if the Cold War was over.

January 1975 Off to Bonn

9

MINISTER IN BONN

1975 – 79

The Minister's Song

(To be sung to the tune of 'I am the very model of a
modern major general')

I'm the one who's given charge of all the innocent activities,
The military meetings and the cultural festivities,
I sit on a committee giving scholarships and bursaries,
I represent the Embassy at awful anniversaries;
At six o'clock I pack it up and climb into the Jaguar
I drive to a Reception for Peru or Nicaragua,
And spend my time in answering the question, whether tacit or
Explicit – what they really mean is 'Where is the Ambassador?'
JULIAN BULLARD Christmas cabaret 1975

'My God! What one does eat for Queen and Country!'
PRINCESS ALEXANDRA – Burma 1961

I HAD thought of the Head of Personnel Department, (invisible and un-
knowable to wives) as a god-like figure who at the touch of a button could
summon every detail of every member of the Foreign Office, his talents,
his past history, the languages spoken, his bad habits, his charm, and having run over these a second time, would let his pen hover for a few moments
between Taiwan and Mogadishu, and decide in which of these the diplomat's
talents would fit most perfectly. It may be that this is how some postings were
decided. Julian's experience in 1966 and 1975 would suggest that the wishes of
the diplomat were not a consideration.

'Not Brussels, but not much further' was the answer Julian got from Personnel Department when he asked about his next posting which he had been expecting for some time. But it turned out to be Bonn. (I later heard that the delay had been due to hesitation whether it should be Bonn or Paris). There is no denying that this was a disappointment. Bonn again! Julian had hoped that his brain would have new problems to deal with, because he couldn't help feeling that Ambassador in Germany was more than likely to be his final post, which would make his total time in its rather dull provincial capital to be almost eleven years. Bonn undeniably lacked the culture of a great city, though, being small, one pleasant feature was that at any large event you could be confident of knowing at least half of the people there. Another compensation was that the Ambassador was Nicko Henderson, with whom, and with Mary we had been friends since Vienna. Sadly for us, but great for the Hendersons, Nicko was very soon transferred to the Embassy in Paris.

There was to be a hiatus of about three months, during which time Julian would be Acting Ambassador. In July after a summer in Castletownshend with the children, we collected our new Sunbeam Rapier and drove to the Minister's house in Fasanenstrasse, a road peppered with Ambassadors and Ministers of several other countries.

Much had changed from the 60's, and not only the value of the pound. At his desk Julian said he found two thirds of the telegrams more or less unintelligible, being mostly about energy and commodities. Even on a subject like Berlin, things were not as they had been. Under Willy Brandt West Germany had abandoned the *Hallstein* Doctrine in favour of *Ostpolitic*, which meant that the Federal German Republic had now recognized the post-war borders of Eastern Europe and opened diplomatic relations with the German Democratic Republic (DDR) for the first time. Every morning a great pile of solid, interesting, thoughtful German newspapers landed on our doorstep. It was clear that Julian would have to get up early and work long hours to catch up with the history and the current political situation.

The Minister's task, apart from representing the Ambassador when he was otherwise engaged, was to be the point of contact between the Embassy and the British Army with its headquarters in Rheindahlen and with the commanding General in Berlin. In addition his role included overseeing the work of the Consulates in Hamburg, Stuttgart, Munich and Dusseldorf and also of the British Council in Cologne, not to mention attending the seemingly endless round of trade fairs and twin town celebrations.

Julian lost no time in paying his official visit to Berlin. This part of his work was pure pleasure. We had a helicopter flight over the city, saw the Wall and the wire and learnt that West Berlin is a great sprawling area of 186 square miles, partly wooded, with two golf courses and 50,000 sailing boats. Suddenly it seemed almost as if we were back in Dubai as we stood on a dais and watched a Welsh regiment beating the retreat under a brilliant setting sun. The General wore an identical hat to the one that Julian used to wear in the Gulf to take the salute from the Commander of the Scots Guards or the Grenadiers. We stayed with Julian Walker, who ran the Embassy's Berlin office, and had some years earlier served in the Trucial States, where he had the job of marking the boundaries between the sheikhdoms. He said he used to put down oil drums filled with concrete, but often found that in some mysterious way they seemed to be in different places the next time he came along. On one occasion he had driven so deeply into the desert that he met two men who had never seen a motorized vehicle before, who asked whether his Land Rover was masculine or feminine, and whether it needed food.

When asked by Walter Momper, the leader of the SPD, the German Socialist Party in the Berlin Parliament, if there was something that he would particularly like to visit in Berlin, Julian asked to see the newly released documents of the Nazi era. Typical were sentences of imprisonment for two months for defeatist remarks or for having sexual relations with non-Aryans. Afterwards we were shown the derelict strip on the west side of the Berlin Wall, then occupied by squatters, and kept empty so that no one could be 'accidentally' shot by the DDR's border guards. We climbed three floors and entered a room with walls painted entirely in purple – bare except for a large poster of Princess Diana. Walter Momper said he doubted that the squatters would be able to offer us any refreshment, so his wife had brought the wherewithal in a shopping bag. The five occupants seemed perfectly content with their life without windows, electricity or water, and told us that all they lacked was a suitable hall where they could play their guitars and make music as loud as they liked. They said that like everyone else of their age, they had no interest in politics, *because the media were entirely interested in negative headlines – scandals and crime*. Afterwards we met the mayors of the Berlin districts in which British troops had barracks. None of them showed any resentment for the fact that the lifestyle enjoyed by the occupying powers in Berlin was paid for by the German taxpayer.

We were hardly back from Berlin when we heard that Michael Foot, then leader of the Labour Party, and his wife, would be occupying our spare room for two nights. He arrived, shabbily dressed, with a large soft zip-bag so full of books there was hardly room for a change of clothes. We invited dinner guests that we hoped he would find interesting, but his conversation was a bit of a disappointment, halting, diffident and with long silences. We had thought he would dominate the evening, but he spoke little. His wife explained that Michael needed an audience of a hundred in front of him to stir him up. He struck us as a typical Hampstead Fabian Socialist who, against all expectations, found himself a Cabinet Minister. Both of them spent every spare moment with their heads in books. Next morning Jill Foot asked me to take her on a tour of the latest newly built suburb. We both agreed that English developers had much to learn from Germany. An important part of the German plan is for new developments to have a central square with school, shops, catholic and evangelical churches, library etc. and for the surrounding housing to be mixed, private housing, rented flats, and social housing. Such an obvious plan, why does that never seem to strike local planners in England?

Tony Benn, who we were expecting the following week, had written to say that he would prefer not to stay with the Ambassador, even an acting one, because that might give the German socialist government the wrong impression. I told Jill Foot that this made me rather nervous. She calmed me down, saying he was really a sweetie. *'Just don't behave as he thinks diplomatic wives behave.'* Tony Benn told Julian that his preference for a hotel was because he liked to work most of the night, and wanted to be able to ring for refreshments. Julian replied that though he might have been able to get night-service in Asia, it was certainly not possible in 1975 Bonn, but we would do our best to fulfil all his demands. I had a small refrigerator moved into his bathroom, and filled it with fruit and sandwiches and put out a line of thermos flasks with assorted hot drinks to accompany the usual alcohol. As he left after breakfast next morning to catch a train to Brussels, he patted his pockets and said that he had much enjoyed the sandwiches, and those he hadn't eaten he was going to take for the journey! His effusive letter of thanks said that though he had stayed with ambassadors all over the world, he had *'never received such imaginative hospitality and he would like to put on record that Bonn does not really need an Ambassador whilst you are in charge of the domestic side of the business.'* A lot of butter goes a long way! It was a good thing that Julian's rank seemed to allow him a cook, a butler, and a couple of maids, otherwise getting the sheets changed and the refrigerator removed before the next visitor would have been a problem.

Christmas 1975 came and with it a house full of children. I am sure the tradition of the dramatic entertainment for the embassy staff in the canteen continued, but my memory is only of the entertainment put on by our daughters and their contemporaries in our large sitting room overlooking the garden.

Julian was glad to have had the experience of having been in Bonn ten years earlier, as otherwise he would have struggled to get a grip on who was doing what. At first glance it seemed as if 10% of the Embassy could be dispensed with without difficulty. In October there were two weeks of lectures and parties in Cologne to celebrate the 50th birthday of British Council. Next item on the agenda was to visit the capitals of all the Länder (regional) capitals and our Consul Generals starting with Dusseldorf. Julian had asked the University Librarian in Dusseldorf to show me his treasures and arranged, while he was with the politicians, for me to meet the founding Director of the Art Museum, Dr Smallenbach. Dusseldorf had now expanded to be the richest city in Nordrheinwestfalen, and the Director told me that the art collection had to be one of which its citizens could be proud. Whatever pictures he chose to buy, no matter how high the price, the city would pay for. His principle was never to buy a mediocre painting, even if by a known name, but only to buy a painting which, when he saw it, immediately made him feel: that is a painting I must have! Then followed a self-praising story of how he managed to persuade Mrs Kandinski to let him buy a painting that she did not want to sell.

In the evening we were given a very smart dinner with all the top people: Dieter Spethmann from Thyssen, Fritz Henkel, whose family invented Persil, and many bankers. My neighbour told me that in Dusseldorf it was difficult to succeed in any profession or career if you don't belong to the CDU, the Conservative party which always gets 60% support in elections. Mrs Thatcher later made it clear that her principles were exactly the same: less state, more free trade.

At the time Julian arrived in Bonn, Britain was financially in a very weak state, not helped by the huge number of strikes led by Arthur Skargill of the United Mineworkers, believed to be supported by the Russians, and Jack Jones, of the Transport and General Workers, said to be regarded by the KGB as 'their' agent. Britain was obliged to go cap in hand to the IMF, which can't have made representing Britain in Germany an envious position.

Julian found his Ministerial role very time-consuming, and not always very interesting. The most important element was representing Britain and getting on good terms with the politicians and notable people in the various German Länder,(regions) as you never knew when in the future you might not need to ask a favour, strike a bargain or explain a painful truth. However it was not easy to be close to the top people in Bonn, Dusseldorf, Münich and Frankfurt at the same time as having to be seen at every Trade Fair, keeping his eye on all the consulates and satisfying the demands of the Army and RAF. He did not want the Chairman of ICI writing to complain that, unlike his predecessor, Bullard never visited the British pavilions. We also had to be present at social events from the Presse Ball, (attended by every dignitary, and which we might have enjoyed had there been any quiet spot where we could have sat down,) to the Anglican Church Bazaar, attended by no dignitaries, but at which it was essential to show one's face and spend money.

We had mixed feelings about the Rev. Mountford, and the Bazaar to raise money for his support. The problem was that the previous vicar had persuaded his flock that it would be better for the congregation to feel themselves independent and self-supporting, and not to rely on the Foreign Office to cover the cost of the vicar's stipend and expenses. Money for both causes had been raised in previous years by dances and concerts, and neither of us were keen to take on both responsibilities, particularly when the congregation was given no choice but to accept the priest whom the Bishop of Gibraltar chose to send to Bonn. The latest priest liked to wear, on top of his surplice, brilliantly coloured stoles which he said were badges of his Indian university. He also chose hymns unknown to many of the congregation – always something that arouses enmity! We could not help thinking that the less successful the Bazaar was, the greater the likelihood that the Rev. Mountford (who we referred to as Rev. Mountebank), would be moved back to where he came from.

Antonia asked for advice about what she should expect when she went for her interview for the civil service. (Foreign Office and Treasury) This was Julian's reply:

'The board will put questions either about current issues, as it might be: What would you do about hunger-strikers if you were Mr Jenkins? Or how should the Iceland fishing dispute be solved? Or what about devolution for Scotland? Alternatively, the question might refer to some experience you have mentioned in the forms you filled in: Why is Germany so successful economically? What will happen in the German elections? Or whether the civil service is overstaffed? Or why economists haven't solved the world's economic problems? It doesn't matter what line you take, just that you speak convincingly, use sensible arguments and adopt a moderate tone. If they dismiss your arguments you might reply with something like: Yes, I am aware of those arguments but personally I find the others more convincing and in line with my own experience.' This advice must have been good because she was offered employment by both of them.

On the occasion of an important local anniversary, most of the Bonn Ambassadors and Ministers were invited to Baden-Wurtemberg for a long weekend visit. We enjoyed the tour of the historical museum where we learnt about the Hohenstaufens, Frederich II being one of the best known, (crusades, papal wars etc.) According to Dante he had heretics wrapped in lead and melted over a slow fire although our encyclopedia thinks he 'was the centre of a cultivated court and founder of the Union of Naples.' We were treated to a Swabian Evening, at which middle-aged women sang funny songs and we ate Griesknockerl, Semmelknodel and Eierschwammerl. On the last day we dozed as the Neckar slipped by, dizzy with folklore, deaf with speeches of welcome and stuffed with fattening finger-food. Police helicopters flew alongside us all the way, disgorging men with dogs and submachine guns every time our boat stopped. It would be difficult to return to normal life after three days of having our every conceivable need taken care of, and receiving bunches of flowers from beautifully dressed girls at every event. Our bags were packed with presents: dolls, scent, books, keyrings, washing up towels, sweets, after-shave, medals, porcelain. The speeches of thanks were delivered by a funny little man who turned out to be the Papal Nuncio, who automatically takes precedence in Roman Catholic regions.

All old Oxonians in Germany were invited to an annual dinner at which our most honoured guest was always the Duke of Hanover, who insisted that 'where he dined he slept.' For his convenience, the Oxford dinner invariably took place in the most expensive hotel in Cologne, adjacent to the railway station. My diary for the period would give support to the opinion of those who think diplomatic life is little more than endless eating and drinking with people who mostly spoke better English than I did German, with just enough time left to type our weekly news bulletin to all the children.

Being the wife of the British Minister in Bonn with a comfortable house and competent servants, seemed a wonderfully spoiling way to live. We had inherited a butler from Montenegro with an exalted idea of how Julian should be served, with a Greek Christian wife who was a marvellous cook, and from whom I learnt a great deal. I did once suggest that I should teach her how to make Queen of Puddings, chiefly because it was a favourite of both James and Robert, but she silenced me with: '*Madame, there are three cuisines: there is the Chinese, there is the Turkish and there is the French. There are no other cuisines.*' I could only agree with her, but I put in a plea that she might have changed her views had she tasted the puddings and roast potatoes made by our cook Chloe in my early years.

Our care-free sybaritic life met with a shock with the arrival of the news that James had unexpectedly (in the eyes of those who had been writing his end of term reports) passed all his O levels with credit, well over the minimum qualification for Seal Hayne Agricultural College, but for which he was one year too young. What was he to do for a year? This was one of the many things that made a Foreign Office career hard for parents. The Headmaster of Marlborough said he could not stay if he was not working for A levels, even though, in the eyes of the Ministry of Education, he was not actually old enough to leave school. I suggested to Julian that he ask Personnel Department to find someone else for Bonn, and give him a job in London – but Julian rejected this as absolutely unthinkable. He managed to find a farmer on the other side of the Rhine willing to give James three months board and lodging in return for help on his farm, after which he said he would give us his opinion on whether James had the making of a farmer.

Problems were not made easier by the number of our visitors. First Foot, then Benn, Lord Harris and Goronwy Roberts, then 16 Trade Union MP's. And then a telephone call to say that Jim Callaghan had been offered a lift back from the UN meeting in New York in a private plane and would be stopping at the Bonn Airport for an hour on his way back.

Julian described this for his father:

'I shook his hand, gave him today's newspapers and told him the good news that the members of his constituency party who wanted to throw him out, had been squashed. He told me that the Special Session on Raw Materials had gone much better than the year before; the Third World realised that they couldn't simply dictate terms to the industrialised countries, since they need us as a source of capital and technology and as a market for their own products. By this time the luggage had been transferred. He got into his plane and flew away together with my Saturday newspapers.

'Callaghan – plain blunt man, but boiled a bit too hard. I heard that in the Office Oliver Wright was considered to have adapted himself too readily from the Heath line on Europe to that of Wilson: it was felt that he couldn't have been so whole--hearted both about the euphoria of 1971-72 and about the 'agnosticism' of 1974-75. His answer I think, would be that officials had to find a strategy which would achieve Mr Callaghan's chief purpose of keeping the Labour Party together, and also the objective of keeping Britain in the Community, and that, ironically enough, he thought the only way of achieving these two things was through a referendum following re-negotiation. A risky strategy, because if either re-negotiation had failed or the referendum had gone the other way, we might have finished with the Labour Party split and Britain leaving the Community. However, it worked, and you will have read about Callaghan's speech in Hamburg. We think it was something to get him to accept the invitation to speak there just at this moment, and still more to get him to choose 'Europe' as his theme, nor was the substance bad'.

Oliver Wright, our new Ambassador, arrived and the gossip columns paid him many compliments. His German was much better than Nicko's, they liked his Jermyn Street shirts and his bushy eyebrows, and he was even invited to appear on a TV talk show. Because his wife had had a brief acting career, she had decorated the Residence with statuettes of Olivier as Lear and Geilgud as Hamlet, and old playbills. He seemed to think everybody and everything absolutely splendid, and was quite content to leave them to get on with their work without consulting him.

James came home for the weekend very contented after two weeks at Herr Reuther's half-timbered farmhouse, during which he had clipped several yards of hedge, sown a field with a tractor and been taken to the Frankfurt Motor Show. James was also very pleased to ride about in the Ambassadorial Rolls Royce with buttons for everything, including summoning the police if Julian should be attacked by terrorists. A letter from Antonia brought the news that she had been awarded a Kennedy scholarship at the Massachusetts Institute of Technology. Julian could not repress the fear that she will meet a good looking American, get married and stay there for the rest of her life.

We had five days in Oxford to celebrate Julian's father's 90th birthday with a splendid party at Lincoln College at which Chapman Andrews made a speech and Sir David Scott told a strange story about Sir Nicholas Henderson and Sir Michael Palliser, now Ambassador in Paris and Permanent Under Secretary at the Foreign Office. Both we learnt only got third class degrees and failed the Foreign Office examination the first time they took it, only getting in at the second attempt when Scott was Chairman of the Final Selection Board! Julian checked this story with Michael Palliser when he came to Bonn, who confessed it was true, but said Scott had not mentioned that it was only on Scott's advice that Palliser had taken the examination a second time. The examiners on both occasions had asked him to explain how he came only to be awarded a Third. The first time he had replied truthfully that he had spent all his time at Christ Church acting instead of working. He could see this made a bad impression, so at his second attempt, when the second lot of examiners put the same question, he explained that it had been difficult to work seriously owing to the threat of war, the O.T.C. and fire-watching duties etc. Result: a triumphant pass and a career leading to Permanent Under Secretary at 54. Julian's comment was that he had given up believing that people described events exactly as they occurred. But everybody simplifies or touches up or alters the balance to improve his own showing. '*Look at Crossman's Diaries.*'

Suddenly in February real winter started. Julian took to leaving his office at 12.30 and inviting all skaters in the Embassy to do the same. About 16 joined him on a pond in the Park but alas on the third day he slipped and pulled a muscle in his shoulder, so it was just as well that the thaw set in or he might have done something worse. February was the month when the Rheinland celebrated Fasching, the carnival the week before Lent starts, and girls come round and snip off men's ties with great delight. The Head of Chancery, Andrew Stark, decided to go and watch the procession and, slamming the heavy door of his own new Jaguar, he nearly cut off his finger. So instead of watching the parade he went to the hospital where the remaining strands were cut off and skin sewn over the join.

In March Harold Wilson resigned, and Jim Callaghan became Prime Minister. He then began to be openly critical of his former boss: how Harold had fancied himself as being in touch with foreign countries about which he really knew nothing except what he had said to Mikoyan in 1947, and how he didn't care for foreigners much, not even the Commonwealth, at whose annual conference he would be found in a corner with his cronies. Callaghan's method of dealing with the long-term economic difficulties involved gambling that holding pay rises at 5% or less for a fifth year would further improve the economy and get him re-elected in 1979. The trade unions rejected continued pay restraint, and a succession of strikes caused it to become known as the 'winter of discontent.' The unrest made his government extremely unpopular, and Callaghan later admitted that he had 'let the country down'.

We tried to get away from Bonn at weekends. Sometimes we followed the Mosel up its valley until we came to a village whose name we remembered seeing on a wine label, and we would ask advice in the main square as to who made the best wine. We would then knock on the recommended door, and ask if we could come and buy a case or two? We were invariably given a tremendous welcome and in half an hour the table in their best room would be covered with opened bottles, none of them with labels. To know from which grape it was made, and on which plot it had grown, the vintner merely put his nose to the neck of the bottle and sniffed. Then we would load our purchases into the boot of the car and he would beg us to come again and bring our friends.

One weekend we visited a town called Kiedrich, not far from Mainz. The organ in its lovely old church was said to be the oldest playable one in Germany, and bore a tablet recording that its restoration had been paid for by 'The English Baron, John Sutton.' John Sutton, we found was a rich, ordained Northampton knight with a passion for organs, and a friend of Pugin and Bodley. He left Jesus College, Cambridge after the college elected an evangelical Master. He became a member of the Roman Catholic church, and decided to end his life living in the Priest's house in the beautiful town of Kiedrich am Rheingau and devoting himself to restoring the 16th century organ.

Julian's diary was full of events to introduce Oliver Wright: lunch for all the Commonwealth Ambassadors, National Day reception for Oman, lunch for the War Graves Commission, (over which we argued whether Pakistan and South Africa should continue to be included) and two separate lunches for the Ambassador to meet first the leader first of the SPD, and then of the CDU, and I rather think we were invited to eat many dinners in his honour in all the German regions as well. One of my favourite invitations every year which did not involve eating, was the wine festival at Koblenz, where the 1594 vineyards on the river Mosel and its tributaries sent in bottles of their wine and two thirds of them received some kind of a medal. The invitees sat at long tables and beautifully dressed girls in dirndls filled our glasses, while the Master of Ceremonies described the wine as elegant, harmonious, inviting, lively and so forth. If you liked the wine you clapped. If you didn't you threw the dregs into a bucket.

I was intrigued that many German academics seem to be in Trade. Dr Oëtger seemed to own most of the grocery stores and many of the travel shops seemed to be run by Dr Tiggis. Since the children's spring holidays loomed, I was tempted to see what Dr Tiggis could offer in the way of an Easter holiday for a family with four children. In no time we spotted a good bargain and booked to take the children to spend two weeks in Yugoslavia, the first week in a hotel not far from Dubrovnik which offered a money-back guarantee if it rained, and the second, partly with a Yugoslav family on the island of Hvar and partly in the only hotel inside the walled city of Dubrovnik. The problem with staying with the family, was that no Yugoslav family could accommodate all of us so we had to spread ourselves between three families. It was a splendid holiday. We all loved the Easter celebrations in Dubrovnik with the stalls of beautiful hand-painted eggs and the barbecued lunches on the beach at Hvar, the cooker being concocted out of flotsam and jetsam we picked up on the beach.

On 22 June 1976 I drove to Oxford in a heat-wave with the car boot full of duty-free German champagne to celebrate Antonia's 21 birthday. I arrived in time for the party on St Hilda's meadow, but not in time to get the champagne iced. In those days before air-conditioning, Germany had a very useful regulation that when the temperature reached 27degrees Centigrade, schools and offices shut and everyone went home. The Ambassador went off to enjoy himself scudding about in yachts during Kieler Woche, leaving Julian to attend the garden party of the President of the German Parliament and the Luxemburg National Day celebration in the heat wave. These were all-male occasions where he said he had discussed French politics in German with a Russian and the Channel Tunnel in German with a Chinese. When I got back to Bonn, I watched Wimbledon with the sound turned down, listened to the English commentary on the radio, and drank a lot of iced water.

Astonishingly Germany had a printers' strike – the second in 25 years. Julian was lost without newspapers to work through. On account of the UK's disastrous financial condition, Whitehall had decided to cancel all the parties to commemorate the Queen's Birthday. Oliver Wright decided to send an invitation for an all-male drink before lunch, and Julian had the excellent idea of having a charity concert in the evening of the same day, tickets DM 15 including refreshments. It turned out we were not short of talent and the concert was a fantastic success. We had a terrific Queen of the Night and an unexpectedly talented solo bassoonist. Rather less good were the vicar and his friends who played the recorder and the viol. We raised something like DM 1,000 for the school and the church, as a great many people sent donations to avoid having to sit through what they expected to be very amateur performances. I hoped they heard what a great evening they had missed. Julian and I contributed a percentage of the proceeds to the church with reluctance. The vicar had just circulated a leaflet against the ordination of women. The argument, dressed up in fancy words like christological and docetic, was: a) to be a priest is not a job, but a sacrament through the unity of god and man in maleness., b) If He had wanted women to be priests He would have chosen a female apostle. c) The pope was against it. d) It would impede our valuable progress towards unity with Rome and the Orthodox Church. We considered cancelling our monthly offering as well.

On one of his visits to Rheindahlen, the British Army headquarters, Julian chanced to learn that one of the ways young soldiers were trained was to send them out in quite large sailing boats without any back-up engine. Julian was urged to make use of the Army Yacht Club with the children when they were on holiday. We took them up on the offer, stipulating that the boat should come with a skipper. So on the first of September 1976 we boarded the *Heron* in Kiel, with Charlie Banks as skipper, and set sail in the direction of the Danish islands for a long holiday weekend.

After little more than 30 minutes, I brightly asked Corporal Banks what that huge black blob in the sky was. Charlie glanced over his shoulder and instantly said '*Women and children below decks at once and attach your harnesses to the rings.*' Hardly had we had time to do this, when the wind rose to about Force 9 driving stinging hail in front of it. Julian stayed on deck, standing in the lurching bows, clinging with one hand to a piece of the rigging and with the other struggling to haul in the jib. Meanwhile Charlie was reefing the mainsail. He knew his stuff, and somehow about two hours later, we limped into a place called DAMP 2000 having lost no children, only our rudder! The following day Charlie refused to take us out at all. We fought our way along the beach, bought some bread, and exchanged weather reports with other mariners in the same situation, wondering if we would ever get back to Kiel, still less to any Danish Islands. But on the second morning we woke to find the storm had passed, Charlie had managed to replace the rudder, and after a good breakfast, we gingerly set sail, and that night paid our harbour dues in kroner. The following day we sailed into the harbours of Aeroskobing and Marstal – all spotless – ship repairers, bakers and pastrycooks open from 7am, even on Sundays. By the time our home port hove in sight, we had experienced every kind of weather except fog, and had had all the sails up – even the Spinnaker. There was never any question of capsizing or falling in, but lots of chance of misjudging the weather, damaging the boat or getting tangled up in the gear and the rigging. Old memories were revived in October 1984, when the headlines in our newspaper said: '250 members of the German aristocracy were present yesterday at the wedding of the Kaiser's grandson to Countess Nina von Reventlow in DAMP 2000!

All in all, we enjoyed the sailing trip enormously and booked a larger and grander boat which had belonged to Field Marshal Gőéring for the coming year, hoping that some of our nephews and nieces would join us. Moral: don't try to repeat a success. The following year God sent no wind so we felt like the Ancient Mariner except that unlike us, he was not under orders to keep large quantities of brass up to standard with rags and metal polish.

Out of the blue Julian had a letter asking him if he was willing to have his name put forward to succeed John Sparrow as the Warden of All Souls. I thought he would make an excellent Warden, but of course he replied that he was quite certain of his unfitness for the job. I think he felt that he had a good prospect of more exciting work if he stayed in the Foreign Office.

In the German elections in October 1976 the conservative CDU/CSU alliance won the most seats, but Helmut Schmidt remained Chancellor thanks to an alliance with the Free Democratic Party of which Herr Genscher was Leader. German politics were mainly a battle of personalities; it was quite difficult to tell the difference between the parties, which were subsidised by the taxpayer, without limit on election expenses, which meant that every lamppost was plastered with portraits.

At an unexpectedly interesting dinner at the Turkish Embassy we met Edward Sutro, the brother of John Sutro, who appears in biographies of Evelyn Waugh. His chief occupation and interest in life was backing plays. It cost about £30,000 to put on a play, he said, but *Donkey's Years* was making £4,000 a week. A friend persuaded Sutro to put some money into '*No Sex Please. We're British*' and he had already had his money back 152 times.

When Julian had to go on long drives, he used to encourage his driver to tell him about his wartime experiences. On one trip Herr Patt told him how he and a friend had bribed a Luftwaffe pilot with 20 litres of sunflower seed oil to fly them from somewhere in Russia where they were about to be captured, to somewhere in Poland from where they walked home. They then took part in the last desperate offensive in the Ardennes in December 1944 for which they were given enough petrol for their tanks for one day and told that they would have to manage afterwards with what they captured. For the first few days it was too misty for the British and Americans to see them, but after that they were sunk. (I think that meant captured).

Six members of the Downing Street Think Tank (Central Policy Review Staff) descended on us to see if it was true that all we did was stand about at cocktail parties, spend millions of taxpayer's money uselessly, and visit exotic places at the expense of the British taxpayer. Julian was strongly against the sweeping changes which, it was rumoured, the Think Tank would like to see introduced: among them the abolition of the Foreign Office, and its merger into the Home Civil Service Travelling Force, (which he thought would just be the same people dealing with the same problems under a different name). They talked of privatising the civil service and wanted young diplomats to be sent to work in the City to see how businesses are run and make them more efficient. The Foreign Office thought of itself as a Service rather than a Business and these ideas were not popular. Julian spent half the night thinking about statistics he might bring up: the whole FO overseas establishment plus the World Service of the BBC only costing the same as the Fire Brigade, or half what was spent on tobacco. ICI's tax bill would pay the cost of the Foreign Office single handed. Even the cost of re-financing export credit, (i.e. borrowing at 15% to lend to the Russians at 7%) was double the Foreign Office budget. But it was difficult to say whether a country in the state ours was in, could not manage, for example, with an establishment more similar to what the Italians had in Bonn, except that if we were becoming a second-rate power, perhaps we needed an even better Foreign Office, not a second rate one.

Julian organized a working lunch with the Think Tank, inviting two or three of the brightest members of his staff, and an equal number from the German foreign ministry, and me. The team from London, which included two good-looking young women, with no experience of the civil service, were invited to put their proposals, on which the English and German officials were to comment. Later Julian had a letter from Sir Kenneth Berrill, head of the Think Tank, who congratulated Julian on 'How well the German foot-soldiers had fought under their British Officers.'

We were relieved that their report was slashed in the Press. It ran into a brick wall in the shape of the British Council and the BBC lobbies. Financial arguments also played their part: the cost of the Foreign Office was very little in proportion to other expenditure, and their proposal to cut posts and close facilities took no account of future government policies which might need them. Julian thought the Think Tank posed three questions and answered them all wrong:

Whether diplomacy should adapt itself to the national weaknesses or try to compensate for them:

Whether there is such a thing as a country's stock, standing, image, reputation, which may be invisible but has an influence for good or ill.

Whether talent is more important than qualifications or the other way about. Would the work be done better if it were done by someone with a Red-brick degree in anthropology who spent more than 40% of his career abroad?

Or in brief:

that the FO did things that didn't need to be done and did them too well,

that the board should try to recruit people of medium ability instead of the best,

that the FO should be half as large again and staffed by the Home as well as the Foreign Service.

I thought if the proposed cuts were adopted, and the Service were required to do the same functions with less money and facilities, what had once been a dedicated, confident and loyal Service, would become one over-stretched, under-resourced and hardy likely to attract talented graduates. But sometimes it did seem that what the government service lacked was people who had the mental courage to look a little outside the boundaries of their job and see the connection between what they were doing and what went on elsewhere, and draw practical conclusions. In an excellent Reith Lecture, Andrew Shonfield suggested that members of the EEC should pool their resources for representation in small or unimportant countries instead of each maintaining its own Embassy with its own overheads. A suggestion which, not long after, was taken on board.

The visit of the Think Tank was succeeded by two young members of the Foreign Office sent to consult us on whether it would be a good idea for Embassies to have a Fund called 'Reinforce Success' so that if a junior member of the Embassy became friends with the daughter of the President or Chancellor, it would provide the money for him to send her orchids every day! Julian said if he had such a fund, he would spend it sending a huge bouquet to the Scottish Opera who had given a performance of Britten's Midsummer Night's Dream at Wiesbaden, because nothing could have been more splendidly played, acted or sung. Altogether it was that rare thing: an evening of modern British music to be proud of. It blotted out our shame at the pound falling from 5.50 to 4.85 and rumoured to fall further. I tried not to spend anything in marks, which translated to more and more pounds every time. The TV was full of stories of the ferries packed with Germans and Dutch and Belgians descending on London and fighting for camel-haired coats. It looked likely that the Conservatives would win the next British election and I was not looking forward to it. Meanwhile we basked in beautiful autumn sunshine and tried not to think about the pound

Anthony Crosland, now Foreign Secretary, came to stay on a visit to meet Helmut Schmidt. Before he arrived we were told to replace the water in the carafe in his bedroom with gin. He told us he knew nothing of foreign affairs and didn't want to be Foreign Secretary, but he found he liked it and admired the Service for its talent, efficiency and sheer good humour. I think that is why Julian enjoys it. He thinks *esprit de corps* must be lacking in the Home Office or they wouldn't have so many disasters. Julian was extremely tired of opening British Weeks, and showing interest in British stalls at Confectionary Trade Fairs and Book Fairs. At the British Week at Baden-Baden he had to blush for the quality of the exhibits, hideous tea towels, overpriced carpets, and mock-oak, mock-cottage, mock-furniture. Wiesbaden was just as bad. I walked round the exhibits beside him wearing my best clothes and trying to smile.

Either Oliver Wright had another engagement or he was not interested in poetry, because we were allowed to take his place in Hamburg, where Philip Larkin was being awarded a literary prize. Julian was a great admirer of Larkin's poem about withdrawal from the Gulf. From Larkin's speech of thanks we learnt that he had never been on television or read his poems in public, or lectured on the subject, or in fact ever made speeches at all. It seemed the visit to Hamburg was only the second time he had been out of England since 1945! He was travelling with `Miss Jones' round whom he had his arm from time to time. She was no beauty and no younger than Julian. The Ambassador also allowed Julian to take his place again a few days later and lecture all the top brass of the British Army on *Germany Today*.

We were summoned home again for Julian to be knighted on 9 November with accompanying music by the 1st battalion of the Grenadier Guards: *Kiss Me Kate*, *The Sound of Music*, *South Pacific*. Julian suggested that perhaps the music was deliberately chosen by Her Majesty to express her contempt for the people her Prime Minister wanted her to pin honours on! We got back to Bonn in time to give lunch to the Chief of Air Staff. Next day it was drinks for the Royal Philharmonic Orchestra, (which would have been pleasant had they not wanted their reception to be after their concert, at 10.30 pm by which time our only desire was for bed.)

James refused to come home for the weekends until after lunch on Saturdays because on that day the Reuters' menu was his favourite – what the children called 'Politzeisuppe' (policemen's soup). During our first posting in Bonn there had been a meeting between General de Gaulle and Adenauer. Inevitably there were enormous quantities of police in attendance, and in Germany the police were always accompanied by huge vehicles from which dishes of pea soup with slices of sausage floating in it were handed out to anyone who was cold or hungry. Our children were always in the front of the queue. Not everybody in the Embassy was as keen on German food. I went to visit the wife of one of the Chancery guards in hospital and asked whether the food was good. She replied: '*Well, it's what you might call German. They brought me a sausage which was – well, curved, not straight like ours, I couldn't eat it.*'

In September of 1977 the papers were filled with the dastardly doings of a group that the media referred to as 'the Baader Meinhof Gang' and sometimes 'The Red Army Faction.' They had captured Hans Martin Schleyer, a leading businessman, and killed his bodyguards. A month later Schleyer's body was found in the boot of a car. Earlier they had killed the head of the Dresdner Bank. They claimed that their action was a protest against capitalism, whose leaders were no better than the Nazis. Three of their leaders later committed suicide in prison.

Vicky stayed with us until Marlborough term started and I took her to see some of the sights of Bonn – chief of which was Beethoven's birthplace: a modest house with a small exhibition of manuscripts, over which one can shake one's head in incomprehension at his illegible writing, and wonder about the tone of his piano, which one is not allowed to try. We then walked to the theatre which announced an 11am performance of Don Carlos: (entry free to encourage people to buy a season ticket). Someone asked why Don Carlos was not being sung in Italian, and was told that if it were, it would have meant paying the chorus two extra fees, one for singing in a foreign language and one because the original libretto was in French!

The British Embassy wives were invited to visit the Eau de Cologne factory, no doubt to encourage us to buy some of their products for Christmas presents. The visit gave me an interesting insight into the workings of a paternalistic capitalist system. It had been run by the same family since 1798. The eldest son takes over when he reaches 34, at which age the secret of the recipe is revealed to him. Almost all the employees were women, each of whom is given 50 Deutsch marks on the birth of a son. (nothing for daughters) and 25% discount at Christmastime. The firm was the first business to run its own medical centre, which they said helped the firm as well as the employees because they did not waste time going to the doctor. I do not know if the system survived elsewhere, but in Cologne the firm has since had several international owners.

Anthony Acland, Ambassador in Luxemburg, invited us to stay for the weekend in his elegant old-fashioned Residence, with long windows, panelled rooms and commodes in red lacquer once given to Mrs Keppel by Edward VII. His wife Ann was spending her days inspecting lavatories, flowers and menus as The Queen was expected the following month, She had to buy herself three hats for the visit as Her Majesty always wears a hat until 6pm.

The Military Attaché at the Embassy, Brigadier Hoerder, retired, and Brigadier Andrew Mayes was sent in his place. The welcoming party for him was in full swing when suddenly the new Brigadier fell flat on the floor, having, he explained, tripped over someone's shoe. Two months' later his wife Monica dashed across the road and shut herself up with the wife of the Air Attaché in the house opposite as yells of fury echoed behind her. It was noticed that Andrew looked the worse for something, had a quivery hand, and was not making much sense. I was asked to see if I could find out what was the matter. I was knocked flat to hear that Andrew had bursts of drunkenness which accounted for Monica's black eye. She said that the fault was hers, really. 'I *annoy him*'. It made me very angry to see what she put up with. Andrew's regiment had decided to get rid of him on account of his drink problem, and thought becoming a Military Attaché would suit him admirably, ignoring the fact that in a country where Britain had 25,000 soldiers, the work was not a sinecure. I wondered why Monica had married him in the first place. Do people change that much in 24 years? Julian had not changed. He had never been full of youthful high spirits, and I did think he had been a bit depressed and low spirited lately, perhaps because several jobs he would have liked have had, had been given to not very brilliant people.

To cheer Julian up I gave him a year's membership of the Embassy fishing syndicate for his 50th birthday on 8 March. The only snag was the two-hour drive each way to the Embassy's stretch of the River Ahr. He had not been warned that the first fishing weekend was the annual river-bank cutting and cleaning-out day. There was so much that needed doing that we feared we might have to spend every weekend on the river banks with little time for fishing.

A few weeks later we met an embassy colleague, John Boyd, on the bank with his newly pregnant wife. John went off to get some lunch for her, but had not returned when we had to leave. I was led to reflect on the selfishness of most people? Most males? And the long suffering of love! I am inclined to think that most husbands secretly or openly regard their wife's life as peripheral and subsidiary; and the older I got the more I slightly regretted not having had a career, and felt I was really just passing the time as a dogsbody. Renate Blech, the wife of a German diplomat, came back from a trip to Washington saying that what struck her most was that every American woman she met from Mrs Vance downwards, asked her what she did, and she felt very self-conscious repeating that she ran her house, dug her garden, and tried to educate her children, and this took all her time. The obvious problem for Foreign Office wives was that for the half of the time you are living abroad with servants, you have time to spare, but it is less easy to pursue a career, unless you are lucky enough to have one that does not require living in the UK and allows you to move from place to place. At home with no help and children having half terms and other needs, it is difficult to fit in anything except teaching. The wives of German diplomats took a leaf out of our book and started their own Trade Union asking for holiday fares for their children and the right to return to their job when posted back to Germany. A new female third secretary arrived with a spouse who said he intended to look for employment. He put up a notice in the American Club: 'Open to any offers for any kind of job'.

Julian thought it unsporting of John Boyd to make Julia watch him fish without buying Julia a rod and teaching her how to use it, so he gave her a spare one of ours. The next week she was still sitting waiting on the bank, not using the rod, because John had not got round to buying a reel for it. When Julian made a rather threatening remark to him about it being rather boring for Julia just sitting waiting, he replied with a wolfish grin: '*She's so marvellously malleable, she doesn't mind at all.*'

I was asked to organize a lunch for the Diplomatic Wives Emergency Fund, which leant money without interest to wives if their husbands dropped dead or left them. I asked everyone to bring a dish of some sort, which we laid out on the billiard table, and I provided soup and wine and pudding and organized a raffle. I remember this event, but I never before or after came across an emergency fund which helped widowed wives. I hope it was taken over and became the responsibility of those who paid our salaries.

In the summer of 1978 the Queen paid a state visit to Germany. Those who were to be presented to her were summoned for a practice at the Residence and told to curtsey and shake hands, both at the same time, keeping our backs straight. Julian was to escort David Owen (now Foreign Secretary), and I was to take his American wife to the Beethoven House, for which I had 7 minutes, and not a second more. I had to cut every possible flower from our garden to decorate the Residence, and also at Marjorie's request, had to cover the Kleenex box in the loo with wallpaper to match the walls so that Her Majesty would not have to see a vulgar commercial pattern.

In July 1978 the 4th G7 Summit conference was held in Bonn. Julian summarised it in his usual pithy way. The US want growth, the Germans, monetary discipline and Callaghan, more protection for industry and less for agriculture. They agreed on a concerted approach to the chief problems of the time. Inflation, unemployment, energy and terrorism. Callaghan got on well with Schmidt. The Ambassador hosted Jim Callaghan, Roy Jenkins, Dennis Healey, David Owen, Sir John Hunt and Sir Michael Palliser and we were left with a lot of private secretaries and typists and duty officers!. Afterwards we treated ourselves to four days of hiking in Switzerland to compensate.

Yet more visitors! Raymond Carr, Warden of St Antony's, and one of our more interesting visitors, Reginald Jones, whose wrote *Most Secret War*, an account of his part in British Scientific Intelligence between 1939 and 1949. During the war it had been his responsibility to anticipate German applications of science to warfare, so that their new weapons could be countered before they were used. Early on in the war he managed to find out how an early German radar system worked, and he invented ` jammers' which 'bent' the beams along which the German bombers were flying, so that bomb loads were scattered over the British countryside instead of hitting London. Now that our enemies were now our allies, the experts on both sides had a happy time comparing when and how each team had made new advances, and the ways they had invented of defeating the other side's inventions. One of his ideas was to drop strips of metal foil from aircraft cut to a length appropriate to the radar's wavelength, which then appeared on enemy radar screens as 'false bombers'.

I thought Reginald Jones might be interested in Caroline Herschel, and told him about the *Memoir and Correspondence of Caroline Herschel,* (the book I had bought from Oxfam at the cost of £1), and what I had discovered about her. Her brother regarded her as his cook, his housekeeper, as well as his astronomical assistant, and told her that when he was away she might use his telescope and sweep for comets, but must keep a journal with details of all she saw. In one year she recorded that she had made 14 observations, including 3 nebulae, which her brother included in a paper he presented to the Royal Society in April 1786. She was the first woman to discover a comet, (she found eight). She regretted that her lack of enthusiasm for spending the night on damp grass and that the time she had devoted to her brother, had prevented her finding more!

Mr Jones was a delightful man, and so encouraging that I later wrote to tell him that I had discovered Caroline's telescope in the storeroom of the Hanover Historical museum, and asked if he thought anyone would be interested if I wrote about it. After her brother died, Caroline had returned to live in Hanover, where they were born, taking with her the instrument she referred to as 'My little sweeper'. Before she died, she dismantled the telescope and put it in a box, and, what I found particularly interesting, left her handwritten instructions inside with details of exactly how to sweep for comets. In 1988 The Royal Society published my nine-page article. A reproduction of her note was printed at the end of my article.

Julian was in despair about the state of England. A dismal Treasury official was keen we should not surrender the priceless weapon of sovereignty over our rate of exchange, but much good that had done us in the last two decades. To Antonia Julian wrote: '*What a dismal country! I still have another nine and a half years of service to go. Even the bakers are on strike*' I heard a tourist on the radio saying that he would never go to England again because the food and the litter were so frightful. The City thought we should have joined the European Monetary System at the start. It was a mystery to me why, if sovereignty over the exchange rate was so important, President Giscard d'Estaing thought France, with worse inflation than Britain, should join the EMS. A Director of ICI told the CBI annual conference that British Industry produced less then 1% more than in 1973 and paid itself 113% more for doing so. *The Times* was on strike, but so was IG Metall in one part of Germany, and the employers had locked out the employees in another part. At such a time it seemed unbelievable that our Administration officer in the Embassy was advertising a sale of old beds, having decided to replace everyone's beds with metric sized ones!

On 5 Nov 1978 rioters attacked the British Embassy in Teheran. Ambassador Tony Parsons (who had been in Amman with us) had urged the British Government to back the Shah up to the last minute, and reported to London that there was not any serious revolutionary feeling in the country. It was ironic that Tony, who had always thought of himself as a revolutionary, should now have his own Chancery burnt under him. He excused himself for not foreseeing this on the grounds that the Shah would have been furious if his secret service had reported that the British Ambassador was talking to anyone likely to be opposed to the Shah.

Julian and I were delighted that Richard von Weizsäcker would become the next President of Germany after all. The CDU candidate who won the election, was revealed to have had been a member of the Nazi party. It was the familiar story of German's past refusing to lie down.

Our last visit to Berlin included grand dinners with the British General and the German President followed by the opening of Michael Frayn's play *Noises Off*, after which Michael and his wife Claire Tomalin took us to a back-stage party, and next morning we took them sailing. On the jetty we received a message that Geoffrey Howe would after all be expecting a dinner party a couple of hours after we return from Berlin! Fortunately, nothing remained to be done when I got home but to swap a couple of table places. I must have drunk too much because I woke up in the night convinced that Julian had said the Queen was coming to lunch tomorrow but he could not at the moment tell me how many others! Perhaps I was just reacting to the busy week ahead. After Geoffrey Howe left, Julian went to Rheindahlen for Exercise Lionheart (The largest British Army exercise since the war). He got back just in time for a dinner dance in Bonn. On Thursday Julian opened a photographic exhibition in Cologne, on Friday we gave 90 people a buffet, followed on Saturday by the annual dinner for British and German old Oxonians. What a last week!

Julian went to Paris for talks, leaving me to supervise the packers. Exhausted after so many farewell dinners and the packers being here, I filled the car with what we had forgotten to pack, and went to bed early to be ready to make an early start for the drive back to London next morning. I was woken shortly before midnight by a crash in the bathroom, and I found a man standing at the bottom of my bed, somewhat surprised at finding the house occupied. I jumped out of bed screaming *'Who are you? What the hell do you want?'* He turned and fled and I followed him, leaping down the stairs in my nightdress. At the bottom he could have turned to the left or right into the kitchen. I hoped that he would turn into the cloakroom, and I saw myself getting hold of the key, locking him in, and handing him over to justice. But he turned into the kitchen, and once again there was a terrific crash. He had jumped onto the cupboards and smashed the windows, leapt over a couple of bushes and run into the road. It all happened so quickly that I was standing at the front door, looking to see if he was still in sight, and wondering what to do next, when a police security car came past (an advantage of living in a road with the Ambassadors of Ireland and the USA). I hailed them. They said: *'Did he take anything? Did he rape you'*? And then said: *'That's all right then'* and drove on. I left a message with the guard at the Embassy, telling them what had happened and warning them that I would have to leave the house empty at 4.30am in order to catch the Ferry at Dunkirk.

And that was my last night as the wife of the Minister in Bonn.

IO

FOREIGN OFFICE, LONDON

DEPUTY UNDER-SECRETARY OF STATE 1979-1982

POLITICAL DIRECTOR AND SENIOR DEPUTY TO THE
PERMANENT UNDER-SECRETARY 1982-84

*There is nothing dramatic in the success of a diplomat. His victories are made
up of a series of microscopic advantages: of a judicious suggestion here, or an
opportune civility there, of a wise concession at one moment, and a far-sighted
persistence at another; of sleepless tact, immovable calmness, and patience that
no folly, no provocation, no blunder can shake.*

LORD SALISBURY

IT was Boxing Day 1978 and about 7.30am. I was in bed and half asleep in
our Cotswold cottage when the telephone rang. It was Peter Carrington to
say that the Russians had invaded Afghanistan and could Julian come to
the Foreign Office as soon as possible. After he had downed a hasty breakfast,
I drove him to Burford to catch the London bus. When I got home, I saw the
keys of our London flat on the hall table. By ignoring the speed limits, I just
managed to catch the bus in Witney. That was more or less the end of our
Christmas celebrations.

When we left Bonn, James had to leave his German farm. He found himself
a temporary job as a night porter at the Goring Hotel, a ten-minute walk from
our flat in Lowndes Close. It gave him great satisfaction to have the run of the
kitchens and be allowed to help himself from the refrigerators during the night,
and even more having visitors fling the keys of extremely expensive cars to him
with instructions to park them. One evening after we had been dining with the

Governor of the Bank of England, where the waiters serving us wore salmon pink frock coats, we stopped at the Goring Hotel and ordered a drink – and were served by James!

Julian was now working for Lord Carrington, which he enjoyed: 'a dashed sight more than he ever did Dr. Owen.' The new Conservative Foreign Minister had no ambition, no vanity, no fits of bad temper, no suspicion of officials just because they were officials, no humbug, and no illusions. His new post involved a good deal of accompanying Lord Carrington to meetings – the first of that year being at Lancaster House with 10 European Foreign Ministers and five south east Asian Foreign Ministers to discuss how to get the invaders out of Afghanistan and Cambodia, and afterwards a discussion about rubber and tin and why the prices weren't higher. The ruling party in Afghanistan had close ties with the Soviet Union but were not popular with either the devoutly Muslim or the tribal groups, known as mujāhidūn. The Soviets' aim in invading the country was to topple Hafizullah Amin and set up Babrak Karmal, as leader, but the Afghan army was not effective in dealing with the opposition and the mujahideen rebellion, backed by the US, had grown.

Britain's financial situation was still bad. The abolition of exchange control had pushed down sterling, so the pound was high, interest rates and share prices low. To help the financial crisis Julian was given a pay rise 'abated in the national interest,' and not payable until the coming year. There was to be no recruiting of civil servants for three months, and the price of drink and tobacco was raised. Twenty-three consulates were to be closed on the theory that the drunks and castaways would look after themselves when they couldn't find British Consulate in the phone book. Surveys in the USA showed that half the new jobs come from firms employing fewer than 20 people, so we have to put our faith in the entrepreneur and new small businesses, and hope they would relieve the financial situation.

Our flat in Lowndes Close was very convenient for Julian during the week, and I had converted the garage into a book-binding studio. It had been when Julian was Minister in Bonn that I had become totally carried away by bookbinding, to which I was introduced by the French wife of the Swiss Minister. From the first day I enjoyed working with paper and glue, and loved working with elegant French tools. In fact I soon became totally passionate about it. Aside from the tactile pleasure, there was the desire to make something beautiful, though this was not easy. The words of the book have to be worth the trouble, and equally the paper on which it is printed. The layout must satisfy the eyes, and the material and design of the cover be appropriate to the subject. If one aims to do the complete work oneself, one needs to have access to the printed and unbound texts which are very hard to come by. My first book, with which I had a great deal of help from my kind Swiss friend, was a slim volume of poetry written by Charles Johnston, who had been our Ambassador in Amman, part of which was a verse translation of Pushkin's *Eugene Onegin*. Looking back, I wish the pleasure of bookbinding had not overtaken me to the exclusion of being interested in Julian's work, especially in the three following years in London when Julian was Political Director., I spent a year at Morley College and then two years at the London College of Printing and Bookbinding. I became blind to other things and although Julian did a lot to help me, I did very little to help him. When Julian went back to Bonn as Ambassador, with no space for a studio, equipment and the paraphernalia which goes with it, I gave it up totally. How strange that after my total dedication, I should have as few regrets as I had had on giving up smoking.

We decided to give up digging our vegetable patch and going for long walks in the Cotswolds, sold our cottage in Filkins, and bought a more convenient house in St John Street, Oxford. Hardly had I finished getting the new house straight, when I opened a letter demanding that I report for Jury service in the Oxford Crown Court. I put on a suit and made myself look respectable. The barrister for the defence stood up and objected to me. I rather crossly prepared to go home, but I was told to come back again in two days' time not looking so posh. At my second appearance there were no objections, and I went into the jury box to listen to the case of a man who had illegally reconnected his electricity supply several times after the company had disconnected it for not paying his bills. We had to decide whether in so doing he was acting dishonestly or not. Alarmed by being brought to court, he had paid all he owed. Three of us thought his action dishonest, the rest not. We were told we were required to reach a unanimous verdict and that we must remain in the Jury room until we had reached one. Our jury room was small and water dripped slowly through the ceiling into a tin bowl. We were given sleeping bags but no food or drink. The judge, in his summing up, gave his opinion that SEB had no right to cut off the electricity supply as the customer had a genuine dispute. I had been elected leader of the Jury and decided to announce that our unanimous decision was to agree with the judge, and find him Not Guilty. I wondered if this was perjury, as I and two others really thought that reconnecting his gas supply had been an illegal act, but I thought the conditions of life in the jury room such that to have to live there until our verdict was truly unanimous, warranted my action, and he had after all finally paid his bill in full. We were thanked for our services and told that we would not be required to serve on a jury again for the next 20 years. The Government paid us all a small sum for our services.

Julian's diary was as usual punishingly full: Dinner at Admiralty House. Reception for Ambassadors of Colombia, Tanzania, Burma and Cameroons. And a great deal of accompanying Ambassadors to Buckingham Palace to present their credentials. When it was decided that the Catholic Archbishop who represented the Vatican was to be given diplomatic status, it was naturally Julian's business to receive a call from him in his new office. When President Bush visited London, accompanying him turned out also to be his responsibility. Next day he had to fly to Brussels.

Julian had secretly hoped he would be made Permanent Under Secretary at the Foreign Office in succession to Michael Palliser. Peter Carrington told him that he had proposed Julian for the top job, but Mrs Thatcher had objected. He added '*I could have insisted, but she could have made it very uncomfortable for you in many ways if I had.*' Julian wondered if the Prime Minister did not think him 'one of us' because he did not share her dismay at French and German plans for greater integration, a Central Bank, single currency and borderless utopias. Or could it have been that Julian's cousin, Dorothy Hodgkin annoyed her? She continually asked Julian to try to persuade Mrs Thatcher to change her views on Nuclear Disarmament, but I doubt he ever tried to. Could *I* have been to blame for trying to persuade her of the merits of proportional representation?

Since we had joined the EU, Britain needed also to have a Political Director, un-British as the title seemed at first. His task would be to coordinate policy advice to the Foreign Secretary and accompany him abroad, and also to represent Great Britain at numerous European and other conferences and summits. Lord Carrington told Julian that he particularly wanted him instead to be the first Political Director, as well as being a Deputy Under Secretary, as Julian was firmly convinced of the value to Britain of being part of the European Union.

For a change Julian did not complain of not having enough work. A sample week might include having to spend Sunday night in London in order to be on hand to argue on Monday morning with the Americans who wanted us not to have talks with the PLO but to have every kind of consideration for Israeli sensibilities. The next day it was the Italian Prime Minister, then the Norwegian Foreign Minister, and on Wednesday a Meeting of all 10 EU Political Directors. The week ended with a Conference of all our Ambassadors to eastern European countries (which included his brother Giles, who was Ambassador in Bulgaria). Another week might have been spent discussing with the other EU Political Directors whether the British, French, Dutch and Italians should contribute troops to keep the peace when the Israelis hand back the last bit of the Sinai desert to Egypt next April, and if so, how.

The Polish situation was also a problem. The Poles like to think tanks are no match for the lances of the Polish Hussars, that Poland is situated west of the GDR and that there is a large pot of gold in London marked 'reserved for Poland.' He found it very difficult to please so many different governments, though Ewen Fergusson told me that Julian never chaired a meeting without knowing just what he wanted to achieve – and getting it.

On Friday 11 December, Julian had spent the day in Brussels and, as Heathrow was closed after a snow-storm, had to come back by train and boat. We had been invited to dinner at St Antony's, but the M40 had turned to ice and traffic on the roads moved about a foot a minute. We only just managed to reach St Antony's before grace was said. After a very short sleep we were woken at 3.00 am in the morning by roaring engines, shouting and spade digging outside our window. Another snowstorm! We put on boots and coats and tried in vain to help the driver. We went back to bed hoping for a little sleep, but at 7.am Lord Carrington rang. *'I want you to get to Brussels at once. Get the RAF to fly you. We have a meeting about Poland – joint statement about what we are prepared to do about giving them help.'* (just like Boxing Day 1979 all over again!). Julian managed to make it by midday. The military regime in Poland, seeing themselves threatened by the success of Lech Walensa's Solidarity movement, on 13 December had imposed martial law.

The media left us in no doubt of the inadequacies of our economy. There were continual shortages, strikes and power cuts and at the end of May the great petrol panic broke out. The news of a 3% fall in supply was converted by the general public into a 60% famine as everybody stopped at every filling station to top up. It almost seemed as if the wedding of Prince Charles and Princess Diana was inserted to improve the country's spirits. Julian took James with him to the Mall where they were lucky and managed to get a good view standing on some boxes which a friend had brought with her. I was sceptical and said I was too busy to go and anyway I would see more on the TV.

James had enjoyed being a night porter, but he thought longingly of farm life, and saw an advertisement to work for a farmer in Canada. Not long after he arrived, he was taken to a Dairy Show, where his eye was taken by the good-looking daughter of another farmer, who was leading young calves round the show ring. Three years later they were married.

I had now passed my examinations and was a qualified bookbinder. My problem was to decide how much time I wanted to spend repairing or rebinding the old books which were continually brought to me, and which brought in useful cash, when what I really enjoyed was designing something original which I could display in exhibitions and enter in competitions. On the other hand, there seemed to be no shortage of friends bringing round leather-bound books in poor condition. My workbench had a large pile of these belonging to Lord Darnley and Lady Wills and also all Fergus Hughes Onslow's Wisden cricketing annuals which he wanted rebound in blue. Most of my daylight hours were spent on this. The evenings were rather a contrast. I smartened myself up and accompanied Julian to receptions and dinners. At the annual diplomatic party at the Palace, for which one is invited to arrive at 10pm, I found myself sitting next to a blaze of emeralds and diamonds which revealed itself as Princess Diana's stepmother, the daughter of Barbara Cartland.

The Political Directors of the European Union 1982. Only Julian has his arms crossed

In January 1982 Julian was promoted to be Senior Deputy Permanent Under Secretary as well as being Political Director, and was given a proportionately grand new office, a very splendid room with gigantic windows with blinds, huge mahogany cupboards, a washbasin behind a screen, and a concealed door hidden behind the backs of books labelled Naval Memoirs Vol. XXII. Anthony Acland, junior to Julian, had been promoted to Permanent Under Secretary, which made Julian ask himself why he seemed to be passed over for jobs that he had hoped would be his, and to ask himself again exactly what Mrs Thatcher had against him. By this time Mrs Thatcher would surely have outgrown her opinion that 'The Foreign Office was a nest of Pinkos.'

I think it was on account of feeling rather disappointed at not being promoted to PUS, that led him to go to see Lord Carrington the next day and ask if he could be considered for some of the jobs that were coming up, in particular: New York, Athens or Delhi. Lord Carrington replied: *'You can have anything you want, but you've got much more power where you are, and much more interesting work. I depend on you utterly. But it's your career. Just let me know tomorrow at 9.a.m'*. Julian thought about it overnight, and next day told him he would take his advice, stop thinking that the grass on the other side of the fence was greener, and stay where he was. I was told by one member of the 22 Committee that when the Conservative party Think Tank proposed some new course of action, Peter Carrington had often said: *'Has this been run past Julian? What does he think?'* Lord Kerr wrote to me after Julian died describing him as 'The best Permanent Under Secretary we never had.'

It is hard to think that any appointment would have suited him as well as Political Director, or any that would have provided as much scope for his many talents. He loved being at the centre of policy-making, and was delighted to have fewer ceremonial administrative and financial duties. Julian was an extraordinarily talented man. After he died one of his contemporaries told me that his intellect was combined with absolute integrity, a clear eye for the truth, great humility, kindness and an underlying strength of purpose. Another that he was totally devoid of arrogance and could correct an error or a misquotation without making you feel put down. He was respected and much loved, not only by his fellow countrymen, but also by the group of EC Political Directors. On his departure for Bonn as Ambassador, he earned warm tributes from his European colleagues. his Belgian colleague wrote: 'You have been for me…dear Julian, an inspiring example… I will always remember your great kindness, your admirable sense of humour, your vast knowledge of the problems…your frankness and patience…your lucid intelligence and your splendid human qualities. We will miss you.'

It was in May 1979 that *The Economist* published Nicko Henderson's leaked valedictory report on his retirement from Paris. It had become Foreign Office custom for Ambassadors to write a frank account of their views on the country they were leaving, sometimes including the conditions of life they had to put up with, and sometimes of the wisdom of the policy of HMG. A great deal of effort. was always put into their composition. The reports were written in confidence to the Foreign Secretary, but widely circulated within the Foreign Office and beyond. Nicko's Valedictory report deplored how we had sunk from our position at the end of the war to becoming not even in the first rank as a European power, and that our economic decline, combined with our policy towards the EU, had contributed to undermine our rightful position as a leader, which we let slip when we failed to join the Coal and Steel community when it was set up in the 1950's.

Nicko's recommendation was that we should take notice of how poor and unproud the British had become, going cap in hand to the IMF without noticing that our European neighbours were all getting richer. With North Sea Oil behind us, we should have behaved as if we were fully committed to Europe, and we should have tried to restore a sense of purpose such as had transformed France and Germany since 1945. Margaret Thatcher was so struck by this, in spite of its call for closer ties with Europe, that she recalled him from retirement and sent him as our Ambassador to Washington – a very happy accident, because he was exactly the right man for the job when the Falklands were invaded.

It was less often now that we had engagements together, but I did go with Julian to a delightful production of *La Boheme* at Covent Garden with the Bulgarian Ambassador and Foreign Minister. We had seats in a splendid box, with a private room behind, where refreshments were brought to us in the interval. At the dinner afterwards I found the Ambassador difficult to talk to, and was reduced to asking how he spent his free evenings. He told me he liked to watch TV and in particular a programme called *Nanny*, a nostalgic programme about pre-war nursery life, suitable for children's bedtimes, 'because it was so unlike anything he had experienced'. Julian and I went to a farewell dinner for Nicko Henderson at the French Embassy before he left for Washington, at which Julian was sitting next to Son Altesse Imperiale, la Princesse Napoleon. On the way home I commented on the exceptionally delicious food, to which Julian replied, that all he could think about was the number of fingers that had been involved in the cooking and decoration of it. Julian never had much flesh to spare, but even he took to doing exercises in the morning, not because he was getting fat, but in order to make himself hold back on late-night drinking by reminding himself that at 7.30am he would have to touch his toes! The Danish Ambassador told us that, in order to keep fit, he drank absolutely no alcohol and biked two miles to a gym twice a week.

Eating seemed to take a big place in his new job. Any trip to Brussels always included a magnificent lunch. One night Julian accompanied Peter Carrington to a mediaeval banquet in Hamburg. The Mayor of London gave a splendid dinner at the Mansion House for Frau Finnbogadóttir, the President of Iceland, who wore a gold Norse/Viking head-piece like an upside-down saucepan. At City dinners husbands were always placed next to their wives, apparently an ancient custom. I thought it amazingly lacking in imagination to invite guests to put on full dress with medals and then seat them next to their wives. Julian used to arrive early in order to do some adjusting of the place cards which no one seemed to notice. One day he spoke to the Duke of Wellington's dining club at Apsley House. The Italian ambassador invited us to a dinner to which he had also invited Princess Ann and Captain Mark Phillips. Julian asked them about their preferences when on foreign visits. Would they prefer the Foreign Office to arrange for them to open an exhibition or to cut a ribbon? Her Majesty's son-in-law replied that, personally he was very happy to be asked anywhere and do anything to get away from boys' clubs and farming. I remember little about these dinners except the splendour of the surroundings. During the day I had plenty of work to keep me busy. I had a new commission to make boxes and wrappers for rare manuscripts bought as an investment by British Rail Pension Fund and I had also been asked by a dealer to do some urgent work for the Frankfurt Book Fair.

The winter in England seemed never ending. I thought we both needed some Mediterranean sunshine, and I booked a fly/drive holiday in Sicily. Easter was early that year and Julian said the Office was going to be shut down for an extra day as nothing very much seemed to be afoot, so 2nd April 1982 found us finishing our breakfast in Palermo. Horrified, we saw the headlines in the Italian papers. General Galtieri was clearly planning to invade the Falkland Islands. Julian had seen reports from Anthony Williams, our Ambassador in the Argentine, saying that there was no likelihood of imminent military action over the ownership of the Falklands, so the Foreign Office could be excused for thinking they had another few years to negotiate a solution. Julian thought we ought to return straight away. Our problem was that our travel insurance was not covered by Acts of War. Julian phoned the Foreign Office and was told that he need not return at once, but should phone in daily, and they would let him know if he were needed. I had no idea of the seriousness of what was first reported as the action of a group of scrap metal merchants, and I was very reluctant to have to cut short our holiday in the lovely spring weather. I had rented a very small car, so small that we had to reduce our suitcases to just one plastic bag each. Sicily was now circled with a new motorway, by courtesy of Brussels, which led us from one ancient site to another. Not far from Agrigento our guide book said: 'Find a small boy and get him to show you the Chief's tombs.' We turned off up a goat track, for the first time glad of our minute car, and found masses of caverns beautifully chiselled out of the hillside, the stones in front rolled away. We crawled in and out of the caves, in which the treasures, taken to the museum at Agrigento, had once been buried alongside the chiefs. Julian was very concerned about what would happen to those 17,000 British subjects in their Estancias in Argentina, and indeed in other sympathetic Latin countries, and felt guilty about the way we have managed the islands for so long without establishing a naval base or a fishery, and actively discouraging contact with their nearest neighbour except when it suited us, such as letting the Argies take over the air service and the oil supply. As we lay on the flower-covered mountainside, the still, golden evening broken only by the sound of goats and sheep, the Falklands really did seem a million miles away. I tried not to let Julian worry about them too much.

Back in London on the Wednesday after Easter, Julian found the Foreign Office 'knocked for six and reeling'. Julian's task was to discuss the situation with all the other EU Political Directors and hope they could persuade their governments to support our stance vis a vis the Argentinians. He said that this went well, even the Italian Political Director was not sympathetic with Galtieri's action. Julian thought Parliament were much to blame. A compromise leaseback proposal had been proposed by the Foreign Office and was debated in parliament. However, Peter Shore, then shadow Foreign Secretary, seeing that there were few Conservatives in the Chamber, put the leaseback proposal to the vote, his interest being primarily the chance of defeating the government. Both parties knew quite well that the islands had been made indefensible by the reduction in the navy vote, and by Parliament refusing to take uncomfortable decisions or to face facts. Julian told me how unlikely it was that we should ever find a satisfactory long-term outcome. Even if a naval action were to be successful, we couldn't keep the fleet defending the Falklands for ever.

Robin Fearn, Head of News Department, told me that at the height of the Falklands war, when white-faced and exhausted diplomats were working long hours in the Emergency room in shifts, Julian was unique among senior staff in regularly dropping by in the late evening to see how things were, and more often than not, bringing a few bottles of wine to cheer everybody up. Robin wrote in his memoir that at first, if anyone was to be held responsible for the invasion, it seemed it <u>had</u> to be Peter Carrington, but as the Falklands war went on, it became clear that to have had Peter Carrington as Foreign Secretary, with the confidence in which he was held in Europe and in Washington, would have been a major asset. Peter decided that he had to resign because his was the final responsibility for not foreseeing the Argentinian action.

On 11 April Julian wrote to Antonia:

'Most of the errors which resulted in the Argentinian action were those of the Foreign

Office, (our Ambassador in Buenos Aires for one), but nevertheless I think Carrington was right to go, the principle of Ministerial responsibility was important, and Francis Pym sat in the Commons, the only place where confidence in the government can be restored.'

To his brother Giles he wrote:`

'That was the blackest day of my whole career. It seemed to me that half a dozen officials (not exactly including me but I was close enough to have done something about it if I had twigged, but I didn't), had by their negligence brought about not only a national humiliation and a first-class international crisis, but also the downfall of one of the best Foreign Ministers we have ever had, or are ever likely to have. We said a painful goodbye to him on Monday, and within 24 hours the whole machine had switched to serving Francis Pym who, I must say, made an excellent start: courteous, modest and exceptionally hard-working. He doesn't show his feelings, even though a Times article says he is most likely to be dropped by Mrs Thatcher in favour of Geoffrey Howe.'

I have no record of what Julian wrote to Peter Carrington, but part of Peter's reply ran: *'I have relied so much on your wisdom and intelligence in these last three years and I have been very lucky to have had someone of your quality as Political Director and to have had your friendship as well.'* Inside his book *'Reflection on Things Past'* he wrote: 'To Julian who taught me a lot'

Julian told me he couldn't deny that the blame really fell on successive governments and parliaments who should, over the last 15 or so years, have decided either to protect the islands or encouraged them to choose between emigration or making friends with the Argies. Now that the worst had happened, it was absolutely essential for the sake of small weak territories everywhere, that the Argies shouldn't get away with it, but on the contrary should be made to pay for it. The world should follow what the European community had done: ban all arms sales, stop all credit, and prohibit all imports from Argentina. In retrospect the war would not have gone so well for us had Nicko Henderson not been Ambassador in the USA. It was to his good relations with officials in Washington that we owed our access to valuable intelligence and being able to obtain fuel, ammunition and missiles at Ascension Island. This did something to relieve the shame Julian felt for the collective performance of the Diplomatic Service.

Over the sinking of the Belgrano, Julian disagreed with Tam Dalyell who thought this to have been a mistake, `because its purpose was primarily to torpedo a peace deal which was on the point of being made'. Julian considered that there was no such peace deal likely of success, and that sinking the Belgrano had had the good effect of making the Argies keep their navy in port, for fear of losing ships. He argued that if you are at war you can't wear kid glove and he was particularly critical of Mrs Thatcher's refusal ever either to negotiate or alternatively, to put a great deal of money into Fortress Falklands.

On 19 April Julian travelled to Washington with Francis Pym travelling in an RAF VC10. Being given a made-up bed with sheets helped him to get four hours sleep, after which he had to write notes for Francis Pym on what had been learned and agreed in Washington, followed by having to be in Downing Street at 10 am, where Mrs Thatcher was in a combative mood. Julian told her that it was his view that the fossil-like existence of the 1800 sheep farmers could not continue as it was – bearing in mind the 170,000 British citizens living in Argentina, not counting those with dual nationality. Nor did he think that the Falklands should be put under the Argentinian flag. The only way forward was for us to support and encourage the slow growth of mutual confidence.

In May Julian wrote to Antonia: '*A terrible madness seems to have descended on government civil servants since the Falklands Crisis, everyone ignoring Saturdays and Sundays and merely pretending that every day is a working day, and most evenings as well. The whole affair is very trying on the nerves, early mornings, late nights and constant changes of scene and general air of never quite knowing what is going to happen in the next hour, let alone tomorrow.*'

Julian gave me a flavour of what the daily meeting of the war cabinet was like:

On one side the Military saying it is essential to give them authorisation to do X Y Z at their discretion, ' for operational reasons' (which they are good at making sound convincing) because unless they can carry out their plans British lives and ships and aircraft will be in danger.

Opposite them sit the officials in civilian suits (which puts them at a disadvantage), saying: 'Of course British lives first, but X Y Z could just make a difference between failure and success. A diplomatic initiative has certain promising features, though details are far from complete, but ideally it ought to be pursued.

Antonia wrote from New York to tell us that Nicko was featured daily on the news. She said Americans admired him because he looked like a crumbling stately home. Nicko said he thought that was rather hard on the stately home. Since Julian had had to go to Brussels (again!), I went alone to a party given by George Weidenfeld for Henry Kissinger which included the Carringtons, Palliser, Heath, Soames, David Steel, Jim Callaghan, the French Ambassador, Harold Evans, Frank Giles, Isaiah Berlin and Lady Eden! Julian went on to Paris, then Bonn, then Luxemburg and was not coming to Oxford at all that weekend.

In May Thomas Hodgkin died, and a memorial service was held in Balliol chapel, packed with friends of all colours, shapes and sizes. In the 1930's he had enjoyed travelling in the Middle East and had asked Julian's father for advice on getting a job there. My father-in-law had replied: '*Get into the colonial service and go to Palestine. See what you can do to reconcile Arab and Jew. It is probably impossible, but it is worth trying*'. I was told he became a communist because, when he was in Palestine, he found it was the only milieu where Jews and Arabs met.

On 31 May I accompanied Julian to Helsinki. He had talks with the Foreign Ministry about disarmament and Namibia, and also wanted to discuss lessons which should be learnt from the Falklands Crisis. The Junior official present, who kept a record of such talks and was conscious of having mangled a record of Julian's discussion with his Dutch opposite number, told me that Julian had called him into his office and deftly taught him how to write indirect speech. Polite, straightforward, leaving him in no doubt that he had done something wrong and also in no doubt that he was trusted to learn quickly from his mistake.

Having now joined the EU there followed a series of Summits. There was a special meeting of the European Council in Paris attended by Heads of State and Government, Foreign Ministers and Finance Ministers, ending with a magnificent banquet at Versailles followed by fireworks. Michael Hall the Conference officer to the UK Delegation, wrote an amusing account of the Finale:

7 June. Julian Bullard, Tom Bridges, Nick Fenn and an interpreter accompanied the Prime Minister to a Special Summit meeting in Paris. Towards the end of the Gala Dinner in the Hall of Mirrors, the Prime Minister suddenly decided that she and Francis Pym, would leave early as she thought it inappropriate for them to be watching fireworks while her troops were at war. The four FO officials, seated slightly behind a pillar, did not see her leave and missed the cortege to the heli-pad. Unsuccessful attempts were made to hold the cars but once French motorcycle outriders have started they are like greyhounds unleashed. There were two cars, but the drivers had no idea where to go. Suddenly the noise of helicopters was heard from behind some trees. The car passengers rushed forward making frantic gestures but these were ignored and the machines disappeared out of sight. The four figures in dinner jackets were left standing, transfixed, staring after them. Directed by the French police, the four mandarins leapt into the car, in which John Fretwell (British Ambassador) was sitting, and tore up the motorway with motorcycle escort attempting to reach Orly in time for the take-off. The speedometer registered 180 km per hour. The traffic parted like the waters of the Red Sea. Half way along the autoroute a police car drew level, an officer in the front seats vigorously indicating that we should stop. The message was quite clear. The Iron Lady was not going to wait. The motor-cycle escort led the two cars into a lay-by. A meeting involving an odd mix of men in dinner jackets and policemen in leathers was held against the background of traffic hurtling towards Paris. John Fretwell seemed stunned as if he could not believe what had happened. He had not been long in Paris. Fenn was furious at being abandoned. '*After all that we have done for that woman!*'

Bullard was the first to take full stock of the situation and to remember that none of them had a passport, a suitcase, a razor or a toothbrush (their luggage had gone on ahead to Orly airport) and to realize that if they caught the early plane to Gatwick, they would have to travel to Victoria in the attire they stood up in – the commuters assuming no doubt we were some kind of musical quartet. '*Or a group of elderly revellers who have not been to bed*', said Bridges with some feeling. It had not been a very good trip for Bridges. His late addition to the Foreign Office group had also meant that he had had to sleep in a Paris motel seven kilometers away where the support staff were accommodated, and where a discoteque blasting away until 3am had prevented him from sleeping.

Fenn commented again on the ruthless manner in which the four of them had been discarded. However, once back at the Trianon Palace Hotel where beds for the night (including toothbrushes) were provided, and seats on the morning plane to Gatwick obtained, the whole quartet, including Fenn, visibly began to brighten up and see the funny side. Bullard said: '*I can just imagine what the Prime Minister is saying now: Typical Foreign Office, slow off the mark as usual*'.

At the next meeting in Bruges, Mrs Thatcher won her demand to 'get her money back'. The other EU states were not content with the way that they had been obliged to cave in to Mrs Thatcher over the budget. The French and the Germans then consulted the Italians who held the Presidency, as to how best they should act. It was unacceptable that the majority of the EU should give way to the minority, particularly on the movement for greater unity, on which most of the rest agreed. So, without consulting Mrs Thatcher, they prepared a document to be put to a vote, which created the very thing that she most wished to avoid: a 'Treaty on European Union'. Interviewed by *Die Welt*, Mrs Thatcher said: '*I do not know what political union means. I do not believe in a United States of Europe. We do not want to bury the Mother of Parliaments in a United States of Europe*'. These being her strongly felt feelings, and, confident as she always was in the justice of her own views, it was not surprising that from Summit to Summit she felt the other countries were ganging up on her. The Foreign Office did their best to avoid any open confrontation, to stop her being isolated, and in particular not to get left behind any forward movements planned on the other side of the Channel. But compromise was not in her book, nor was she encouraged in that direction by Charles Powell.

In mid-September we booked ourselves to stay for a week in the Nietzsche House in Sils Maria, in Switzerland, not long after it had been opened as a memorial to preserve the legacy of the great philosopher, and also as a guest house. It was from there that we visited the Diavoletzza, and, as I described earlier, encouraged by me, we foolishly set off on a dangerous walk down the glacier without a guide.

Julian found himself struggling to catch up with the work when he got back to the office, and decided he could just about manage if he got up an hour earlier and wrote a great many drafts and minutes before breakfast. The main problem of the moment was still Poland, as it was at Christmas 1980. A solution needed to be found that would hurt the Polish regime but not the Polish people, please the Pope and not damage any western interests, bring Solidarity back to life and sound good on the News Bulletin.

Kenneth Kaunda came on a state visit. Mrs Thatcher was his guest of honour at the dinner which he gave in a restaurant, as his embassy was small. When we had taken our seats, we were asked to stand and join in the Zambian national anthem. Our host then said: '*Stand up Mr Ambassador!*' He folllowed this by praising the embarrassed Ambassador for all that he had done, for all the help he had given, and so on for some time with much warmth. The Ambassador was physically a small and insignificant looking man, who had clearly done his best and made a very good impression on Kenneth Kaunda. Mrs. Thatcher, who doesn't try to hide her opinion that Ambassadors are just for dressing up in ostrich feathers and a waste of money, could clearly not believe what she was hearing.

On 17 October, Julian had to go to Lisbon, and I went with him as the Ambassador, Hugh Byatt, was an old friend who we had known at Oxford. John Shakespeare was on Hugh's staff, and while we were there, a phone call came from the Headmaster of Marlborough to say John must come and take his son away at once, because he had been caught dealing in drugs. John said his son had not been dealing in drugs when term had started, and he thought it was not his fault if his son had started to take drugs while the Headmaster was in *loco parentis*. The boy's story was that a pusher had got in from outside and persuaded the boys to buy the stuff. Marlborough won, and I later heard that the son had been taken on at Winchester as a day boy. When one is abroad teenager trouble was one of the commonest and most difficult to manage.

Faber and Faber agreed to my request that they would offer 100 unbound texts of Philip Larkin's *Required Writing* for the next bookbinding prize. I was delighted. As none of my clients were waiting impatiently for their books to be ready for collection, I stuck to my plan to stay with my sister-in-law in Lewes and spend a week at the Brighton College of Art. We had lectures and demonstrations all day long and I met some talented bookbinders who had interesting ideas about how one could make the cover of a book beautiful without making the cost prohibitive. I also learnt a lot about French methods. They apply gold leaf differently, and their bookbinders specialise, not training to be an all-rounder as in England, so that paring leather is the task of someone who does nothing else, another only does the designing, and another the gilding. The outer cover, whether cloth or leather, is someone else again. In Germany, perhaps unsurprisingly, you have to have eight years of training and pass several exams before you are allowed to charge any money for your work.

Julian went to Moscow on 17 November for Brezhnev's funeral, chiefly because it would give him an opportunity to spend half an hour with Francis
Pym and Gromyko and also be able to speak to George Shultz and various European Foreign Ministers. The Franks report on the invasion of the Falklands
had been published, clearing the Government of responsibility for not having
prevented, or failed to foresee it. Not a verdict which was widely held in the
Foreign Office.

In March 1983 President Reagan publicly described the Soviet Union as an
'evil empire' and proposed his Strategic Defence Initiative as part of the struggle between right and wrong. This led the Foreign Office to consider that relations between the superpowers were becoming too fraught and persuaded Mrs
Thatcher to convene a seminar to discuss future policy in our relations with
the Soviet Union, also to discuss weapons and why we need them. Hitherto
the view had been that the West and the Soviet block should maintain a parity
of weaponry as the best defence against war. What was not publicly known,
was that at least on four occasions, we had very nearly had a nuclear war by
mismanagement. During the Cuban missile crisis, a Soviet nuclear torpedo was
only just prevented from being launched by mistake. In November 1979, a US
computer was thought to indicate that 200 Intercontinental ballistic missiles
were in flight to land in the US, but fortunately it was discovered in time that a
training tape had been mistakenly inserted into the computer. Both sides made
mistakes. On 1 September 1983 a Korean passenger aircraft, way off course, was
mistakenly shot down by the Russians and 269 passengers killed. Unfortunately an American spy plane was also in the vicinity and the local commander had
confused the two. For a week both sides thought this might be a prelude to war,
particularly as the Soviets refused to admit that they had had anything to do
with the disaster. The danger of human error was brought home to both sides.

A day's meeting at Chequers was convened to discuss the way forward. The
Prime Minister asked for invitations to be sent to academics rather than to the
Foreign Office, who were only told to submit a paper. Julian showed me some
notes he had written for it.:

> 1. Nuclear Weapons can't be dis-invented so wars must be avoided to prevent
> them being used. Recent wars have only been between countries without Nuclear
> Weapons, so that it follows that nuclear weapons have been responsible for 37
> years of peace. Proof of this is that in 1945 there might well have been a war be-
> tween Russia and the West had Nuclear Weapons not been only in the hands of
> the West.
>
> 2. If we scrapped our Nuclear Weapons, would this make Russia, China and
> the USA (India, Israel etc.) scrap theirs?
>
> 3. The idea that the peace of the world rests on the balance of terror is horrible,

but the countries of the world will not stay at peace with each other if one side terrorizes the other.

4. The danger of accident or miscalculation is serious, particularly bearing in mind China's attitude to human life, which is why close contact with other powers and the talks which were going on in Geneva were so important.

5. It was no coincidence that the Soviet Union strongly backed CND in the West, but did not allow it in Russia. The Russians saw the demands made by CND in Britain as useful for themselves. For Julian this was almost a conclusive argument in itself.

6. What is the alternative? No cruise missiles? No British Nuclear Weapons? No NATO? Total pacifism? Consider the danger: The six communist countries in Europe were all controlled by Russia. Suppose they were tempted to snuff out Berlin, compel Italy to let Communists into the government, force Norway to hand over Svalbard or demilitarise her Arctic frontier, or drag Yugoslavia into the Warsaw pact, or impose a military alliance on Finland, or make Germany reduce the size of American troops there, or in some other way dictate terms to western Europe – What held Russia back from doing any of these things? Only because she knew that the US would use her greater strength in reply.

7. Britain and France needed to remain Nuclear Powers because, although we were a mini player in their development, were we to renounce Nuclear Weapons, this would be unlikely to cause other countries to do the same. We should consider that the day might come when the US might have a President who might decide it is not worth risking New York for the sake of protecting London.

8. Nuclear Weapons should be seen as weapons of defence not as weapons of attack. During world War II Germany had the V1 and V2 and we did not. That was the reason why Germany decided to use them. The atomic bomb was used against the side which did not possess it. Poison gas, which both sides had developed, was not used by either. Peace was kept by keeping sufficient balance to deter our enemies in all the circumstances we could think of.

9. Wars were not caused by weapons but by one side believing it was stronger than their enemies and being reckless enough to put this to the test. A good example of this was the Falklands affair. The Argentinians surely would not have invaded the Falklands had they not thought Britain was crippled with miner's strikes and economic problems and not strong enough to launch a naval attack or to throw them out afterwards.

All this pointed to what our policy had to be: We had already negotiated 18 two-sided agreements since the war; Test Ban Treaty, Non-Proliferation Treaty etc., and we should negotiate more. Russia supported Nuclear Disarmament in her own interest only, therefore, as long as Russia remained a threat, it was not likely to be in our interest. Since the risk of war came from one side thinking they have military superiority, we needed to maintain and keep modernising our weapons.

Peter Carrington's view had been: '*It is a hard but important truth that a*

Nuclear War which doesn't happen is better than a conventional one that does.'. Mrs Thatcher won the general election on June 9 with a big majority.

Julian came back from a very cold visit to Stockholm, from which he brought back lots of fishy eats. Gromyko had not been as grumpy as usual. He found Geoffrey Howe rather like a 10,000-meter runner, never varying his pace. He went on steadily talking, listening, writing and especially reading. However thick the book, he had read to the last page by breakfast-time. Julian's next visit was to Brussels. Then to Paris, where he had to speak at a conference on the Gulf. The European Union were appealing to the belligerents to stop fighting, conduct peaceful negotiations, spare civilian targets and comply with the Geneva Conventions of 1949 on the treatment of prisoners of war.

Early in February 1984 the policy of Engagement with the Communist countries of Eastern Europe, discussed at Chequers began to be carried out. The Prime Minister and Geoffrey Howe, now Foreign Minister, planned to visit all the East European capitals, starting with a trip to Budapest, on which Julian accompanied Mrs Thatcher. Julian told me that she had put an unusual amount of effort into making the trip a success, and he hoped it might lead to some good results. John Birch, though Head of the Department, was not included in the trip, at which he was very disappointed. Julian spotted this, and on his return telephoned him to give him an account of the visit and thank him for the preparation. John Birch told me that it was this kind of gesture that made Julian so loved in the service. At the weekend he accompanied Mrs Thatcher on a visit to Rome. On his return, Julian's appointment as Ambassador in Bonn was announced. We intended to arrive in August, so Julian signed on for German lessons and a BBC course on speaking on the radio. I was delegated to go the Rolls Royce show room in Park Lane and choose the colour of our new car. I chose walnut.

For the last four years I had had few occasions during the day to wear anything more than a jumper and skirt and a large brown overall so it was clear that I had to get some appropriate Ambassadorial clothes that would not disgrace Julian. Mary Henderson advised me to write to Jean Muir and ask her help. That was an introduction to a new kind of shopping. One rang the bell of what seemed a private house in Mayfair and climbed the stairs to the showroom. I was invited to choose from the rails on which hung the designs unsold from previous years. Not only were these offered at prices I could afford, but they had much more style than the offerings of the London shops. I was nervous the first time I approached store managers at Jaeger and Burberry and asked for a discount, but I don't remember it was ever refused!

In April I was referred by my local doctor to the Chelsea Hospital for Women and after a few tests, a week later I had my reproductive organs removed, a cancerous growth having been found. We were six women in a Victorian room with huge windows which had been nailed up and sealed to keep the heat in and the draught out during the winter months. Over the Easter Weekend the sun came out and it became like an oven. Our request to have the windows open was rebuffed. 'Not until the workmen returned on Easter Tuesday.' Until then we would just have to sweat and bear it. Julian and another husband came in on Easter Saturday with a bag of tools, and we were able to breathe again! He was always so talented in unexpected ways. After about 10 days I was released from hospital and went back to Oxford. Julian borrowed a wheelchair and pushed me to the Parks to watch cricket with him. My kind next-door neighbours made me a soup and cheese lunch every day. David Cornwell invited us to use his chalet in Wengen in August, by which time I was once more ready for mountain walks and soon after felt well enough to do the hundred and one things that had to be cancelled, re-organized and packed, and also find tenants for London and Oxford. We were also commanded to present ourselves at Buckingham Palace.

II

BRITISH AMBASSADOR, BONN

1984 – 88

For a British Ambassador it requires great, not to say gymnastic, efforts to try to bridge the gulf between the British people's lively remembrance of the past and the Germans' total oblivion of it.

SIR NICHOLAS HENDERSON 1984

Whereas it appears to Us expedient to nominate some Person of approved Wisdom, Loyalty, Diligence and Circumspection to represent Us in the character of Our Ambassador Extraordinary and Plenipotentiary to Our Good Brother the President of the Federal Republic of Germany: Now Know that We, reposing special trust and confidence in the discretion and faithfulness of our Trusty and Well-beloved Sir Julian Leonard Bullard, Knight Grand Cross of the Most Distinguished Order of Saint Michael and Saint George, have nominated, constituted and appointed, as We do by these Presents nominate, constitute and appoint him, the said Sir Julian Leonard Bullard to be Our Ambassador Extraordinary and Plenipotentiary to Our Good Brother the President of the Federal Republic of Germany as aforesaid. Giving and Granting to him in that character all Power and Authority to do and perform all proper acts, matters and things which may be desirable or necessary for the promotion of relations of friendship, good understanding, and harmonious intercourse between Our Realm and the Republic of Germany and for the protection and furtherance of the interests confided to his care; by the diligent and discreet accomplishment of which acts, matters and things aforementioned he shall gain Our approval and show himself worthy of Our high confidence. And we therefore request all those whom it may concern to receive and acknowledge Our said Trusty and Well-beloved Sir Julian Leonard Bullard as such Extraordinary and Plenipotentiary as aforesaid and freely to communicate with him upon all matters which might appertain to the objects of the high Mission whereto he is hereby appointed.

I T remained for both of us to go to Buckingham Palace and for Her Majesty to present Julian with this scroll. She offered her hand and Julian brushed his lips over it. All went very smoothly, unlike Julian's father's experience on being appointed as Minister in Jedda in 1936 during Edward VIII's short reign. A full hour after the appointed time, he had asked whether the new king was frequently so late, to which one of the Palace staff replied, rather unhappily, that the king was at Fort Belvedere and that when he was with Mrs Simpson he ignored anything that might be classed as duty. Julian told the attendant courtiers about his father's experience, and they told us about an occasion early in the reign of George VI, when His Majesty George VI had received Herr Ribbentrop as German Ambassador in London, accompanied by his most senior diplomats, all of whom greeted the King with the Nazi salute. His Majesty was rather startled but said: '*Actually I am very accustomed to strange native greetings, which I am frequently given by people of my Empire*'.

Two days later we drove to Bonn in our own new car, a brown Ford Sierra. The Rolls Royce was used only for official occasions, in which case we were accompanied by Julian's personal protection officer, with the boot full of a selection of other number plates in case we should at any time need to throw the IRA off the scent. This was not long after they had murdered Sir Richard Sykes, our Ambassador in the Hague. We were immediately struck with how much wealthier Germany seemed than England: the well-tended gardens, the tidiness and cleanliness, the impression of comfort and affluence created by the clean cars, buses and lorries, and the well-stocked shops. One surprising thing was to find that opening hours were still what they had been in 1963: anything that you had failed to buy by lunch time on Saturday, you would not be able to get until breakfast time on Monday, a law which dated from 1937, designed to restrict consumer spending.

Next morning the German President received Julian. Richard von Weizsäcker had a patrician manner and exceptional grace and distinction, and was well known to us, as he came regularly to the annual Königswinter conferences, which gathered politicians, journalists, academics and civil servants for discussions designed to improve Anglo-German understanding. The President never wavered in his long-standing belief in German unity, and after the wall fell, he was quick to see its implications, and to assume his new role as President of the entire German nation – an idea which had already figured in a speech he made in the summer of 1984.

The British Ambassador was lucky to have one of the best situated residences in Bonn, even though it was not actually in Bonn itself, but seven kilometres further south where the majority of diplomatic staff lived, in the spa town of Bad Godesberg, (the berg being the rock out of which sprang particularly unpleasant natural mineral water). The Residence had been built at the turn of the century for Johanna Cappel, the mistress of a rich Ruhr industrialist, and stood high above the Rhine looking directly across towards the Siebengebirge (seven mountains). Below its windows and terraces chugged a continuous stream of barges, each displaying the flag of one of the many countries bordering on the Rhine and also other flags identifying the barge's owner and other details. Overlooking the Rhine was a new pleasure for us and Julian spent his spare moments at breakfast adjusting the focus of his binoculars to puzzle out what the barges carried and what the different flags and numbers signified. Julian liked to be able to answer the questions inevitably asked by official visitors, but found it fascinating himself. The Naval Attaché explained that vessels travelling *upstream* were allowed to use the inside of any bend in the river in order to use less fuel and make better time, and vessels going *downstream* had to use the outside. Consequently, the barges were constantly changing sides, sometimes being on the left, sometimes on the right. (What a good thing road travel did not demand this!) When the barges hauled up a plain square blue flag, this indicated it was about to change sides. To make it more confusing, a vessel travelling in the opposite direction hoisted the same blue flag to acknowledge that they had seen the flag of the oncoming barge. I can't say whether spending her life trying to understand the flag system of the Rhine barges had anything to do with Fraulein Cappel going mad, but in 1920 she threw herself into the river.

Julian's arrival was given a good deal of prominence in the local papers and he enjoyed the experience of having a General and an Air Marshall treating him as if he were the Queen herself. Less pleasant was having German policemen with submachine guns scanning the rose bushes. My first day was spent rehanging all the pictures in the Residence including the Winterhalter portraits of Victoria and Albert soon after their marriage, which we had found in the store of the government art collection. I was the first casualty of the new security doors (9 inches thick and weighing about what our eldest son did). A gentle pull resulted in a bony crunch and a violet-coloured middle finger nail before I had time to scream. This made it impossible to give a cheerful smile to accompany my painful handshaking when I called on the Chef du Protocol that afternoon. The editor of a glossy magazine *Impression* asked if they could come and interview me and take pictures, and the next edition began with seven pages of views of the Residence, including the butler putting finishing touches to the table for a dinner party and the chef decorating a Scottish salmon. We had inherited both a first-class chef and a splendid butler who curiously addressed each other as Herr Schlatt and Herr Justus, though they had worked together at the Residence for six years.

After his years as Political Director, Julian was very conscious that Anglo-German relations were not all they might be. He thought a good deal of the blame for this lay with the Prime Minister, and he was determined to improve them. Mrs Thatcher had no doubt that the Berlin Wall was the Russians' fault, but she was never happy about the possibility that Germany might one day become reunited and strong. She also distrusted any talk of Europeanisation or of the warmth the Germans seemed to feel for Europe. Julian had nothing to do with Community activities except to promote understanding, if not friendship, between Kohl and Thatcher, and to do what he could to prevent her being isolated, which led her to feel that the other Europeans were united against her.

Charles Powell, who had worked for Julian earlier when he was Minister, was now the Prime Minister's private secretary, and Julian hoped that Charles would be able to make her letters to Kohl a little warmer, perhaps by beginning 'Dear Helmut'. But the next one began as usual: 'Dear Chancellor.' Julian did his best to get her to realise that both halves of Germany and the other countries all foresaw that one day the time would come when it would not any longer be possible to resist a united Germany, though very few expected it to come so soon. On the bottom of a despatch on the subject which Julian had sent to No. 10, Charles Powell wrote: *'German reunification is an area where we have to say one thing and think another'*. Charles seemed to have become more of a devoted courtier than her adviser on foreign affairs, and where Foreign Office views differed from hers, he knew whose side he was on.

A few days after arriving in Bonn, Julian wrote to the children:

> *'Life has been mostly short rides in the ambassadorial Rolls Royce with a tiny piece of paper to remind me of the answers if asked why Britain doesn't . . . anything from 'join the Exchange rate mechanism of the European Monetary System' to 'teach more German in schools'. Then one long ride to the RAF headquarters in Rheindahlen for an evening of 'The Queen' 'HM Ambassador' . . . chef and bandmaster brought in for a glass of port and a chat, speech after speech and my watch showing 11.27 pm when it was finally my turn to reply on behalf of the guests. A long day, because it had begun with an appointment at 8 am in the heart of that thick wood to the west of Bonn to see the dying forests with our own eyes. We went open-minded and came away shocked, not just at the sight of all those dead and dying trees, blackberry leaves showing the yellow spots of chlorophyll deficiency etc. But at the acceleration of the symptoms as witnessed by this young Forstmeister in only three years at his post. The most moving thing is the instinctive efforts made by the trees which sense that they are losing. They respond by sprouting needles in unnatural directions, producing huge crops of acorns and beech nuts every year instead of every six or seven years and oozing resin to try to protect themselves against whatever it may be in the air that makes them feel unwell.*

By chance I read that Jo Grimond (then Head of the Liberal party), was opening an exhibition in Cologne of paintings of British Liberal politicians: Gladstone, Asquith etc. I went along, unannounced. In no time I was given the most fantastic reception: photographed with Jo Grimond, with Karl-Günther von Hase, with the head of the Neumann Stiftung; invited to lunch with David Steel; and escorted to my car. I could quite understand how Ambassador's wives get a bit above themselves. My next excitement was to open the Jaeger boutique in Munich. Julian received huge numbers of less exciting invitations: speaking at a dinner for the International Chamber of Commerce, giving talks to the Nuremberg Chamber of Commerce and Royal College of Defence Studies, being interviewed by the Stüttgarter Nachrichten newspaper about the Libyan affair, and presenting a medal to a lady who has run the German/English Friendship Association for 35 years. Sometimes there were more interesting ones: breakfast with Franz Josef Strauss, the Minister-President of Bavaria, being guest of honour at the Eiswette dinner in Bremen (a men's club that has taken bets every year since 1829 on whether the Weser River will freeze), and opening night of *Das Rheingold* in Berlin. There were also promises of an invitation to visit the Frisian Islands.

When Julian had been Minster in Bonn four years earlier, everyone's lips were closed on the subject of Germany's Nazi past. Then almost overnight everything changed. German television showed a serial called *Heimat* covering rural life in the village of Schabbach in the Hunsrück, covering the time from the Great War with veterans returning home, to the rise of Fascism, WWII and the occupation and division of Germany. Suddenly everyone wanted to talk about the past. No one, Germans or foreigners, accepted invitations for the evenings when *Heimat* was on the screen. For sixteen weeks everyone watched one of the most moving TV series imaginable. Some of the telling facts emerged out of the corner of one's eye, as it were, from the patient accumulation of unobtrusive detail. We both thought this was just about the very best historical television we had ever seen.

It could be that the series was timed to connect with the media's frequent features on what was called the German Question, the discussion of the territorial changes that should happen in the future when Germany was no longer divided, after the armies of the conquerors had left, but more likely it was the approach of the 40th anniversary of the ending of the war in Europe, in England called VE Day, a day on which I remember we had been let out of school and allowed to dance in the Market Place in Wells. In Germany the 1984 celebration of the anniversary of the end of the war in Europe, was regarded as special, because it was the 40th anniversary, and therefore of special significance, forty representing the life-span of man, the length of time needed for transfer of responsibility from the generation of the fathers to that of the sons. On 8 May 1985 Richard von Weizäscker made a moving speech in the Parliament building in Bonn, which was followed by a service in Cologne Cathedral. He reminded listeners how too many Germans had denied knowing about the Holocaust, and did not accept responsibility for the war. Four months before declaring war, Hitler had made a speech on the necessity to conquer Poland '*Neither right nor wrong nor treaties matter*'. Who had resisted? He urged the German people to honour freedom, peace and justice and to face up to the truth.

At about that time the Parliamentary Secretary to the Minister of Health was staying with us and we invited his German opposite number for dinner. They were sitting on either side of me. The English official leant towards the German and said that we in Britain were very concerned with the number of people who had some form of severe disablement, and we realised that to deal with the problem we needed to know the actual numbers involved and the details of the disablement and asked if Germany was doing the same? The German answered that such a thing would not be possible in Germany. There was a good deal of nervousness in his voice as he explained that the last time this was done was in the 30s...... His voice trailed off and we realised he was remembering that Hitler's intentions then were rather different from the purposes of the British Ministry of Health.

I have a feeling that every British Ambassador was held in high regard in Germany, but they certainly made it clear that they liked and admired Julian. There were many references to his 'fine head' (said to have been admired by the President!). His appearance was said 'to reflect the distinction of his mind'. They respected his knowledge and judgement and were delighted that he was so interested in Germany and German history and culture. I don't know whether they expected very much of ambassadors' wives, and when I found that my neighbours at dinner tended to ask: 'How many children do you have?' I decided to set myself a hurdle: to know enough about subjects that would interest my neighbours for them not to resort to that question. This I counted as Victory for me. Otherwise Defeat. What did seem to be expected of Ambassadors' wives is that they would unendingly accept 'Schirmherrschaft' (patronage, but literally 'umbrella domination') of this or that bazaar or society. But this seemed to require little more than smiling acceptance, my best dress and a visit to the hairdresser.

Not every diplomatic wife enjoys being away from home, friends and family, and many would prefer to have a career of their own. But I had to accept that without a workbench and a studio, bookbinding was not practical, so I shut the door on what had occupied me every day for the previous four years, and threw myself into trying to run the Residence and the catering as well as I could, look after the guests, and be a good Ambassador's wife, which in truth was a great pleasure. Some days the programme would include being taken down a mine in the Ruhr, some days we went behind the scenes to a rehearsal at the opera. We were invited to private views of the most interesting exhibitions without having to queue or jump up and down to look over the heads of tall men as in the National Gallery. We travelled all over the country staying

Julian with Chancellor Helmut Kohl

Julian with Lord Carrington when Foreirn Secretary 1986

in Renaissance castles, and dining in erstwhile royal palaces. Perhaps the most enjoyable invitations were to stay with Princess Peg, who was English, and the widow of Prince Louis of Hesse (the son of Queen Victoria's daughter Alice). When we stayed there our bedroom was the former billiard room of the grand hunting lodge of the ruined castle of Wolfsgarten. In the corner was a slate not wiped since a billiards match played between Tsar Nicholas II, Kaiser Wilhelm II and Prince Louis of Hesse Our bedspread had been embroidered as a wedding present by Queen Victoria's daughter Beatrice. There were of course duller moments. I remember a British Week at Wiesbaden at which Julian had to speak. The Mayor wanted to do his very best to please the Ambassador and ordered a traditional 'English' meal of roast beef. What we got was a thick slice of hardly cooked beef, running with blood and covered with sweet English custard. The chef had been told that in England roast beef was served rare with Yorkshire pudding and unfortunately in Germany the word `pudding' describes what was called custard in England.

The newspapers always seemed to have a new scandal. One day the headlines screamed that wines produced by 31 different vineyards had been found to have been doctored with glycol (antifreeze) to reduce their acidity. It chanced that we had bought a case of a wine which contained this additive. After having a couple of glasses (before reading about the glycol) my face swelled so I could hardly see out of my eyes. I was given injections but they had little effect. After three weeks of suffering, I was normal again, with the name of the vineyard firmly imprinted on my brain. Strangely the glycol seemed not to have affected Julian.

In October 1983 we found time for a holiday in Greece. First we spent an evening envying Tom Bridges his lovely Residence in Athens, and next day gratefully accepted a guide-book and the keys of his car and caught the ferry to Karystos on the southern tip of Euboea (now called Evia) where we found a charming inn charging end-of-season prices. It was clearly dangerous for us to go on holiday: we always seemed to attract a diplomatic crisis. This time, while we were lying in the sun reading our books, U.S. troops invaded Grenada. Grenada was within the territory of Julian's brother Giles, by then High Commissioner to Barbados and the Eastern Caribbean. Rather like the Suez Canal situation in Amman, Giles was told nothing until it was all over. He had had no warning from Washington, but assumed London knew, but had not thought it necessary to tell him. Or perhaps, in retaliation for Anthony Eden keeping Washington in the dark about Suez, the State Department had not warned London about Grenada? Mrs Thatcher had been kept in the dark until the last minute. President Reagan sent two telegrams to Mrs Thatcher, the first asking her advice, the second, an hour later, saying: 'Our forces will establish themselves in Grenada.' The Prime Minister was wounded that Reagan, in whom she had total trust (she was rather apt to give her trust to charming, well dressed men who flattered her, like Cecil Parkinson) had not been totally straight with her. She also did not enjoy her interview with the Queen, who had made it clear that she was less than pleased that no action was being taken about the American invasion of her territory (the Queen remained Grenada's Head of State after the island's independence in 1974). Defending herself on the BBC, Mrs Thatcher said:

> 'I am totally against communism and terrorism, but if you are pronouncing a new law that wherever communism reigns against the will of the people, there the United States shall enter, then we are going to have really terrible wars in the world. The West has defensive forces in order to defend our own way of life and when things happen in other countries which we don't like, we don't just march in'.

After this both sides made an attempt to mend fences.

One of the best perks about being Ambassador in Bonn was that we had a whole establishment in Berlin that we could use whenever we chose. This consisted of an elegant house in Berlin's Grunewald, a large Daimler flying the Union Jack, a British Army security detail, and the Mayor's office begging us to ask them to arrange anything we wanted to do. The house, dating from the Thirties and now the Residence of the British Ambassador, had a shower which sprayed water at you from all angles, and a conservatory whose glass walls went up and down at the press of a button.

Julian's strongly held view was that the separation of Germany into East and West could not and should not last,but exactly what the future would hold for the two Germanies was very much the subject of debate. Julian persuaded the Foreign Office that he needed to have experience of life in the East, and our Ambassador in East Germany should have experience of the West. As soon as there was a space in Julian's diary, we left our comfortable Berlin house and drove through check Point Charlie, (always with the windows closed and not permitting the communist guards to get their hands on our passports) to the much less elegant house of Tim Everard, British Ambassador to the GDR, passing the depressing flats in a triumphal avenue called Karl Marx Allee, where his staff had to live.

Tim had arranged for us to meet some people of interest in the DDR. We had in the boot several boxes of unavailable comestibles sent by his friends in the West for the Bishop of Mecklenburg. The Bishop's sister was married to a senior member of the Stasi, the East German security service. This connection was not enough to exempt the bishop's son from the rule that only children of Party members were admitted to university. On a later occasion we met the Stasi brother-in-law, I think his name was Albrecht. I wasted no time in asking him how he could justify admitting children to universities, not on the basis of their ability, but on the political opinion of their fathers? He answered: *'What's wrong with being a carpenter? Jesus was one, wasn't he?'* (After the bishop's son had been denied a university education, he had become a carpenter). We were taken to a meeting of a women's club, who were listening to a talk about poverty and hardship in Africa. A box for contributions was passed round. I asked to whom the money was being sent. *'We always support the ANC.'* We were also promised a meeting with a university professor who Tim knew, and who he said spoke more freely than most. We had been invited to his house for coffee, but we were met by an embarrassed wife who said that 'They' had just phoned to say that the professor must on no account meet the Ambassador from Bonn – not even to shake hands! *'The meeting cannot be registered.'* That things could not be registered was a phrase we were well accustomed to from Moscow.

Next day we went to visit Weimar. Our escorts were determined not to lose sight of us. We had hoped to be able to talk to people we chanced to meet, but this was the opposite of what the Travel Bureau of the GDR wanted. Julian told them that his wife had a headache and, though of course we would certainly have liked to be taken to see the statue of Shakespeare, we would prefer to read our guide-books in our rooms in the Elephant Hotel. Half an hour later we crept out of a side door and looked for a cheerful looking *Bierkeller*. In the GDR restaurants were always full, but as we were tourists, the management persuaded a couple to let us share their table – exactly what we had hoped for. At first the German couple were carefully discreet about criticising anything about life in the GDR, but by the end of the evening they had let down their guard enough to say that now they were able to watch West German television and see how luxurious things were in the West, in comparison with the shabbiness and dreariness of the East, they had started to feel critical of their government. They hated having to queue for everything, bribe someone in order to get a slightly better car or washing machine, and be careful of what they said and did, lest it be reported to the secret police. They found the restriction on travel the hardest to bear, as they longed to have a holiday on the Mediterranean and to see Paris.

On our next visit to West Berlin we were invited to a concert given by the Berlin Philharmonic Orchestra and conducted by Herbert von Karajan, to celebrate their recent reconciliation after a difference of opinion about the management of the orchestra and his membership of the Nazi party during the war. It was a performance of Bach's B Minor Mass, and we were seated in the front row of the Dress Circle, next to the President, (with whom I noticed Julian was now on Christian name terms.) Karajan, very old and stiff, appeared, unsteadily clutching at the railings. While he conducted, he attached something that looked like a belt to a piece of railing. As we left, we found Julian's Berlin security detail, Corporal Grief, sitting in the foyer on the watch for unexploded bombs. It was sad that he did not care for concerts or opera as he had to accompany Julian wherever he went.

We had endless official visitors, something over two thousand a year, (although not all to dine or sleep!) It is the Foreign Office tradition that the Ambassador's house is treated as a hotel. His allowances are liberal, he is supplied with a grand house and competent staff, and HMG is saved the cost of putting up visiting politicians and officials in five-star hotels. The quid pro quo is that is helpful for Ambassadors to have a chance to get on good informal terms with leading figures in politics.

When the Prime Minister stayed with us for the first time she brought with her Geoffrey Howe, Michael Heseltine and their private secretaries. Our butler Harry (his name was really Heinrich, but Mary Henderson had preferred to call him Harry, and Harry he remained) told me confidently that she would want good supplies of whisky, and, for breakfast at eight in the morning, just black coffee. Taking her up to her room, I asked if she would really only take black coffee in her bedroom for breakfast. She asked where the others would be breakfasting. I said that it would have to be downstairs because we had too many guests to serve everyone in their rooms. '*I will do what they do – I wouldn't like to miss anything*'.

One day we had the Minister for Northern Ireland for a night. He arrived wearing a kilt which must have made the evening memorable for our German guests. Harry beckoned to me and whispered '*Come and see his bed.*' Charlie Lyell was occupied talking to Julian so I followed Harry upstairs. The bed was neatly turned down. Tucked in with only their heads showing, was a line of stuffed animals. At that moment the door opened. The Minister had needed some papers from his luggage. He was not as abashed as I was, and he introduced each animal to me in turn. '*Never travel without them. Couldn't sleep if I did.*' Peter Morrison, tipped to be Minister of Agriculture, was our next visitor, whose opening remark was: '*I may as well tell you I am a terrific snob because you'll find it out sooner or later*'.

In July 1985 Oleg Gordievsky, the most valuable spy the West ever had, suspected that his cover had been blown, and he dramatically escaped to Finland by means of a clever scheme involving two women, a baby and a soiled nappy. Not long afterwards he came to meet Julian in Bonn. Julian asked him if he would like to have the collection of well-bound pre-revolutionary Russian classics which Julian's father had bought in Leningrad in 1930. He thanked Julian with tears running down his face. He told us that OPERATION BOOT had been a blow to the KGB from which their London operation never recovered, and which had also damaged its prestige at home as much as internationally. Gordievsky's defection had resulted in a tit-for-tat expulsion crisis between

ulian and Margaret (with yellow parasol) with Graf and Gräfin Schulenburg being driven to lunch at Buckingham Palace

ulian and Margaret

Britain and Moscow, with each country expelling 31 members of the other's Embassy. This had turned out to be a turning point after which the Soviets seemed to take Britain more seriously. Ambassadors in Moscow noticed that the Russians, like other bullies, despise weakness and admire strength.

Julian's main concern during this time was German-UK relations On the world stage the Cold War was coming to an end. This process had taken a leap forward after the December 1984 visit to Britain of Mikhail Gorbachev, then widely seen as the number two in the Communist Party. Inside a week he had had a five-hour discussion with the Prime Minister at Chequers, followed by meetings with ministers, members of parliament and business people which gave a huge boost to the policy of engagement. A Foreign Office minute on the visit reported that '*The PM seemed to go uncharacteristically weak at the knees when she talked to the personable M. Gorbachev.*' Mrs. Thatcher memorably told a BBC interviewer, '*I like Mr. Gorbachev. We can do business together*'. Gorbachev appreciated the way in which the Prime Minister had spoken positively of the recent changes within the USSR, and had related her criticism of past Soviet behaviour to the Politburo. Persuaded by Mrs. Thatcher, Ronald Reagan met Gorbachev (by then General Secretary of the Communist Party) in Reykjavik). In 1988 Gorbachev declared at the UN that people of every country had the right to decide for themselves what kind of system they wished to live under, which indicated a sea-change in relations between East and West.

One evening, after a high-level meeting of some kind, Mrs Thatcher and four of her officials settled round the fire in our sitting room with glasses of whisky and Julian suggested that the Prime Minister should tell us about her conversation with Reagan. There was an uncomfortably long pause, and she then said: '*Oh I asked Ronald if Nancy's anti-drug campaign was going well.*' Perhaps she had had a very tiring day. Perhaps she didn't choose to share what they had discussed, but she gave me the impression of not being accustomed to pay very close attention to other people's views. Julian would have had no difficulty summarising what had been discussed.

Diplomatic life did not make it easy for Julian to keep up with events at All Souls, so he played little part in college affairs, even though an old friend from Magdalen days, Patrick Neill, had been elected to succeed John Sparrow as Warden. In those distant days heads of colleges took it in turns to be Vice Chancellor of the University as well, and it fell to Patrick Neill to propose that the Prime Minister, as the first woman to hold that post, should be given an honorary degree. His proposal was defeated by a large majority, keen to make clear the university's disapproval of her educational policies and the cuts in money for research. The Neills came to stay with us in Bonn and were with us when Julian opened a display of watercolours of the Rhine. Patrick told me how impressed he was with the ease with which Julian was able to move seamlessly from English to French and German. I remember Julian saying to me that he loved listening to perfect German being spoken, though he sometimes thought it was best to savour the words without too much regard to their substance. He 'liked to sit back in his chair and enjoy the cadences, the rise and fall of the complicated sentences, with their parenthetical clauses, waiting with a thrill of anticipation for the main verb'.

The Queen and Prince Philip were paying a visit to Berlin for some Army occasion that autumn, and we flew up from Bonn and stayed with the British Commandant. During lunch Lady Gordon Duff leant forward and said to Prince Philip: '*You must be looking forward to Christmas, Sir.*' To which he replied: '*You must be joking! Christmas means trying to stop the grandchildren killing each other, busting up the furniture, and acting as marriage guidance counsellor to their parents.*' In 1992, which the Queen was to call her *annus horribilis*, he told me that he had invented the science of 'dontopedalogy' (opening your mouth and putting your foot in it).

For Julian's 59th birthday I organized a surprise party and decided we would introduce Rhubarb to some German friends. This was a Victorian version of Charades which involved a lot dressing up. Our guests threw themselves into it with delight and years later, long after Julian had retired, I chanced to meet Otto and Alexandra von Lambsdorff and a rich newspaper magnate, all guests at the birthday party. (Lambsdorff led Germany's FDP party for many years.) They separately reminded me of that evening, and said that they had enjoyed themselves so much that whenever they had a family party in the winter it had become a tradition to play the Bullards' acting game.

On Saturday 26th April 1986 the No. 4 reactor in the Chernobyl Nuclear Power Plant near Pripyat in the Ukraine exploded. Quite soon the media was full of stories of the nuclear disaster having caused radioactive rain which was destroying the forests, so we arranged to see the young Forstmeister who had taught us, soon after we arrived, to recognize the signs of trees under stress. In the markets customers veered away from all green vegetables, sure that contamination would have been blown across from the East.

In July 1986 German President Richard von Weizsäcker, paid a state visit to Britain. As was the custom, the British Ambassador and spouse were included. The visit included lunch with Mrs Thatcher at No. 10, and dinner at Buckingham Palace. Some weeks before the event Julian and I were walking down Bond Street and we passed S.J. Phillips, a shop which buys and sells antique jewellery. I suggested that we ask if one could hire a piece of jewellery. They asked on what occasion it would it be worn. When I replied that it was for dinner at the Palace, they said I might choose anything I liked and there would be no charge! We selected a brooch with W IV in diamonds surrounded by blue enamel. William IV had been made to marry a German princess in the hope of providing England with a legitimate male heir and avoid the throne going to Princess Victoria. He was so sorry to leave his actress mistress (Mrs Jordan) that he had brooches and buckles made for his many daughters and sons with the same insignia. During the evening at the Palace, Prince Philip noticed my brooch and asked its history. I did not tell him it was on loan. Eighteen months later, when Prince Charles and Princess Diana visited Germany, Julian went to Phillips, and finding the brooch still unsold, bought it for me as an anniversary present. Sadly, after Julian died and I moved into a flat, it was stolen by a burglar.

Taken from Julian's letter to the children:

'Our diaries are unbelievably full, but with events of varying interest. Some days it is `Walk in the woods and tea with the Telchiks' (Horst Telchik was the Chancellor's private secretary) or 'Queen's Birthday party' '70 ladies to tea with violin and piano duo' (me very nervous lest it should rain). Then three brilliant days during which we had medieval jousting and were invited to lunch by Graf and Gräfin Spee in the Barbarossa Saal of Schloss Helstedt. After which we walked through the rhododendron woods of which he was so proud. In spare moments he mounted a digger and replanted the rhododendron to get new effects. The weather collapsed, and returned to 6 degrees, thick grey sky and rain, rain, rain, which was a pity because we had the Patties staying, (the Minister for Science and Technology) and planned to take them on the Rhine. They were both good value and restored the hope that there are one or two people in Westminster who are not self-seeking ignorant odd balls, although Lady Pattie confidentially told me that most of the Cabinet and Junior Ministers spent as much watching each other and trying to do the other down, as they did on their own work'.

Then came the Grand Army Anniversary Parade in the stadium where the Berlin Olympic Games had been held in 1938, at which the salute was to be taken by Princess Margaret, but HRH took to her bed with a cold and Julian had to take her place. He looked very elegant with his sword and cocked hat. We were at Buckingham Palace shortly after this and the Queen thanked Julian for taking her sister's place and said: *'Silly girl! She could easily have got out of bed and taken the salute.'*

Vicky kept one of the longest letters I ever wrote her and as I have quoted liberally from Julian's, perhaps it is time I included one of my own:

'Two months ago we received an invitation decorated with seals and tassels for a whole-day event to celebrate the 60th birthday of Prince von Thurn and Taxis, said to be extremely rich as a result of an ancestor being made postmaster general of the Holy Roman Empire in 1595. For the final dinner we were asked to wear eighteenth-century costume. As the Prince's birthday was on the same day as mine, I persuaded Julian to accept, even though it meant going all the way to Regensburg. His resistance collapsed when he heard that we could borrow costumes from the wardrobe of the Opera House. (I chose silvery grey and rubbed half a jar of talcum powder into my hair). It was not

long before we learned about the disreputable life the Prince led and also heard various stories about his newly married 23-year-old Princess, whose friends on the Punk Rock scene were equally outrageous. The German aristocracy in general accused them both of bringing the Nobility into Disrepute, and they all said they wouldn't be seen dead at his birthday party. But we had met the Princess at that party near Bonn where we watched the mock medieval jousting contest, and Julian and I liked her, young, direct, decided, serious, but penniless – happy to marry an undesirable very rich man who was a distant relative and needed an heir.

The day began with all the guests boarding river steamers. Along with Hapsburg Archdukes and their Duchesses, I met a lot of people called Guinness with swimming blue eyes from outside Dublin, the Begum Aly Khan and one or two younger sons of European noble families with names like Hohenlohe, Fürstenberg, Schönborn, and Schaumburg-Lippe, and soon we seemed to be promising to come and stay in castles in various parts of the world with Bobbie and Fifi, and Gaza and Monika, and did we remember that evening when they had all flown over to Palm Beach for that Barbecue with Babs, the one when Gigi said such terrible things to dear Klaus? The weather was kind to us for about 15 minutes as we made our way through the steep gorge cut by the Danube through the Bavarian Jura.

After changing into our borrowed costumes and powdering our hair we drove to Schloss St. Emmeram, seat of the Thurn and Taxis family, and somewhat larger than Versailles. We were greeted by dancers pretending to be eighteenth-century wind-up figures like Coppélia. Then we moved into a courtyard of wooden farm carts and blazing fires and curtseying children and chickens being slaughtered and horses being shoe-ed and old women making lace – Bruegel in fact. Then – into the hall where we saw a vision of waving white plumes and Marie Antionette shaped dresses and little negro pages with umbrella canes . . . who could this be? None other than the entire Khashoggi family, about whose doings Private Eye was so full.

What followed next was a shortened performance of Don Giovanni sung by the Munich State Opera, which, at the moment when the Don should vanish into the flames of hell for his sins, dissolved into a vision of our hostess shrieking, 'No!' whereupon the music swung into pop and most people danced. We needed refreshment and moved into rooms lined with revolving mirrors, with tables set up with fabulous flower arrangements where we ate lobster and samphire and asparagus and drank champagne ad lib – only somehow one's appetite for such things was less keen between midnight and one a.m., and gradually a mood of depression rather than elation set in. A lot of those who came didn't know our hosts any better than we did, and had been gathered from all corners of the world: Spain, France, America, one or two shooting farmers from Norfolk, Italy, Saudi Arabia, Sweden, in fact, I was hard put to it to find any decent German who had accepted.

Surely Gunther Sachs was a name I had read in gossip columns? Who was he apart from being an elderly gent, not wildly thrilled to find me sitting next to him, wearing a faultless outfit in shades of pale blue and gold and shouting across the room at

Mick Jagger and his girl-friend who I did not know either? I saw no signs of drugs but there were plenty of men of doubtful sex. The fact that the Prince and I shared the same birthday had seemed a reason to accept the invitation, although I had a pretty good idea of the kind of company we were in for. But I am glad we experienced it, though I didn't fancy a repeat. Julian did not like to think what it had cost the British taxpayer to fly us there and send the Rolls to drive us back to Bonn, or what the German taxpayer had to fork out for six policemen – and still more what it must have cost the Prince. 'Wenn Schon Denn Schon' was his parting words to us, which means roughly 'If you're going to do a thing, do it properly'. On Thursday we flew to London for a memorial service for Charles Johnston, on Friday we dined at St Anthony's, on Saturday it was All Soul's Gaudy (ladies also invited). I believe we are having what would be called a spiffing time if only it would stop raining'.

In August 1987 Rudolf Hess, for the last 20 years the sole inmate of Spandau Prison, killed himself by winding an electric flex round his neck. Hess was by then 93 years old and during the previous 20 years Britain had made eleven attempts to allow him to return to his family, to which the Americans and the French had agreed, but to the Russians a life sentence was a sentence for life. Julian and I had always felt curious about some of the aspects of the mysterious appearance in Scotland of Hitler's deputy. Julian would be nominally in charge of him while he was in Spandau prison, because it was in the British sector. Before he left London Julian had asked to see all the documents about Hess. What exactly did Rudolph Hess hope to achieve and what was the reaction in Germany to the news that a senior member of the government had flown to Britain? Was the flight on Hitler's orders or, as Hess maintained at his trial, was it his own plan? We found no answer to these questions because all papers on the subject had been ordered to be taken to the Royal Archives in Windsor Castle.

One curious thing about the flight was that it took place at exactly the same time as messages reached the Foreign Office, via the Bishop of Chichester, asking whether the Allies would be interested in peace negotiations if Hitler and his cronies could be got rid of. There was no evidence in the archives that any reply was sent. How much resistance was there against the Nazis? Julian thought that although small groups of clergy, Socialists, Trades Unionists and Communists disliked the Nazis, no steps were actually taken until Army officers became dissatisfied with the conduct of the war, and wanted peace in order to put a stop to the bombing of German cities so that all Germany's energies could be devoted to fighting Russia. In punishment for the 20 July plot, Hitler ordered several good men like Dietrich Bonhoeffer, a distinguished priest, together with their families, to be rounded up in the final months of the war. They were actually still being hung by the Gestapo while the sound of American and Russian guns could already be heard.

Soon after this Julian brought home the news that Prince Charles and Princess Diana were coming to visit Germany in November for a week and would be spending two nights with us in Bonn and one in Berlin. A letter came from the Foreign Ministry asking about the royal couple's favourite dishes and what they should not be offered. This question was sent to Prince Charles' office, and we learnt that HRH liked bits in his orange juice, and that her favourite foods were lobster and caviar. Julian and I nearly came to blows. He thought it his duty to pass on the information just as sent by the royal couple, (or perhaps by a member of their staff without their knowledge). I thought it his duty to change this to the standard reply as sent by the Queen's office: 'Anything you think it appropriate to offer her, Her Majesty will be pleased to eat.' We had to move out of our bedrooms in Bonn and in Berlin as they were not prepared to share a bedroom even despite the newspaper headline of 'TOGETHER AGAIN!'

We were piloted by Prince Charles between our various destinations. He did the taking off and landing a good deal more smoothly than British Airways pilots, and in between we shared a table in the aeroplane with HRH and his Private Secretary, John Riddell, who presented him each morning with a resumé of the reports about him in that day's papers. I cannot remember the words I used, but I tried my best to suggest politely that, given the attitude of the gutter press to the royal family, reading the headlines in the tabloids would be certain to make one start the day in a bad mood. He replied: '*I have to know what they are thinking about me. Do you know how many people read this stuff?*' From time to time he asked Julian how to say something in German, but after a day or two, he was able to manage not too badly and with increasing confidence, which earned him extremely good press. (I am not sure who started the rumours that Princess Diana was polishing up her German – an announcement which made everyone on the Prince's staff roar with laughter.) It puzzled us why all the members of the household including her husband treated her so dismissively, even in front of us. Whatever their private marital differences it would surely have been better had he kept his feelings hidden. The only people in the royal party who I saw speaking to her were her lady-in-waiting and her policemen, (large and fat and drank a lot of gin in their bedrooms), who behaved as if they were on very intimate terms with her. She criticised their shirts and they her hair in front of the rest of us. She was not unaware that she was annoying her husband.

Munich won hands down for splendour. We had lunch in the Nymphenburg Palace seated on chairs that had belonged to Eugénie de Beauharnais and embroidered with her monogram. We ate off 1807 Paris porcelain surrounded by furniture that had been made for Napoleon's victory dinner in Moscow, but the Wittelsbach of the time, doubtful that Moscow would be captured, had held on to the baggage train in case its contents should not be needed. Our host, Prinz Franz, we learnt, was Heir General to the British throne. That is to say, had a law not been passed requiring the British monarch to be a Protestant, he would have a better claim to it than Queen Victoria. (In Hanover, our last stop, the Minister President said in his speech: 'The Wittelsbachs may have had the better claim, but it was the Hanoverians that won')

That evening we sat in the royal box for *Marriage of Figaro,* and the next night ate dinner by candlelight in the richly painted seventeenth-century Antiquarium, the largest Renaissance hall north of the alps. Princess Diana sat on the right of our host, the Minister President of Bavaria. After he had made several abortive attempts at getting a reply other than 'No' or 'Yes', he gave up and turned to me on his other side, which meant that she was required to make polite conversation with another German who seemed to her equally fat and uninteresting. Bored, she turned her chair round and chatted to someone nearer her age at another table; her blackest moment of the trip in my eyes. It was perhaps a report of this that reached Marianne von Weizsäcker and caused her to say to me, after the visit was over: *'Margaret, could not the Queen teach Princess Diana how to behave?'* I had read that she had referred to herself as 'Thick as a plank' and also heard that Prince Charles had found her a tutor for grammar and spelling in order that her thank you letters would not disgrace her. But even if she was unlikely to contribute much intelligence to the royal family's genetic inheritance, she was extremely pretty, and did a lot for the prestige of Britain in Germany.

In order to boost British trade (and because we had Princess Diana of course) a fashion show was included in the visit. I didn't have much hope of the clothes, and it is difficult to think that it would contribute to a boost in sales – or certainly not as well as seeing them being worn by the Princess of Wales would have. My contribution was to ask the Director of the Museum Ludwig, (the modern art museum in Cologne) if we could hold the Fashion show in their largest gallery, and to persuade the manager of the Kaufhof department store to provide the reception eats. Dinner followed at our house. We had to seat 80 guests at round tables and I asked the Military Attaché if he could arrange for us to borrow silver candelabra from the regiments stationed in Germany. This might have been hugely expensive in candles, but I found the Roman Catholic church have a cheap source of supply. With variegated ivy ferns and small yellow and white flowers hanging down from them, the effect was good. We ate our way through consommé royale, lobster quenelles, roast venison from Scotland with chanterelles, Stilton cheese and finally a concoction by Herr Schlatt of mango and blackcurrant sorbets and exotic sliced fruits. Then Justus Franz went to the piano and played Mozart, Chopin and finally Beethoven's Appassionata. Then came a big surprise. Diana rose and went to the piano and played some Schumann very fluently by heart – for quite a short time – but enough for us to see that perhaps she was not just a pretty face.

When she was saying goodbye to us, she announced that playing the piano at our house had been the high spot of the trip. I fear she really meant that the whole week had been a crashing bore and she wished she could have stayed at home and played the piano and swum. I thought it was a most interesting week. Julian thought it would have been better had the sun shone throughout, if the royal butler had not been allowed to play the part of Private Secretary, or the giggling royal secretaries that of ladies-in-waiting. The Prince needed a royal Jeeves to steal the coloured silk handkerchief out of the breast pocket of his dinner jacket and the museum should have put out another hundred chairs so as to be sure of covering the cost of the fashion show. And of course, the British press should have been towed out beyond the 12-mile limit and sunk.

Shortly before Christmas Julian had a letter from Frau Albrecht, the sister-in-law of the Bishop of Mecklenburg whom we had earlier met on our GDR excursion, She was here on her own to visit her elderly parents, and could we meet? She came to lunch and I asked what struck her most about the West and how did she feel about being here. Her look and her reply stayed in my mind: 'Guilty'. I think she meant that she felt guilty because she was conscious that she was allowed to travel and visit her mother only because she was the wife of a senior man in the most hated and feared institution in the DDR.

Bonn had a small theatre, not really an opera house, but to make a splash, they decided to have a performance of Mozart's *Idomeneo* over the Christmas period and somehow persuaded Yehudi Menuhin to conduct it. He was feeling his age (about 70) and had ceased to give violin performances. On evenings when he was not conducting, he would appear at receptions or dinners given by neighbouring bigwigs, to which we were often invited. A few days before our last Christmas in Bonn, he telephoned to say that the hotel where he was staying would have no staff on Christmas Day and could he throw himself on our mercy for lunch? I tried not to show my reluctance to welcome him, but I did make it clear that he would perhaps do better to find a Turkish or Chinese restaurant to feed him, as our four children would be celebrating Christmas with us. The next day he phoned again: his wife was flying out to join him and he knew we would like to meet her . . . I could hardly believe it when the day before Christmas Eve he phoned to ask if he could bring his very old friend, a marvellous pianist . . . . . . This time I did say no.

I have since wondered why he behaved as he did: not saying one word to any of our children, both of them talking exclusively to us about themselves, and not bringing even a token small present for our children or flowers for me. During lunch, his wife pulled up her skirt and flung her leg into the air to show us the leather boots which had been her Christmas present. Next day he did send a small bunch of flowers with a card 'From your fellow countryman, your fellow subject, Yehudi'. I concluded that Christmas and other people's children meant nothing to him, but that since he had British nationality, he thought himself entitled to free meals at British embassies in exchange for the extortionate taxes Britain demanded from him.

Just before Julian's 60th birthday, in the spring of 1988, I was invited to join a group of ladies for a week's trip to Egypt. The Egyptian government had asked its ambassador in Bonn to do something to boost tourism from Germany. Until I arrived at Bonn station to catch the train to Frankfurt airport, I had no idea who else was invited. There, all was pandemonium. A closely packed crowd of politicians, senior civil servants, members of the aristocracy, and Ambassadors, including the Israeli Ambassador, were wishing their wives *bon voyage*. Deutsche Bahn trains stop at Bonn station for no more than two minutes and as Mr Ben Ari was unable to push his way out of the packed train, he was forced to stay and have an unexpected journey to Frankfurt.

The entire Ministry of Tourism greeted us in Cairo with refreshment and flowers. I had a double room overlooking the Nile in a hotel built for Napoleon, but the refrigerator was out of order. We watched a camel and horse display. Plentiful buffet. Everyone except me wore stunning outfits. Next day down came the rain. Ran to Egyptian museum. Good guide, yelling for all she was worth. Wonderful objects. We boarded a boat on the Nile. Enormous meal served to music of ouds and drums. Roses, gold cartouche key rings and calendars distributed all round. Ran to bus through rain. Streets awash. Taken protesting to Muhammed Ali Mosque. Fifteen minutes to change for reception at German Embassy. Bus to reception at more elegant British Residence. British ambassador old school friend of Julian. Left hotel at 8.00 a.m. for Memphis and Saqqara. No time to stop long because invited for tea, coffee and sticky cakes with Mrs Mubarak. Visited three libraries. Streets awash. Tea with wife of Foreign Minister. Sank into bed. Wednesday very successful: visited suq, blue glass factory and Ibn Tulun Mosque with wife of French Ambassador. Arrived too late for lunch so no sustenance until 7.00 p.m. Next day left 7.30 a.m. for Valley of the Kings. Bumped into a former girlfriend of King Hussein who I knew in Amman, who kissed me warmly. Visited the tombs of Seti I, Ramses III and VI and Prince Amenhotep. It was hot. Our group continued to astonish me with new outfits every half hour. Bus to Son et Lumière at Karnak At the Esna lock next day we overtook a long queue of boats waiting to pass. Angry shouts from all sides. Our captain shouted loudly: '*All the passengers on this boat are princesses!*' At 7 p.m. we docked at Edfu and saw the carved figures in the temple of Horus the falcon by the light of moon and stars. Very romantic. Told to appear suitably dressed for last night Oriental Banquet and Nubian dancing. Everyone (except me) in new glamourous filmy outfits. Trixie bought

Julian with Margaret

Margaret bookbinding

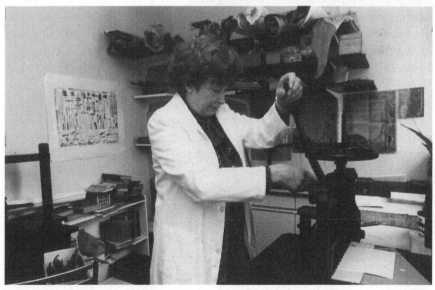

a bottle of sekt at some stage in the evening. On Saturday, we set off from Aswan in several feluccas. No wind. The Swedish ambassador's wife and I took over the oars. We went backwards. Police boat appeared and towed us to the house of the Begum Aga Khan for orange and mango juice. Watched sun go down from Old Cataract Hotel. I thought it sad not to see the temple of Philae (the temple that was rescued, moved and rebuilt) by night. No one else had the energy to join me, so I hired taxi and boat, and set off alone. Breathtaking. Almost the best part of the trip.

Last Day: Visited quarry at Aswan. Flew to Abu Simbel. Usual chaos at airport'.Abu Simbel certainly very fine, the Prussian blue and gold colours splendid. The figures enormous, elsewhere a whole wall is given over to hundreds of soldiers, battles, captures and prisoners. It struck me that the Pharaohs' desire to destroy the cartouches of their predecessors and substitute their own, and after them the Christians with a similar desire to destroy all possibility of worshipping earlier gods, was all a bit like the instinctive dislike of Ambassadors to hear anything good about their predecessors!

It was not until March 1989, twenty months after Julian retired, that the Berlin Wall was torn down and all the frontier posts between the DDR and the Federal Republic opened. How sad that we should so narrowly miss that shattering event! During our last year in Germany, the question of the future of Germany was already being hotly debated. The Foreign Office had begun discussing the appropriate territorial settlement for Germany during the war, and after 1945 the East and the West struggled openly over a solution. Few would have bet on German reunification coming so quickly, but Julian was on record that he saw the collapse of the DDR as being inevitable because of the huge unpopularity of the Stasi which had penetrated every sector of society, Erich Honecker's failing health, and the ruling group that showed more interest in retaining power than in ideological fervour. The economy was clearly in financial straits and it was unlikely the Russians would come to their rescue. For ordinary citizens the main grumble was the contrast between the conditions of their life and the Federal Republic. When the news broke that Hungary had opened its borders to the GDR, the fate of the Wall was inevitable. Euphoria and disbelief followed. I knew many people in Bonn with connections in the East who rushed over as soon as they could, but returned rather puzzled and slightly indignant. '*We had expected to be gratefully greeted with open arms. But they thought they were the good Germans and we the baddies led astray by the wicked Americans'*.

Before Julian retired it had already become clear that the situation of the GDR was difficult, and Mrs Thatcher's suspicion of all things German became more vociferous. In the *Spectator*, Charles Moore said she saw German unification as a cloak for German power. Julian had to steer a tricky course between the consequences of the Prime Minister's dislike of Chancellor Kohl and the latter's opinion that Margaret Thatcher's problem was her resentment that Britain had lost its empire and wrecked its economy even though it had won the war. Kremlin records later revealed that two months before the Berlin Wall came down, Margaret Thatcher told President Gorbachev that neither Britain nor Western Europe wanted German reunification and she made it clear that she wanted the Soviet leader to do what he could to stop it. Six days before the Wall came down, the Politburo themselves discussed pulling down the Wall. The Prime Minister in her memoirs wrote that the one policy on which she had met with unambiguous failure was her desire to prevent reunification. She had done what she could to prevent it, but only a year later, without bloodshed and on acceptable political and financial terms, the river of unification simply flowed downhill, surmounting all obstacles and brushing aside such little resistance as it encountered. The Soviet forces in the GDR had been the spearhead of the Warsaw Pact, held in check only by the strength of the Atlantic Alliance and the commitment of the United States. In little more than a year they were 'poor devils' engaged in black market deals, contemplating desertion and unenthusiastic about having to return to a Soviet Union that no longer existed.

On 8th March 1988 we had a party to mark Julian's retirement, to say farewell to Bonn and to celebrate his sixtieth birthday, a day whose significance had yet to stamp itself on him. No longer would a secretary give him a daily list of engagements, or the even more daunting longer list of engagements which lay in wait for him during the forthcoming week. There would be no more requests for interviews or speeches, or invitations to trade fairs, or conferences, or requests to open British week. But nobody had suspected what a hellish card fate had in store for him. He drew me to him and showed me that he could not hold his glass of champagne in one hand without support, and without a tremor – a totally unexpected and stunning shock: Parkinson's Disease was making itself felt.

A few days later we said a regretful goodbye to all our staff and drove to the Dutch frontier accompanied by our German personal protection officer, Michael Kirchstein, who had guarded Julian throughout his years in Bonn. He made a slight bow, shook hands and handed him a fat envelope. Not a farewell gift, but close-up pictures of each ear, finger and toe which would have come in useful for identification had Julian been kidnapped by terrorists. So goodbye bullet-proof car, goodbye armed personal protection officer, and goodbye Germany!

ENVOI

1988 – 2006

There is no career in the world in which a man's work is so much shared by a woman as is a married diplomatic by his wife. A woman with the right personal gifts married to a diplomat or consular officer and conscientious about the performance of her duties, is invaluable to the public service.

LORD TYRRELL 1933

Oxford – a place where a certain kind of England comes to die.

Irish Times

WRITING this book has been a very happy voyage through thirty-five years as a diplomatic wife in which I moved house eighteen times (though not always on orders from Whitehall). If we moved to an unknown house in an unknown country, I tried, not always very successfully, to learn the language, to make friends and to explore the country. And for most of the 35 years between my marriage and Julian's retirement I enjoyed a life style in my opinion, more interesting, comfortable and enjoyable, than many of my contemporaries at home - and with more job satisfaction. As Julian rose in rank, I enjoyed meeting people at the top of their profession, both from the country where we were posted and from my own. Julian may have been the guest of honour, but I got to sit next to the host. Had I not been married to Julian it was unlikely that I would ever have been on chatting terms with members of the British Cabinet, been driven down the Mall in a horse-drawn carriage, met so many interesting people or seen as much of the world. I never failed to find something to enjoy in any post, though there were some less enjoyable than others. It was not until Julian reached retiring age in 1988 that I felt regret at not having a career of my own to occupy my time, and for a moment or two wondered if I had wasted my talents. But I did regret spending so many years being interested in little besides bookbinding. For one reason because it is a very solitary occupation, and I had spent too many years bent over my workbench, thinking about little except what needed to be done next and listening to the radio. And to be honest, not even my best work had filled me with total satisfaction.

Julian did not lack offers of employment after his sixtieth birthday, though most of them did not come with emoluments. He was nominated by the Privy Council as their representative on the board of Birmingham University, and was very soon elected Chairman and after that Pro Vice-Chancellor. He set up the Foreign Policy Studies Programme at All Souls, and was in demand to lecture on International Relations in Britain, Germany and elsewhere in Europe. Roy Jenkins persuaded him to take on the somewhat poisoned chalice of the Oxford Society. Papers about the Trilateral Commission piled up on his desk. Both All Souls and St Antony's made him Honorary Fellows. He was also asked to join the newly inaugurated Campaign for Oxford, to raise money for the University. Julian had no difficulty in filling his time, but what about me?

Out of the blue came an invitation to lunch from Jonathan Taylor, Chief Executive of the Booker Group and an alumnus of Corpus Christi College, who thought that I might be a useful addition to his Committee which was raising money for the Bodleian Library. Booker, which was a wholesale food company, had ingeniously created the Booker literary prize in 1969 as a means to advertise its name and saw the Bodleian as a way to reinforce the connection with books.

I was daunted when I met the other members of Jonathan's group, all male, and I gathered earning large salaries in the City. Fundraising was much harder for the Bodleian Library, the Ashmolean Museum and the Botanic Garden than for the university or the colleges, since none of these had direct alumni contacts. Bodley's Librarian David Vaisey told me they hoped to raise ten million pounds, though at the moment they did not even have enough money to clean the windows. At the group's first meeting, the conversation was about possible donors to be approached, and the sums mentioned were way beyond those that ever appeared on an Ambassador's bank statement. How was I going to start? I went to Mr Feller, my butcher in the covered market, who wrote me out a cheque for £1,000, which I proudly gave to the Librarian. It was enough for the windows anyway.

New College had elected a Reader in Opera Studies, and that year his pupils performed an opera in the Warden's garden to which I was invited. I suggested to Michael Burden that I should pay him £2,000 for the following year's performance and give the Library whatever profit I made from the sale of the tickets. This proved a popular annual fixture in Oxford's cultural scene and every year I put on concerts and plays and operas in different venues and also went

Antonia, Thurston and three daughters visiting Bullards in England.

Group of Bullard descendants of A. L. Smith, Master of Balliol 1916-24, whose whiskery portrait hangs on the wall behind

with a begging bowl to charitable foundations. The goal which I set for myself, was to raise a million pounds for the Bodleian.

With my team of friends to help me, we put on no fewer than 43 fundraising events in nine years; without their help I could never have succeeded. They did the flower arrangements, cut thousands of sandwiches, proof read the invitations and programs, cut stamens out of the lilies so that the singers would not refuse to sing, and averted many disasters. I chanced to meet the head of OUP on the train to London and he offered to print our programmes. I found firms to sponsor most events, some British but also Siemens, Bosch, Deutsche Bank and Metallgesellschaft. Bodley's Librarian asked me no questions, gave me a room and a computer and left me entirely in charge of the organizing and the financial planning.

Perhaps the most splendid of all our events was one of the first. I am not sure how I discovered that 1991 was the bicentenary of the year in which Haydn was awarded an Honorary Degree, and for the occasion had given his most recent composition the name of the *Oxford Symphony*. We planned a three-day event to celebrate the occasion, opening with a performance of *The Creation* in the Sheldonian in the presence of the Prince of Wales. I had decided that our final performance would be a recreation of the programme for Haydn's last concert. I was surprised when Bodley's music librarian told me that the music for many of the items had been lost, so we had to extemporise, and hope that the audience would not be disappointed, or even perhaps notice. Amazingly every year All Souls allowed us to break the silence of the Codrington Library, the most beautiful room in Oxford, with an opera followed by dinner in the Divinity School, the gothic heart of the Bodleian. At the invitation of The Duke of Norfolk, we put on an opera in Arundel Castle. Another splendid event was a concert and dinner in the Banqueting Hall in Whitehall. We even produced a Feydeau Farce in the elegance of Christ Church Old Library.

In those days Toby Blackwell, of the famous bookshop, used to fund an Annual lunch for the friends and supporters of the Bodleian in the Hall of Exeter College. My neighbour at the lunch told me he had just been chosen to become Lord Mayor of London, and would be the first old Oxonian to hold that position since the war. I hastily asked him what he was thinking of doing to help the Bodleian. He offered me the use of the Guildhall, and, as 1992 was coming up, I proposed a dinner to commemorate Columbus' voyage of 1492. *Hello!* magazine sponsored us for £50,000, and one evening, at a dinner in London, I heard that the government, wanting to encourage people to support charities, was introducing an incentive by offering to double any money raised in sponsorship! I must have been one of the few people who knew about this, so I was able to be quick off the mark. Why not double *Hello!*'s sponsorship? Our guests were each given a reproduction of a page of the Codex Mendoza, the Sherry Institute of Spain provided sherry poured from a great height by a *venenciador*, and an Oxford jazz band played for dancing afterwards. The sherry was not a success. One of the guests congratulated me but said: '*Pity you couldn't afford a better sherry.*' I should have explained earlier that it had been specially blended by the Spanish Sherry institute to be what Columbus would have drunk on board the *Santa Maria* (thick and sweet but not so popular with our guests).

Only on one occasion did the Librarian question me. This was about the Columbus Dinner. The University were not pleased with what they saw as the Bodleian trying to attract London money, which they had intended to be their exclusive prerogative. So the Vice Chancellor,,hoping to frighten the Librarian into countermandering my plans, had written warning him that the cost of a jazz band could only result in a sizeable deficit, and the Columbus event was more likely to lose than to make money. I must confess to a certain smugness when I was able to tell Richard Southwood how much we had made, the most we ever made on a single night. The Vice Chancellor had not known about the sponsorship from *Hello!,* of course, or of the government's contribution. Since I begged most things, we had minimum expenses, and the jazz band was taking no fee. In my characteristic way of rushing into things, I decided our menu would be entirely composed of food which had come to Europe from the New World, which did not in fact make our dinner very original, as it featured turkey, tomatoes, potatoes, beans, chocolate and squash!

The hiccoughs happened in the earliest years. I heard that there was an elite club of rich book collectors called the Roxborough, whose members seemed exactly the kind of people who I hoped would be interested in helping the Bodleian. With the cooperation of the colleges owning the rarest and most beautiful books, I offered club members the best part of a week in Oxford during which we would visit the selected colleges, and of course the Bodleian, for a talk, a meal and a specially arranged exhibition. I hesitated to book them in the Randolph, where prices were not for the likes of fund raisers, but, at the Eastgate, which had just been refurbished, and I managed to negotiate a good deal with them for the accommodation. The members of the club were very pleasant, had extremely grand titles and came not only from England but also from Spain, Germany Greece and South America. The Spaniard wrote me a kind letter afterwards, but pointed out that he had been disappointed with the hotel, as he had had to sleep, for the first time in his life, in the same bed as his wife! But after nine years of putting on events, we became experts and all went smoothly.

For ten years I gave my services to Bodley, and with both donations and our takings from the 43 events, the Library was able to do a lot more than keep the windows clean, including cataloguing the incunabula for the first time and digitalising the main catalogue of printed books. The Chancellor of the University, Roy Jenkins, presented me with a scroll declaring that I was now a Distinguished Friend of Oxford University!

❧

On 25th May 2006 Parkinsons finally claimed its victim. The nurse heard him singing and asked if he would like tea. When she brought it, he was lifeless. In the following weeks it seemed that everyone who had known him wanted to send a tribute. I have chosen just four.

We think of him with great respect and gratitude. He did a lot to improve and stabilise the relations between our two countries.

> KARL-GÜNTHER VON HASE, German Ambassador to Britain

I shall always remember his keen insight, his capacity to react to sudden changes, his thorough knowledge of difficult dossiers and of international relations in general. As our President in the Political Committee, he steered the deliberations skilfully into diplomatic action. He will stay in my memory as one of the outstanding British Foreign servants.

> DR FRANZ PFEIFFER, German diplomat

For us as Germans it was very valuable that someone like Julian represented your country here and set out to improve a relationship that cannot always be taken for granted. Discussions with him and invitations to your house were something to be treasured

> PROFESSOR KARL DIETRICH BRACHER, German historian and political scientist

However sombre the situation a flash of humour from Julian would lighten the mood, and in the long years of the cold war he never doubted that there would be a good outcome. When it came it was in great measure due to the steadfastness and the acumen of Julian.

> ALAN BROOKE TURNER, British diplomat

❧

I was asked one day whether I minded not ever having done anything for which I would be remembered after I died. After all, I had spent a much of my life standing quite close to great events, but without playing any part in them. Though this is true, it was even more true of our husbands. They were more likely to be remembered for failing to warn the government of some threatened

Opening of the Dubai Lending Library 1969

50th anniversary of Dubai Library 2019

event than for anything big like averting a war. In the words of Lord Salisbury, diplomats work 'by a series of microscopic actions, a judicious suggestion, and far-sighted persistence...' This is the part Julian felt he had played in his career as a Cold War Warrior.

In the distant past there have been wives of diplomats who made a mark: Lady Wortley Montagu is credited with introducing the practice of inoculation against smallpox to England. Lady Stratford Canning was thanked by the Sultan of the Ottoman Empire for her work amongst the poor. Lady Rodd organized a team of Embassy wives to help the victims of the Messina earthquake in 1908 and was given a gold medal by the King of Italy for her nursing work during the First World War. Lady Peake had a street named after her in recognition of her work after the earthquake in the Ionian islands. Had Lady Duff Cooper not devoted herself to restoring the Paris Embassy to its former glory after the War, future occupants might have had to live with the bright and cheerful chintzes which the Ministry of Works was so fond of selecting.

Perhaps one reason why some wives think longingly of a career at home is the fact that as a diplomat's wife you are no longer a totally private person and this takes time to get used to. As your husband gets more senior you will be taken as representative of your country, whether you like it or not. Britain will be judged by what you say and how you behave. And for giving up doing what you might choose to do, the 30% extra on your husband's salary may not seem sufficient.

Something else which you may not have anticipated when you walked up the aisle with your budding diplomat, is that you might be signing on as the catering manager of an establishment serving over two thousand meals a year. I was a guest at a lunch for twelve given by a British Ambassador at which, when our hostess had finished eating, she pushed her plate forward, lit a cigarette, and said 'God, wasn't that an awful meal!' This doesn't go down well in most capitals. In some countries it does not matter if you are not yourself a good cook because there will be no shortage of good cooks delighted to work for you. In some countries it does not matter at all if you cannot speak any language but English because, perhaps by chance, your husband may serve entirely either in London, the US or Commonwealth countries. But in other countries, if you aren't reasonably fluent in the local language, you may be cut off from culture and friendships and it may lead to boredom and loneliness. Being a married to a diplomat principally means that you have to be prepared for anything. but should your husband become Head of a Mission life will become exhausting, demanding, thrilling, spoiling, challenging, but memorable, varied and incomparable

I remember reading an essay titled *In Praise of Mistakes*. Robert Lynd's conclusion was that 'it was not only human but wise to err.' The wisdom lay in giving the reader a feeling of satisfaction that he knew more than the writer, even better if it also gave him a chuckle. He quoted a sentence in a novel in which the hero rowed in the Oxford and Cambridge Boat Race: '*All rowed fast, but none so fast as he*'. I am very conscious of my ignorance in the workings of the Foreign Office, and I am sure that there are also many other errors and inaccuracies in what I have written about politics and even more in my account of the part Julian played in them. But I hope *Endangered Species* will also raise an occasional smile.